Many Rivers to Run

Dave Manby

First published in Great Britain 1999
by
Coruh River Press
Copyright © 1999 Dave Manby.

ISBN 0-9537007-0-4

Dedications

Those friends who eddied out too soon:-
Mike Jones.
Marty Sinclair.
Pete Collins.
"Diesel" Dave Coles.
Adrian Mills.
Wolf Hopp.
Roberto Travato.

Thanks

Michael Manby.
Ian Beecroft.
Peter Knowles.
Steve Rudd.
Steve Crozier.
Ian Macdonald.
Beverly Merricks.
Paul Grogan.

Printed by Technographic, Colchester, Essex CO7 0SX.

Front cover   Humla Kanarli   Francesco Salvato
Back cover   The Indus   Dave Allardice.

CONTENTS

WORKING TITLES

Thinking of a title for this book was hard and many ideas were rejected. For a long time it had a working title of, "So you come all this way just to get wet"; a comment by an English tourist getting out of a tour bus in the car park in Landeck, Austria. We too were in the car park, a convenient get-out from the River Inn. After exchanging pleasantries some explanation of our search for whitewater and that the River Ouse in his native Yorkshire was not up to scratch (to which he took mild offence) followed. His comment that "you mean t' tell me thar you 'ave driven all tis way jest t' get wet" was an almost Mallory like conclusion as to why we paddled white water; "because it's there" but without being quite so serious about the issue. Then, I kid you not, he popped open a can of John Smith's beer and poured it into his dimpled pint glass and walked off to view the Tyrolean town!

Another possible title was "Stories Numbers 137 to 164"; funny to a clique of my friends but meaningless to the general public. These friends mock me incessantly about my stories, often repeats, when told around campfires and in bars. But this is an in-joke and this book contains other people's stories which do not deserve to be subjected to the same ridicule as mine.

"Tales from the River Bank" I am sure has been used somewhere else as a title and to me implies an almost "Wind in the Willows" idyll of warm summer evenings and lazy rivers and messing about in boats. This is not what this book is about. "Tales from Midstream" came from here and was rejected too. I finally settled on "Many Rivers to Run". I hope it carries the feeling that all the authors are still paddling out there in the river and are not washed up in an eddy or grounded on the bank. Despite some of us having receding hair lines and that the greying effect of age is now all too visible, we are out in the mainstream and still enjoying the paddling and its ebb and flow, its good and bad days, life on the river, life.

The vast majority of the authors are of the same generation as me and are friends of mine and those whom I have not met I am sure would quickly fit into my community of friends around the world. This accounts for the age of the stories; this was not deliberate, and now I feel old as I type this; some of the younger generation of paddlers who are my friends were asked but declined. Whether this was because they felt intimidated by the roster of ancients who had been approached or maybe because an epic adventure has to have time to settle in one's mind so that the salient features can permeate to the top and then the judgement of whether to commit it to the page can be made.

Back in Britain after my Braldu solo trip I was laid up at my parents' house while they were away; injured and unable to work I started writing "My Book". Then someone, in an unrelated conversation, said that thirty something was too young to write an autobiography. Later, I reflected on this and put the files of notes and jottings to one side. Maybe one day stories Numbers 1 to ??? will be committed to paper. Many more tales, many more rivers to run.

LANGUAGE AND UNITS

These stories come from around the world and as a result there are slight problems with language. I have tried to use kayak to refer to a kayak and canoe to refer to a canoe but otherwise have kept to English not American spelling and have edited peoples' copy with this in mind. The exception being Donald Bean's account of paddling from the 1930s onwards. See my introduction to him for my reasons.

The other problem was units, not those units your doctor tells you to cut down but metric or imperial units. When I first started paddling, rivers were up or down, occasionally they were tanking; also they were either steep or no one mentioned the gradient. Then I went to the USA and met paddling by numbers. Gradient, volume, length of run, shuttle distance, air temperature, water temperature, river grade all had to be factored into an equation as to whether to paddle. This was strange to me. I was used to a factor, a dither factor of how long it took actually to get onto a North Wales' river, a unit-less calculation derived from the number of pints drunk the night before and how many fishermen could be seen on the banks. Cubic metres or feet per second, (cu.mecs or cfs in paddlers' vernacular) kilometres or miles, feet or metres were never mentioned back in Britain. I set out editing this collection with the idea of being consistent throughout and sticking to metric, objecting to imperialism in all its forms. This did not work: sometimes you just have to use miles instead of kilometres and chang-ing all volumes to cu.mecs would have made a mockery of the rivers where c.f.s are the normal units. If you don't have a calculator to hand just remember that: a mile is a little under two kilometres, if you multiply metres by three and add ten percent you won't be far wrong when it comes to feet, and if you convert cubic metres to cubic feet by multiplying by thirty you will be out by a few percent only.

ALLEGEDLY....

When I first had the idea of putting together this book it was to be a repository for all those old stories that circulate amongst paddlers for a while and then disappear as the generations move on.

Most of these stories are based on "an unimpeachable source", i.e. some bar room conversation where the tale usually begins with the phrase, "So and so told me that so and so did."

So I gathered these stories I had heard out of the recesses of my brain and began jotting them down on paper but as I did this better stories that I had no right to tell popped up in my mind. Stories that I have managed to persuade others to write for this book.

Anyway I was left with all these stories ....

DRY LAND BANDIT RUN

Because of the nature of access to rivers many paddlers end up doing a bandit run, paddling a stretch of river which is forbidden. In Britain paddling white water during the salmon fishing season requires almost all runs to be bandit runs. Accounts of bandit runs down the Grand Canyon exist, despite the problems of sneaking on to the river with several days' supply of food. Other bandit runs have ended in arrest and court appearances. Back in 1957 the world slalom championships were held at Merano, Italy. Milo Duffek from Czechoslovakia was odds-on favourite to win the men's K1. This was back in the days when the Iron Curtain was being drawn tight across the satellite states surrounding Russia. Duffeck had seen the writing on the wall. The day of the event came and Duffeck set off down the course smooth and clear using the Duffeck stroke that he had developed. Then he hit a pole on gate 14. A deliberate penalty? A moment's lapse of concentration? A careless error? Anyway the resulting 50 seconds penalty pushed him down the results list and he ended up out of the medals finishing 27th out of the 62 competitors. That evening when the medal ceremony was taking place Duffeck was not in the crowd cheering the winner: he had slipped his minders and was in the back of the Swiss team's bus heading over the border seeking political asylum. Deliberate penalty or spur of the moment dash to freedom?

He was not the only paddler to escape from the Eastern Block in team mini-buses and cars at various international slaloms.

THEFT

Once again Merano was the site for a Slalom Championships and once again the Eastern Block was dominant. The East German C2 teams were all conquering; when they were competing everyone stopped what they were doing and went to watch them. This dominance obviously had to be because of boat design and not the paddlers' skill! A cunning plan was devised. In those days slalom teams camped, and to keep the Eastern Block paddlers away from the corrupting influence of the western paddlers they camped on the opposite banks. After dark a group of British paddlers snuck across the river and stole the Hartung C2, paddled it back across the river and quickly took a mould off the boat before returning the boat early the following morning without being noticed. A few months later the East German team were in Llangollen competing in the John Player International slalom. Standing on the bridge watching the paddlers practise, the East German coach remarked "Ah I see you have the Hartung C2. How you finding it?" The British coach replied "Well, we're struggling with it but we have only had it for a few weeks. Seems to take some getting used to." The East German coached laughed and remarked that he had been examining the boat the previous day: it appeared that the deck was on the wrong way round. Obviously the speedy moulding job had been a little too speedy and the two flimsy halves had warped as the resin had cured. Back in Britain the perpetrators of the theft had to resort to joining the ill fitting halves together on a "best fit" basis.

9

ESKIMO ROLLS

I organised a slalom back in 1984 for Maurice Rothwell. He had just retired from his last post in the BCU. It seemed a fitting event as Maurice needed more of a "thank you" than the new tie that the BCU had presented to him. This is not to say that the new tie was not needed... I invited to the event anyone who had ever been a member of the British Slalom team whom I could track down and the slalom was run on the River Dee at Trevor Rocks, with the same course and to the same rules (almost) as Maurice had competed to way back in 1939 at the first slalom in Britain. Many of the old boys and girls of slalom turned up and paddled; a good day was had by all. Bill Horseman, who had been in the same team as Paul Ferrant who had won the slalom gold medal for Britain back in 1959 recounted a tale from the old days. Competing in a slalom at Swarkstone on the Trent, he capsized and rolled up and completed his run. On arriving at the finish he was reprimanded by the race official, Oliver Cock. His offence was rolling. Apparently in white water this was a dangerous stunt and should he do it again he would be banned from the BCU. The fact that Bill had learnt to roll whilst competing in slaloms in Europe where "all the continentals were rolling in the rough - even their ladies" cut no ice. It was a dangerous stunt, all right and useful for lakes but a stunt none the less and totally unsuitable for rivers.

PADDLING TO AUSTRALIA

Don Cohen, a friend living on Vancouver Island, once recounted a tale I would love to have had the time to track down. He bumped into an old man, Egon Kuhn, in Victoria on Vancouver Island who had been in the German rowing team for the Olympic games in Melbourne, Australia in 1956. To get to the games Egon and a friend had bought a double kayak and taken two years off and paddled there. Just speculating about the route is enough to set the imagination running riot. Up the Rhine down the Danube along the Black Sea overland to the Euphrates and down it through Turkey and Iraq and then along the Persian Gulf. Did they go up the Indus and then overland across to and down the Ganges? Outlandish? Yes. Impossible? No.

THE ALMOST PERFECT MURDER

Down in the corner of Austria near Salzburg are the Lammaröfen and Salzachöfen. The German word "öfen" literally means oven but here translates to "a gorge". The Lammaröfen is a small tight swirly run which will still get the best paddlers edgy and nervous. The Salzachöfen is a large swirly run which can still get the best paddlers nervous and edgy. They were, however, first run back in the 1950's in fold boats. The Salzachöfen was also the scene of a near perfect murder. The local paddlers had been eyeing the two stretches as a possible run but no one had plucked up the courage to attempt either of them. The local doctor and his wife set out one day to paddle the Salzach and put in some way upstream of the Salzachöfen and paddled down to the take-out just above the "öfen". Here he pushed his wife in and then paddled down to the other end of the gorge and rescued his wife's body. His idea was to claim that his wife, also a noted keen kayak paddler, had fallen in on their attempt and drowned. Unfortunately the push was seen by another local paddler.

THE AMAZON

Everyone has heard of the Amazon. Many people have paddled bits of the Amazon. Few have attempted to paddle its length and of those fewer have succeeded, the expeditions collapsing from interpersonal problems or illness or boredom or a combination of these reasons. Somewhere along the road I heard of someone who had paddled the length of the river solo. The story ran that he had fallen ill, been taken in by a native tribe and nursed back to health, paddled on down the river, fell ill again was taken in again by another tribe and recovered and carried on to the end of the river. This was all I knew of the solo expedition. Tracking down more information was hard:-

Dave,
Steve Bezuk was not really a friend; just one of those many eccentric acquaintances that boating attracts. I, like many others, only paddled with him once. He liked doing rivers only either once or at flood stage. Someone once met him coming down Loon Creek into the Middle Fork of the Salmon doing a three day run down to Heller's Bar. This included a great portion of the middle fork, then the Main, past Riggins, the Lower Salmon and the day or so down to Hellers. He did this to escape getting permits plus he paddled at night. He did the same thing down the Chilco, Chilkotin, Fraser etc. He did write an account of his

11

Amazon run but it was so dry (I understand) that it was totally unreadable. However, I know he carried a gun with him and when asked if, on the Amazon, he ever used it. Bezek answered, "I did what I had to do". He was killed running the Upper Green River Gorge WA. in a monster flood. Although he was wearing a helmet, he had a massive head wound. Only after he died did people find out more about him: that during the Hungarian revolution he showed up at his friends or relatives in a Russian tank that he single-handedly captured. He had tea with them, then left the country. This, I guess, only his wife knew about. He didn't even tell fellow countryman Al Zob (US team 1972) who had machine gun scars on his back. One other thing about Steve that says something for his character; he was a bridge keeper. You know, the guy who holds traffic up to let boats pass.

But to let you know how much I didn't really know him - like everyone else - I'm not even sure I spelled (sic) his name right.

FIRST DESCENTS

A few years ago I bumped into a rafting group on the Çoruh. They were on the second half of an expensive "designer" rafting holiday/expedition. The punters had been sold the trip on the strength of a unique trip to unexplored regions, (but they were happy enough to buy the rafting T-shirts the locals were screen printing). The first half of their trip had been to Albania which had just opened up after the collapse of the communist regime. When they arrived at the proposed put-in there was no water in the river. Donkeys were hired and they finally rejoined the river further downstream where there was sufficient water to float a raft. Several days later the team arrived at the take-out bridge. Here they met the old bridge keeper who had been keeping river level records for over half a century. He confirmed that the river was the lowest it had been in living memory (or since records began which was the same in his case!). This reassured the embarrassed raft guides who had been trying to explain that they had done all the necessary research to the increasingly peeved punters. However the river guides' increased esteem was quickly dashed when the bridge keeper remarked, "I was wondering when some more people would come down the river. We haven't had anyone down this river since a couple of Italians came down in the time of King Zog". So much for the promised first descent!

MILT JINES

Look at this logically:-

1. I have never met Milt.
2. He is a cartoonist.
3. He used to be an commercial airline pilot. He used to play a tape of a model-T Ford starting up when taxiing the plane to the runway. Playing a cockerel crowing as the dawn came up at 40,000ft was not unheard of either.
4. He now is an artist, "doing sculpture in four dimensions, the fourth dimension being humor". This apparently involves sculpturing skulls and then sticking things in them. e.g. a circular saw blade sliced into one with the title of "Skull Saw" an arrow stuck through another and called "Kennedy: The Single Arrow Theory".
5. His letters are just a stream of jokes.
6. His sense of humour is sick, obvious see 3 & 4 above.
7. He is a friend of Whit Deschner.
8. Friends of Whit I have met include:-
    i. an orthopaedic surgeon whose business card used to read "If it's broken call Loken".
    ii. an ex-air traffic controller who drives the long way round, an extra eight hours, to the put-in on Hell's Canyon on the Snake to see if a friend is in a bar and then phones him from the bar and finds out that he is away on business.
    iii. a gillnetter (trawler to most people but apparently this is an important difference) owner who fishes off Bristol Bay and thinks nothing of constructing a golf course at the harbour to while away the time waiting for fish. The tee for the first hole was on one side of the estuary and the green on the other over 500m away. He argues that this saves time: you never have to look for the balls. (Why you would want to save time when whiling away time I have never worked out.)
    iv. Xxxxxxxx xxxx, xxxxxxxx x xxxx.

Something in the list does not add up.
It makes me unsure if I want to meet him.
Ergo I don't think that you will want to meet him.
Therefore I don't need to write an introduction to him.

KAYAK SPELLED BACKWARDS
IS KAYAK. THE WORD,
LIKE THE BOAT IT DESCRIBES
AND THE PADDLE USED TO
PROPEL IT LOOKS ABOUT TH'
SAME NO MATTER WHICH
END YOU ARE LOOKING AT.
COME TO THINK OF IT, SO
DO A LOT OF THE PEOPLE
WHO SQUEEZE INTO THESE
WIERD LITTLE CRAFT TO SPEND
WEEKENDS BOUNCING THEM
OFF'N ROCKS AND STUFF...
SOME EVEN ATTACK OCEANS!

WELL, IT IS TO THIS
GROUP OF WIERDO'S THAT
THIS COLLECTION OF CAR-
TOONS IS DEDICATED.

MILT JINES

COLIN HILL

Chill, as Colin is almost universally known, won't thank me for mentioning that he is the holder of three world rolling records in that book of pointless facts, The Guinness Book of Records. Better than goldfish swallowing but still ... He will, however, be pleased if I mention that he was the first person to paddle the white-water stretches of both the Blue and White Nile. He is the master of under-statement. Any time Chill says a river was a little serious or a particular rapid was tough I know that it is to be avoided; even if he says it is a great fun run I feel nervous. It just just makes me wonder whether other paddlers, bereft of this piece of information about his character, have gone and got themselves into serious trouble! Understatement is not uncommon for Brits and once, giving a brief scribbled guide to west coast rivers, I mentioned that Tumwater canyon in Washington "had a little something on it". I did not, however, mention that it had only around 2,000 cfs in it when I ran it. Mike, Ross and the others soon discovered that there was a big "little something down there" at this level, 15,000cfs. No real problem, a bad swim granted, but the road runs alongside. With Chill these under-statements tend to be about some remote river in East Africa, Papua New Guinea, or some other expensive air-ticket destination and the river will be in the middle of a jungle and miles from anywhere.

Chill sent me a CV of his paddling experience. Two pages of small type. This is a summary. Take a look:-

The following destinations include eight rivers that were successful first descents. Papua New Guinea, Sikkim, Ethiopia, Vietnam, Uganda, Japan, Ecuador, Canada (Yukon), Alaska, New Zealand, Mozambique, Pakistan, South Africa, USA, India, Zimbabwe, Nepal and extensively in Europe.

Last time I saw Chill he was operations manager for "Ultimate Descents" in Katmandu and Jacquie his wife was pregnant; this was going to change his life I thought ..... His daughter was christened *Indus* Jade Hill; I think the paddling will continue!

THE SLIDE SHOW

It was a change to be doing a slide show where I wasn't trying to sell the audience a rafting trip. It was just a group of friends, some of whom were trying to decide if they should buy a house or go travelling again. As the first slide flickered onto the sheet pinned to the wall, I felt myself smile with the memories as I was transported back in time. The image on the screen and in my mind's eye was of Rob Hind, unconscious on the bed with a bottle of cheap vodka on his chest and a kayaking helmet on his head: that was a strange trip.

1993 Vietnam – "I'm afraid you cannot go on the river, and must accompany me to the police station". All of our hopes of a quick getaway were dashed as we heard the police officer speak in perfect English. Up to that point we were doing quite well at acting stupid. OK, I admit that the problem was that we had forged our permits to get near the Chinese border. I guess that we were a little naive in thinking nobody would check, as we were probably the first tourists in that area for a long, long time. The town itself was a ferry point for the Song Hong river and like most border towns it wasn't high on the beauty list. Loa Cai had a ferry, a few tea houses (with dog soup specials) and of course the police station.

Here are a few hints about travelling in countries which haven't seen kayaks before:

1. Think about inflatable kayaks. I hate seeing the dollar signs in the eyes of bus men, taxi drivers, porters, train guards and egotistical check-in people at airports.

2. Take a photo of yourself kayaking on some white water so they can comprehend what you want to do.

3. Never, and I repeat, never, think that by not taking your Walkman you will save weight and get to experience the culture a little more!

The police guard, whose uniform was complemented with a rack of bullets and a big gun, told us what was going to happen …. "unless he heard otherwise from his superiors we were going to be held under arrest". Rob and Greg Bell decided that I had the best smile and so they sent me off back down South to try to gain permission for us to leave the area. This meant, I guess, that if I failed in my mission we were going to be stuck there! I was driven down by a wee police man on a motorbike. He was eager to impress me with how fast we could go without wiping out on the corners. It was at a slightly different pace from that we had taken to get there. That had been a slow moving, hard-seated train, which took 8 hours, and for the pleasure we had to pay 10 times local rate. The journey was a little strange in that every time I tried to sleep a beautiful Vietnamese lady would wake me and say "mustn't sleep, they steal from you" and then look knowingly at the other passengers. Rob and Greg were already dead to the world, so I tried duck taping my eyelids back. Stealing was a bit of a pastime on that train as the conductor got in on the act with his hand in our bag whilst checking our tickets.

Happy to be off the bike, I still had to get through a full day of interrogation: this consisted mostly of me smiling and drawing kayaks on paper. It was finally agreed that we could in fact leave the area, but by bus, not by the river.

When I returned to my comrades, who were a little relieved to see that I hadn't done a runner on them, we had New Year to celebrate. The guards were a little happier knowing they could get rid of us, so we all had something to celebrate. Sadly the boys overstepped the line after a few too many rice wines when they started to toast "the first kayak decent of the Song Hong". So Greg took his leave and left the room, then blacked out in the kitchen sending the pots and pans everywhere. The boys' plan of getting the guards drunk enough so that they would agree to let us paddle away failed.

So at 5 am I awoke with a slightly different plan: "let's paddle off while everyone was sleeping"! I have to admit that as plans go it was slightly flawed, but I figured that they would be glad that we were gone. Rob's red eyes managed to make an appearance between the slits of his eyelids. "Piss off", he said as he saw me dressed in my paddling gear. Twenty minutes later we crept from the police station, under stars fading into the morning sky, to the bank of the river. What a pleasant surprise it was to see one of the police guards taking his large gun for a morning stroll. The boys were on brink of blaming the whole thing on me when he shook his head, smiled and shouted out a "good luck". I thanked any God who was listening that we were free again to paddle and wouldn't be shot that day.

That was the start of our paddling in 'Nam, and the start of our search for white water. We found big surf by the ocean, paddled past villages on the Saigon River but didn't find that grade V anywhere or any grade III for that matter. But then again, that wasn't what this little trip was all about. We enjoyed exploring the country as we searched and this was as much of a thrill as scaring the wet-suit pants off yourself is; I just wish

they would stop putting dog in the soup.

As the slide show went on, I realised that I loved each country I had visited or lived in for different reasons. Ethiopia; where a short Kiwi bloke had his raft savaged by a hippo not twenty feet ahead of me and that was only day three of the twenty-one day trip down the Omo. After that, the same short Kiwi asked me to run a commercial raft trip down the Blue Nile.

Oh, what a sense of humour one must have for a trip with an option of either a grade VI rapid or grade V+ portage. That is a different story for another slide show. Anyway at the end of my third 21 day Omo trip which, I must add right here, had run like clockwork avoiding hippos, crocs and heat stroke (there's no avoiding tsetse flies), we arrived at the take-out. Now as far as take-outs go this is pretty wild one, with tribes living there adorned with lip plates, scarification on their bodies and either a spear or an AK 47 in hand. All very interesting, but the only thing we really wanted to see, and the thing that was really missing, was our 4x4 vehicles to take us to an airstrip. "Not a problem", I told my clients; that kind of worked for the first three days. By day four they were a little bit nervous. Meanwhile I was carving myself my own spear as I tried to work out which tribe had the nicest girls with the smallest lip plates! Five days later the vehicles showed, with the news that the aeroplane would not be there. It took another three days to drive back to Addis Ababa, so if anyone ever complains about a late shuttle within earshot of me then I launch in to my Omo tale (ignoring the groans from other guides).

The slides flicked on..

Ecuador 96 – Another epic mission trying to find rivers suitable for a pre-sold rafting trip! Getting 600 kg worth of rafting gear through customs was a fun start to a roller coaster of three months' work. This trip led to a turning point in my life. There comes a time when you have to stare mortality in the face. This is the guts of the deep conversation I had with myself as I swung from a vine over a waterfall I was trying to inspect and back into the cave where my kayak was tied up.

Like many of the more famous epics you hear about in the kayak world it started with a swim, Steve Nomchong's swim in fact (I'm a great one for naming names). We could find no information about anyone having paddled this fast steep gorge, but off we went anyway. We were doing pretty well until after lunch, when the river started to gather momentum and we were faced with the old steep drop with boulders either side of the deep hole scene. After getting Nomie to the side on the back of my kayak, I thought I'd better go and find his boat. With a quick smile off I went, unknowingly into "The Gorge Of Doom". It was after the third close call from running drops blind that I managed to pull into a cave just in time; the water disappeared entirely from view. My heart raced as the fall sounded 'bad'. I attached my kayak to a tree root and climbed around a rock wall over the fall to a ledge where I could get a good view at something I wished I wasn't seeing. It was not good, in fact it was very bad; this was not runnable.

Then things became worse as I tried to climb back to my kayak. I just couldn't climb down and back into the cave, without falling into the waterfall. This is when I started to think about my fiancée, 'Whoops', I thought, 'she'll kill Steve if I don't make it back.' After some time had passed and a lot of lateral thinking, I saw the vine. It held after a few

20

tugs. Boy, if someone could see me now, I thought to myself as I swung around the rock wall (I would have given a Tarzan call if I hadn't been so scared).

The rest was a continuation of the nightmare, attaching a throw bag to the boat, climbing back around, pulling the boat out above the fall and pulling it back in and up the ledge. By this stage the muscle fatigue was starting to win the battle over any adrenalin that was still flowing. The grand finale was the launch back into the river below the falls and pulling away from the tow back. I ran a few more rapids I shouldn't have and was glad to see a track waiting to take me to South American dancing music. Well, that was one possible rafting river off our list, only another ten to check out.

Another country flashes onto the screen –

Uganda 95 – As Andy and I launched into the source of the Victoria Nile, we both felt as if we were making a wee bit of history being the first humans to paddle both sources of the Nile. We had heard of one Swiss guy who had tried to kayak the top section of the Victorian Nile in an inflatable but he was never seen again. Running this first descent led to both of us getting our butts kicked at one time or another, but what a hoot. Andy Copestake later returned with some rafts and kayakers to give the lower section a go but that, as they say, is another story.

I'm in my groove now as the carousel is changed…

Nepal 91, Mozambique, Sikkim, Zimbabwe blah, blah, blah, etc. etc. etc…….In the back of my mind I think about the first show I went to. I was 14 and it was given by Nigel Timmins on a trip he had done on the Marsyangdi. Cool, I thought, I want to go to Nepal, even though I didn't have a clue where on Earth it was. There are people in one's life, who, without that person realising, can inspire you enough to change the course of your life forever.

Two weeks later the couple who were thinking about a mortgage, bought a ticket to Nepal to go rafting and trekking. My wife and I, who were half thinking about settling in New Zealand as we now have a little baby girl (named Indus), decided on one more season, just one more….Then Jono and Teresa who had hosted the slide show were so impressed they decided to get the discovery channel! Ach well....You can't win them all!

OK so Steve Nomchong; (I had to ask what happened to him, Ed.)

As it happens Steve found his kayak only 10m downstream of where I had dumped him on the bank. He decided to call it a day there and then and hitched a ride downstream to a hotel where we had arranged to meet. He got the driver to stop a few times on the way to see if he could spot me. As he peered down into the gorge what he could see of the river made him really worried. After dropping his boat off at the hotel, he spent the next few hours trekking up and down the road looking into the gorge hoping he wouldn't see me and that I had walked out a long way above what he could see. I was probably swinging off vines below him, out of sight at the time. He was in a truck hitching a ride back down to the hotel when I eventually broke cover from the bush onto the road looking a little worse for wear. We called a break in our exploring for a few day and headed back to Quito to dance the Salsa with the ever eager to teach South American girls.

MICK HOPKINSON

Most of Mick's introduction is in his story of the Blue Nile. He sent me a list of facts to turn into a smooth flowing piece. He bought his first kayak, a second hand KW4 in 1965. He cites his first serious attempt at drowning himself as "1967 Shipley weir in flood". His first new kayak was a KW7 bought also in 1967. He didn't say in which order these two events happened! Many other notable achievements followed.

I first met him back in 1975 on a trip paddling around Landek in the Austrian Tyrol. He, along with Mike Jones, John Liddell, and Rob Hastings, were the experienced paddlers; I just followed them. When choosing between the different lines offered by them all disappearing over some horizon line, Mick's back was the one I followed, the one I trusted. Later that year I called at his house in Bradford. The house, two small back-to-back houses knocked together, was logically arranged and dedicated to the outdoors; the kayaks suspended in place of the kitchen airer, the climbing gear stored upstairs in the spare bedroom and the caving equipment in its rightful place, the cellar. The walls were covered with caving maps and climbing pictures. (White-water kayaking and canoeing was in its infancy and as such visually impoverished.) At the time Mick was a geography teacher but even term time failed to slow down his pursuit of the outdoors. Accounts of making it out of some Yorkshire pot or back from a paddling exploit just in time to get cleaned up, changed and into assembly ahead of his pupils were legend.

Mick has a presence; he can dominate a gathering, but normally will sit in the background watching and listening and then with a few precise words bring the discussion back down to earth. But this is not to say he doesn't have a lighter side to his character. Some of his bawdier tales were rated in pints; the number of pints before the, often self-incriminating, tale would be told. The tale behind his need to return across Bradford by the early morning bus still dressed in a wet suit after an extended night out rated five pints; I don't think I ever heard the oft asked for "ten pint story."

Along with Mike Jones the two of them stood head and shoulders above me at this paddling game. The two were a formidable team.

Whilst Mike was the eternal optimist whose plans often seemed to require all traffic lights to be green, all flights to leave on time unless he was late, and all assumptions correct, (though he was never depressed nor surprised when they were dashed by these reasonable demands). Mick, on the other hand, would listen to Mike's synopsis of the expedition's proposed logistics, and then restate the plan, this time with several ifs, buts, perhapses, maybes and possiblies. Mike's enthusiasm just dragged you along. Mick, he just has a better grasp of reality.

While I was putting this book together Pete Livesey, a friend of Mick's and probably the most influential British climber of the seventies, died and Mick reflected in one of his letters to me "I can still remember watching Pete soloing E2s in Hush Puppies! Guess we are getting to that stage in our lives when our peers are dying of natural causes as opposed to just falling off things or drowning." Mick's peers, not mine. I don't claim to be at that level but I rate Mick up there.

MIKE JONES & MICK HOPKINSON 1976

Mick was up there "Pushing the Limits" long before Leo Dickinson's TV series with the same title featured Mick, John Wasson, Rob Lesser and myself in the "A Breath of white-water" episode or before we "starred" in "Dudh Kosi: Relentless River of Everest". He was the first person I know to paddle the Finstermünz rapid on the Inn; he led our first descent of the Oetz from Sölden to Huben, and was the first down the "Inn Shoot" below the dam at Prutz. These descents were in 4m long fibreglass boats, that's what we paddled in then; plastic boats and specialised equipment had yet to be developed. Nearly twenty years later he made the first descent at natural flows of "Nevis Bluff" New Zealand's mega classic on the Kawarau River. Still at the leading edge. Still pushing.

Now married and the father of a future world kayak champion, Mick has set up and runs "New Zealand Kayak School" in Murchison.

THE BLUE NILE

Everything happens in cycles. First a sarcastic postcard from Slime showing the Shafartak Bridge with the words "Three commercial trips a day and the locals are tubing it! Where was that film footage shot?" Then a glossy "Adrift" brochure from Cam Maclay advertising their trips on the Blue Nile and a small photograph in the Prijon catalogue of a Polish expedition. Just warming me up for Dave Manby's "Can you just write 5,000 words on the true story of the Blue Nile just to prove that you have not got Old-timers' disease?"

The irony is that the Slime postcard from Ethiopia is the identical one I sent back from Bahadur in 1972. There must still be only one type of postcard there. Except the postcard of '72 had me complaining about the altitude and quoting the locals as saying the crocodiles were 6 metres long but that "They went away if you clapped your hands". How naive we were in hindsight.

The true story of the Blue Nile? The bare bones are there for all in Chris Bonington's "Quest for Adventure" coffee-table-size tome where for the first time kayaking got star billing, up with the Everest trips and Polar exploration.

But Chris kept it clean and none of the human drama, the internecine strife, was there.

Did it really happen? I guess we have the 16mm. footage and the slides. I had all the gear nicked from the car whilst lecturing on the "Blue Nile" to Leeds Canoe Club in 1972. No souvenirs there. The kayaks are probably still hanging up in the garage in Addis Ababa. But I still have the paddles, a pair of wooden Prijons that I bought second hand from Ken Langford because they were too heavy for slalom racing. They hang in mute testimony on the wall at home. I never used them again after the trip, perhaps I had an inkling they were going to be of historical value!! But they do tell a little story. One blade has deep grooves gouged in it from the sharp volcanic rocks of the riverbed. I can remember doing a back deck roll with the blade in front of my face and thinking that the paddle had probably saved me a set of facial stitches from the ever-keen young house surgeon Mike Jones who was still practising on Saturday night drunks.

How did Mike get hold of me? I think we were both survivors of dwindling peer groups whose continued enthusiasm for kayaking was being diluted by the onset of responsibility and marriage - an ever present threat to the young male kayaker of the seventies. For some reason you seemed to have to do one or the other. Not mutually compatible. Women kayakers were as rare as rocking horse shit and were snapped up with alacrity. We had a bit in common ..Yorkshire background.. "trouble at t'mill" and all that stuff. We were both "never wases" in the First Division Slalom scene. I think he was 14th. in the ranking list and I was 10th. (Pity I can't just ring up Maurice Rothwell and check!) We both had British Team aspirations but were built like rugby players. We drank a fair bit. It became one of the selection criteria for our later exploratory teams. "In Vino Veritas!"

Mike had made a name for himself as a young tyro on the River Inn expedition and he had been a member of the famous Hawksworth Paymore Grand Canyon trip.. the film of which was pretty mind-blowing in those days.

I had trodden another path. A delayed weaning from the St. Bede's Canoe club led to paddling with pretty much the same team of slalom paddlers for 4 years, to the point that we formed the nucleus of the first British youth team tour which, under the management of Mick Colgan, travelled to Yugoslavia and Austria in 1971.

Fortunately in those days one's slalom boat was also one's play boat and "big water boat". Most of us were paddling Prijon "Iseres", the Gaybo version of the "Inn", with the exception of Alan Edge who paddled a "Hartung" in honour of his East German slalom hero Sigi Horn. So when we caught the River Inn in huge flood between slaloms we were as fully equipped as we were ever going to be to hit the big water. One of our slaloms was on the Sanna at Landeck and a routine quickly developed... gates in the morning... The Inn in the afternoon... We learned quickly and the Inn was a good teacher providing big holes; at least one of which ate up Alan Edge, Ian "Herman" White and Roger Huyton all at the same time. I developed a fixation for the giant rapid just below the dam. It had never been paddled, was in the German guide book as unrunnable and was given the ultimate accolade by Ian Pendleton, a member of the British Canoe Union Committee who happened to be there. He threatened to have me banned from the

BCU, (probably in memory of Sicksmith and his partner who had drowned on the Isel), if I killed myself on the rapid, thereby giving British canoeing a bad name.

Faced with such enticements who could turn it down? So, armed with two spray decks and a calor gas bungy cord, (no neoprene decks yet!), I launched onto the rapid in my 24 pound fibre-glass race boat wearing the lifejacket that my mother had made and ran my first grade 6 rapid. (OK it is only grade 5 now and everybody runs it but in 1971 the guide book had grades 1-6 and X for impossible. That rapid "Big Landeck" was classed X. Is it my fault the grading system is screwed up??) I was super fit and could roll like clockwork and most of all I was an invincible twenty-two year old. However I do remember being absolutely terrified at the start of the descent and thinking, not for the last time, "It didn't look this big from the road"!

I also learned about the adrenalin syndrome; I could carry on being terrified and wobble down the river into oblivion or I could get a grip and attack the line I intended to make. I chose the latter course and survived the run which was immortalised on super 8 film. I also had my picture in the BCU magazine doing this important first descent. The caption read "Mick Hopkinson of Manchester Canoe Club paddling on the River Lieser in Austria". At the time this was a severe blow to my ego! I still remember, five years later arguing in broken German and English, with a member of the German Slalom team that Yes I had run that rapid in 1971. He didn't believe me though in actual fact I had run it again in 1973 with Mike Jones and in 1974 with Alan Hall and John Liddell.

But enough: I had become a "big water kayaker" and achieved a certain cachet in the small world of slalom, enough for Mike to invite me on the Nile expedition.

In 1972 I was a first year teacher under pressure, mostly self imposed, trying to meet the demands of my new profession, lesson preparation and marking homework, but kayaking every day and going to white-water races and slaloms every weekend. Life was fun and hectic. I had just purchased a Mini Minor to replace the Morris 1000 that had seen me through my student days. Sadly it wasn't the racing machine of my Monte Carlo fantasies and I became adept at overloading it and burning out the valves. Fortunately I also became adept at fixing it. Now I was suitably independent, the spring slaloms that year became the planning grounds for our Blue Nile expedition. We even once had a meeting, probably the first and last time Mike used this tactic.

The meeting was in North Wales and the occasion was auspicious because Mike and I got a ride there from Yorkshire in Chris Hawkesworth's E-type Jaguar. I remember sweeping down the newly opened M62 motorway at 130 mph. being faced with a huge bill for the petrol and thinking it was all a major waste of time. Chris pulled out of the trip with about three weeks to go and Jim Hargreaves, who was in the army, had his political clearance withdrawn after Mike had an argument with Blashford-Snell over the phone.

I never got the full details of the conversation but the gist of it was that Mike's major ploy was that we were about to attempt the first descent of the Blue Nile, a not unreasonable raison d'être as the British Army Expedition of 1968, led by then Captain John Blashford-Snell, had not in our eyes completed the first descent of the river. They were not white-water experts and had used very small rafts with little success and in the end had not attempted large sections of the river, opting to portage below the Tississiat falls and to use the, what we considered unethical, tactic of throwing their rafts in above the gorge leading to the Portuguese bridge and having a second party pick up the remains. Obviously egos had clashed. After all they were a large and well organised military expedition and we were a bunch of young know-nothing kayakers trying to usurp their best effort.

One outcome of Mike's conversation with Blashford Snell and the resulting non-appearance of the military members of our trip was that we lost our access to guns. We had read about the two serious bandit attacks on the British Army Expedition and about the 1962 Swiss expedition from the Geneva Canoe Club. They had tried to paddle the stretch of river from the Shafartak Bridge to Khartoum but had been attacked near the Sudanese border by a group of Shifta Bandits and two of their team had been shot and killed. A more successful attempt had been made two years later by Arne Robin, an intrepid Swedish paddler. He had paddled from the Shafartak Bridge to Khartoum in eight days but he had been attacked by crocodiles! Arne also tried to paddle the upper stretch of the river in 1966 with a companion Carl Gustav Forsmark but they lost their double kayak in a whirlpool and had to walk out. The very first expedition in 1905 had also ended in tragedy. An American team had tried to navigate the river in steel boats during the dry season. They had sunk after only five miles and during the subsequent walkout one of their team was caught and castrated before being released – a sort of negative souvenir of his holidays!!

So we knew we had to have guns! Bandits and Crocodiles! Mike had rung the head keeper of London Zoo who was of the opinion, which later proved to be correct, that a .45 bullet was the smallest calibre that would stop a crocodile! Armed with this information Mike and I visited the local sports store, Carters, in Bradford and asked for "some guns please?" "What for?" "To shoot crocodiles," we replied. After numerous visits and Mike explaining to the local police why we needed hand guns, very unusual items in England, we finally obtained two Webley .45s. They were ex-government surplus and clearly marked 1917, officers' pistols from World War 1! We also purchased a double barrelled shotgun that eventually turned out to be neither use nor ornament.

Another drawback to the Services' refusal to grant clearances was that we were down to a team of two. So, out of the blue Mike managed to persuade Dave Burkinshaw and Steve Nash, both fellow division one slalom paddlers, to join us. My only contact with them had been at race weekends. Dave was teaching in Rotherham and Steve worked as an electronics engineer in Reading for a company called Racal. A friend of Mike's, Glen Greer, was to be our support crew. Glen and Mike had met at Birmingham University but Glen was now working as an engineer for Rolls Royce.

Originally the plan was to drive out! Mike had the offer of a Land Rover from British Leyland. Fortunately that plan fell through as we studied the problems involved in driving across Europe, the middle East and half of Africa! (We were to suffer for this failed driving dream of Mike's when in 1976 we got to drive all the way to Nepal instead!) Mike joined the RAF, the university of Birmingham Air Squadron, in a last ditch effort to get the team and the vehicle to Ethiopia. That failed. Finally Mike managed to get some sponsorship from Egypt Airlines and it became slowly apparent that we would probably be going! I visited my doctor and had some shots.. tetanus, typhoid, para typhoid, cholera and Yellow Fever. It all felt very exotic! Well, it did till about nine o'clock that night when, after having several pints with fellow teacher Stan Connell, I passed out in the pub and had to be driven home!

July arrived. I finished school for the summer. Mike disappeared on the Universities' kayak tour to Austria. I puttered around collecting bits of gear. I remember Graham Goldsmith solemnly shaking my hand as he handed over our boats. I began to think .."This is serious!" I took shooting lessons organised by a friend of mine, Bob Hollingworth, our school caretaker. He had connections with the Territorial army. At the time it was all rather surreal. Here I was, a young would-be expeditionary, being taught by a veteran Sergeant Major who listened patiently while I explained about the bandits and the crocodiles!

Mike reappeared and for a while his home in Utley, where his ever-patient parents, Reg and Molly, organised us, fed us and tolerated us, became mission control. We were visited by the local policeman who had been sent to check that the guns were safely under lock and key as Mike's firearms license had dictated. As it happened, when he arrived we had the gear all over the back garden including the two hand guns ... a definite no-no in a small Yorkshire town!

Mike disappeared again on 24th July, this time to Ethiopia with all the gear. I was left in a kind of nether world with last minute instructions to buy the food for the river trip! I filled my time working on a building site to earn some extra cash for the trip. Even that seemed a bit bizarre, explaining to the Irish foreman that I was going to Ethiopia next week. He must have believed me because he gave me a cash bonus to get some gear for the trip.

News filtered through Reg and Molly's. Mike had landed in Cairo in the midst of one of the Arab-Israeli wars carrying two revolvers and a shotgun. He was immediately arrested! Surprise! Surprise! Mike was free; he had talked his way out. Mike was in Addis Ababa.

Two weeks after Mike left, the rest of the team met in Reading at Steve Nash's place. Dave's wife Sue was there and to my surprise I discovered that Steve was the recent father of a baby girl. I also found out that he had persuaded his company Racal to part with some very expensive high-tech radios and to a certain extent he had put himself on the line by bolstering his request for time off by persuading them that the Ethiopian army was a potential market for their equipment!

We finally left from Heathrow on an Egypt Airlines jet and somehow we were given seats in the first class compartment. I had only ever flown once before, aged ten, on a prop-jet from Bradford to Dublin. This seemed like the height of sophistication. However things were not as well as they seemed. Steve had smuggled a .38 revolver, carefully covered in lead foil, in the battery case of one of the radios. Would we be discovered and given the same treatment as Mike? In the end we faced a much bigger problem! As we were about to board our plane from Cairo to Addis Ababa an official took us to one side and showed us the contents of a lockup on the runway... our kayaks! We were about to discover, as Mike had done two weeks previously, that a thirteen foot kayak wouldn't fit into the cargo hold of a Comet jet. We tried everything, including getting them into the passenger compartment.. but they wouldn't fit through the door. It was only when we started investigating removing one of the windows that the pilot lost his patience and took off without us. There followed a nightmare stay in Cairo airport as we tried to persuade a whole series of petty officials that they were actually sponsoring us to get to Ethiopia.

After endless communications between Cairo, Addis Ababa and the Birmingham office of Egypt Air the kayaks were shipped to Ethiopia via Ethiopian Airlines as freight. My personal arrival in Addis Ababa was less than auspicious. I spent the flight chatting to the wife of the British consul in Addis and at the same time I was getting serious food poisoning. I didn't take much interest in anything for the first thirty-six hours except for the location of the hotel toilets!

With the arrival of the boats we were transformed from a pointless bunch of tourists to an expedition again. We had a vehicle rented from the Ethiopian tourist board, complete with driver and interpreter, Mazengi, a cheerful, wiry man in his early thirties, who treated the Land Rover as though it were his own personal status symbol. His driving was atrocious but fortunately there wasn't much other traffic for him to annihilate us on. We also became the subject of numerous jokes which started at the airport and continued all the way to Bahardur. Most were along the lines of how long we would last on the river and a few were punctuated with long flapping arms mimicking the jaws of crocodiles.

The drive to Lake Tana was relatively uneventful and the road was actually tar sealed. At the Shafartak Bridge, a large concrete structure built as part of a Russian aid project, we had our first view into the gorge of the Blue Nile. The river itself was a long way down, a deep brown in colour and relatively placid. A more immediate threat was the sign on the bridge informing us it was moving and likely to cast us into the gorge at no moments' notice.

In the town of Debre Marcos the warnings continued. An Italian colonist who somehow had survived since the Italian invasion of Ethiopia in 1936 and its subsequent liberation by Orde Wingate and Haile Selassie in 1944, pointed out the consequences of the long walk out from the river back to Debre Marcos through what he described as hostile territory. Ominous!

Lake Tana proved to be a large circular crater lake, suitably placid and fringed by reeds. We at last launched our kayaks and I raced around and did a few rolls to impress the crowd that had gathered. My initial euphoria was somewhat deflated after a chat with the local doctor, a German who spoke better English than I. He pointed out that the lake was teaming with Bilharzia and that all the locals had this debilitating intestinal disease which was why they didn't rush around as much as us! One of the local boatman, however, showed an interest in our kayaks and we let him have a go. His boat was made entirely of papyrus from the reeds at the lake edge and was constructed to a time immemorial design that looked as if it came from the time of the Pharaohs. He proved to be adept and had good balance, an obvious legacy from poling his reed boat around the lake.

We retired to the local lakeside hotel to make final preparations and to eat our last meal of "enjara and wot" the local too-spicy lamb "delicacy". And to contemplate being in Africa and about to start on a fairly momentous event. I mean... I had spent the first roadside stop outside Addis Ababa gingerly stepping around in the grass looking for snakes! And where were the lions?

The next day we finally got going, sort of! At the outflow of the lake hundreds of people turned up to see us off including the local governor and his officials, conspicuous in suits and ties in the heat. Mike was photographed solemnly loading one of our ancient revolvers and I stood around sweating in a yellow and black rugby shirt that I had deemed tough enough for a would-be explorer. But it was hardly an auspicious start. Dave had spent a lot of the night fitting out his boat, glassing in knee bars, and was short on sleep. Steve, perhaps motivated by his work commitment, wanted to spend the day testing the radio gear. There was already a feeling of unease. The radios were Steve's agenda and not

Mike's. He wanted to get on with it as we were well behind schedule. It was September 3rd. and Mike had left Heathrow on 24 July.

Since this was long before the days of sensitive new age guys and conflict resolution, an argument ensued. I was in the dubious position of middleman since most of the conflict was between Mike and Steve and Dave. In the end Glen Greer took Steve's place for the 30 mile run down to the Tississiat Falls. There was a small hydro station there and a road ran parallel to the river. So Steve and Masengi were to take the Land Rover and meet us that evening.

By any standards that first day was a disaster. This was our shakedown trip except that Glen was paddling instead of Steve. The initial float down from the lake was livened up by an explosion of activity in a large eddy on river right. A herd of hippopotami surfaced like nuclear submarines and gave us a startling display of their rather large dentures. We were definitely in darkest Africa and I, there and then, decided that a kayak was a less than ideal viewing platform for such a large species of wildlife. Thereafter it was all downhill... We quickly discovered that we all paddled at different levels. Mike and I had a similar "go for it" attitude. Dave was as skilful but much more cautious and Glen was brave but struggling. Problems arose immediately. Dave and Glen wanted to scout from the bank. A timeworn adage and sensible (here you see the blind arrogance and invincibility of youth tempered by wisdom and hindsight!) but time-consuming. Some of the rapids were long and continuous class 4, longer than anything Dave and Glen had encountered before. So walking and inspecting miles of rapids was either difficult or impossible. The pressure was on to "boat scout" and keep going. This produced a lot of stress for Dave and Glen. Added to all this we had the 16mm. camera. The clockwork Bolex, Mike's pride and joy, and later nearly the cause of his demise. I did not even possess a still camera! Mike had discovered early, after Chris Bonington's stunning centre-fold photograph of kayaking the river Inn, that media coverage demanded visual proof, and spectacular proof at that, of one's claims to fame. I had tunnel vision in that respect. I just wanted to go kayaking and keep it as simple as possible.

So the scary business of paddling big water rapids in deepest Africa was compounded by the usual trauma of filming - black bags for loading and unloading film in the harsh tropical sun and waiting nervously at the top of some unknown rapid for the go signal.

At one stage the river bifurcated around a whole series of densely vegetated islands. This effectively put paid to scouting and we ended up running some big drops almost blind. It was at the bottom of one of these big drops that Glen disappeared for a while. His boat and paddle reappeared long before he came up gasping for breath a long way down-stream in the boily water. As a consequence his confidence was badly affected and he began to miss his roll. So the afternoon dragged on with rescues and tape jobs on Glen's boat.

At 11 degrees north of the equator night comes hard on the heels of dusk and 6 p.m. found us benighted, fortunately on river right, but a long way from the Tississiat falls. We tried to attract the attention of Steve and Mazengi in the support vehicle by firing our revolvers in the air! It was here that I made a very valuable discovery! Our ammuni-tion was not waterproof! The first four times I squeezed the trigger nothing happened. The fifth time produced a satisfying boom from the ancient revolver. Mike's performed similarly only firing on the fourth attempt. (I told you we were young and inexperienced!) So we walked to the road carrying Glen's lacerated boat and Dave's too. The support team had made the right deductions and driven up from the falls looking for us.

Another evening of regrouping with time for thought back at our lakeside bungalow. How many times can you keep weighing up the pros and cons of starting on a fairly daunting expedition? The next day saw only Mike and me take to the river in an attempt to finish the stretch down to Tississiat Falls. Glen had done his dash and it was obvious that the river was beyond his ability. Besides he had only come along as the support crew and wasn't supposed to be kamikaziing his way down rapids far bigger than he had ever paddled before and in a far-off land. Dave had had another evening of contemplation and decided that running rapids without scouting wasn't for him. Steve had come along on a different trip. He was there for the long run, for an extended paddling trip down to the Sudanese border. In this context he didn't see running individual rapids where there was a good chance of losing all the gear (and your life!) in the first few days of the expedition as part of his remit.

So it was left to the young and brainless to get back on the river. We had fun. No politics.... lots of scary kayaking and I ran my first water-fall... purely by accident. A complex set of big water rapids and my usual problem, impaired vision (I was still wearing glasses to paddle) meant one hand off the paddle to wipe the specs and "What's this horizon line thing?"... "Whoops here we go!"... A mere 20+ footer, nothing on the Shaun Baker scale but enough to get the heart pounding. Fortunately the plunge pool was deep and forgiving and I had time to paddle out and watch Mike frantically back paddling along the lip to a more sensible series of cascades on river left. We portaged one cascade without a second thought: a 25 ft. ledge drop with the whole river falling into the almost man-made looking hole running evilly across the bottom – the joys of paddling in volcanic terrain! Rather happy we pulled into the quiet water on river right above the Tississiat Falls, by the hydro station inflow. A crowd had gathered and the suits were there again. Lots of helping hands to get us out and a soggy cardboard box full of beer from our German doctor friend. It was soggy because we were a day late and the ice had melted.. but it was a nice thought.

That was the end of the nice bits. Mike had to switch from kayaker back to expedition leader of a rapidly diminishing expedition. Dave didn't want to go on and a harrowing shouting match ensued. Dave not unreasonably was frightened of dying and Mike, having organised the whole show and having control of our fragile purse strings, felt he was owed more commitment for his sustained organising effort. I guess that was the problem. Dave, and to a lesser extent Steve, didn't really own the trip. It was Mike's trip and they were merely the players. No, we didn't have a group meeting and appoint a facilitator – none of us had been to Outward Bound. In fact we were having our own group crisis right there and then but without any ground rules and with absolutely no strategies to resolve our conflicts other than hitting each other as they did in the days before anger management and conflict resolution programmes. Mike and Dave didn't come to blows – but it was close!

So-o-o we set off again next day, this time in the narrow gorge below the Tississiat falls. I guess recalling the angst has blinded me to the sheer majesty of it all. I mean, the Tississiat falls is actually the third highest falls in Africa and during the latter end of the monsoon is over half a mile wide dropping dramatically into a huge spray-filled cleft that runs at right angles to the river flow. Somehow all this water squeezes into a narrow gorge about 20 ft wide below the first Portuguese bridge, an ancient brick structure built during the Portuguese attempt to colonise their little bit of Africa. Now we were three, Mike, Steve and I, with our boats filled with 10 days' food, radio, camera gear, guns, spare ammo, sleeping bags, billies. The narrow gorge was rather boily, (that's squirrly to any of our American readers) and Steve immediately looped (performed an involuntary back ender) and cracked his fibre glass boat and proceeded to sink in front of the large crowd who had gathered to see us go, (fulfil their prophecies of imminent death!) or whatever. This produced another strained non–conference on the bank where tempers flared. Steve wasn't prepared to paddle with all the gear in the boat but neither was he prepared to set off into the unknown without it. A conundrum! In the end an unhappy compromise was reached where–in Steve, still with the vision of the long river trip to the Sudan after we had gotten the harder white–water out of the way, suggested that a bank support party make its way down the right bank with all the extra food for the 160 miles from the end of the gorge to the Sharfartak bridge. This we knew to be possible since the British Army Expedition in 1968 had "marched" to the second Portuguese bridge that marked the end of the major rapids, a distance of some 30 river miles. This plan gave Dave an "in" and he agreed to rejoin the team and walk with Steve to the sec–ond Portuguese bridge. So porters and guards were hired and Steve and Dave set off looking like Livingstone or Stanley with their bearers and guards, except that they were carrying kayaks. The guards were there at the insistence of local officials and each came with his own Lee-Enfield .303 and bandoliers of cartridges. Apparently the area we were going into was particularly lawless and in the sway of groups of Shifta bandits.. probably the same bandits that twice attacked the British Army Expedition in 1968. Glen and Masengi were going to drive back upstream to Bahadur and then take the high road to the Shafartak bridge.

Finally and at last Mike and I eventually got going. I think it is a great tribute to our sheer persistence and stupidity that we avoided so many opportunities to sensibly pull out. I guess it was now September 6th and we had been setting off for days! We were getting good, however, at packing and we finally elected for a sleeping bag and a pistol each. Mike got his Bolex and the spare film. By now he was trying to save weight by changing film inside his kayaking cag. at night. I got the radio. I wasn't particularly keen on this since you couldn't eat it and all it did was serve to keep us in touch with both bank parties who did have food. I went along with it however, since everybody seemed to think it was vital. I have subsequently developed a lifelong hatred for the things and have studiously avoided having anything to do with them. In the twenty-first century all would-be adventurers will be required to have micro chip radios surgically inserted into their bodies so that the newly formed World Park Rangers Association can track them on computer and worry about them from a distance. But the radio, with its dipole aerial became one of my little jobs. I had also taken it upon myself to hijack Mike's now rusting revolver and spare ammunition every day. I cleaned the guns but more importantly I tried to dry out the ammo every day, lining up our 49 spare rounds each in the sand to avoid the failures of our first evening. This simple ploy probably saved my life.

Oh yes, and we took some food! Not a lot: a large bar of Kendal Mint cake, an oatmeal block and a Rowntree's Jelly each. You can see why I thought edible radios would be a good idea.

More kayaking of the grade 4/5 variety (1972 grading standards!) led us 12 miles down the river to where it narrowed into a defile about 6 or 7 feet wide through which the whole river was squeezed, a bit like the Serpent's Tail (a North Wales First division slalom site), only two miles longer and quite a bit fiercer. We walked! With amazing foresight Mike had brought a few silver dollars with him and we managed to hire a rather bemused native who was tilling a small field near the river. He carried one kayak and we shared the other. He soon got into the spirit of the thing and shared his dinner with us... some sort of pre-boiled potatoes!

We got back on at the start of a serious-looking gorge where the river widened out but the walls were about 100ft. high and overhanging in places. Two hours of being frightened to death in there was quite enough and fatigue and the coincidence of gathering dusk and a convenient side stream cutting through the overhanging left bank combined to save our skins. It was 5 o'clock and about to get dark when we climbed up the steep rock, passing the boats between us. As if the situation wasn't serious enough Mike tried to finish me off by knocking a large loose boulder in my general direction. Only my lightning fast reflexes and a healthy fear off being killed caused me to dive to one side and hang on to the kayak. (Sound like Harrison Ford yet?) We spent the night under a tree which failed to ward off the standard evening rainstorm. I mean, it's OK to get wet all day on the river when the sun is shining but it's not fair when it rains in the evening and all you can do is lie in a wet sleeping bag and snivel. Coincidentally it was also Mike's 21st. birthday, hardly an auspicious occasion, but I guess it saved him from the monumental hangover he would have had to acquire if we had been in Britain. In the morning he confessed to having woken up with his revolver drawn and pointed at my head. Perhaps the strain was getting to us?

Came the dawn and we were able to see how lucky we had been. Peering into the gorge we could see that the next rapid, after our lucky and timely exit would have been just a bit too steep and difficult even for would-be heroes like us! Another portage and then back into the gorge for some solid class 4 with boils. Mike contrived to disappear on one eddy line in his supposedly boil-proof Olymp 4. Rather daunting. We alternated leads in a sort of rhythmic eddy hopping-dance until quite suddenly the second Portuguese bridge appeared magically in front of us. The bridge was amazing – a narrow Roman-style brick structure with two arches across the gorge, built by the Portuguese in the 18th. century. It did have a 20th. century alteration though. The centre of one of the arches was missing. It had been blown up by the Ethiopian resistance during the Italian occupation in World War 2. However it had been "repaired" by laying logs across the gap. As each generation of logs began to weaken and bend new logs were simply laid on top and eventually the sagging logs at the bottom of the pile fell into the river.

Mike and I pulled into an eddy on river left about 100 yards upstream of the bridge and found a bivvy spot in the rocks. We carefully hid the guns under a boulder, left most of our clothes behind, which was easy because we hardly had any, and sauntered on down to the bridge where we miraculously appeared much to the consternation of the small group of locals who were seated on the low stone wall at the end of the bridge. A group of three older men seemed to be in charge. They were armed to the teeth with World War 2 rifles and one of them possessed a revolver which he periodically took from his waistband to caress! They were the keepers of the bridge! Everybody passing over the bridge had to pay a toll and during the course of the next couple of days we got to see them in action. They struck me as charming brigands and their attitude to us was tempered by their contact with the army expedition of four years ago which had regrouped here after one of their members had drowned attempting to cross the Abaya, a right bank tributary of the Nile. The old guy in charge even had a business card from one of the army team. I think their previous contact with the army and our seeming penury probably saved us from any harassment.

Whatever, I made a great show of mounting the radio that evening.

Actually I didn't have much choice as hanging out 60 feet of wire in a north south direction is not something you can do surreptitiously! But back to my previous snide remarks about radios. They do not change fate. Glen was glad to hear us and happy that we had made it thus far. The bank support team however, were in strife. Their seemingly simple task of walking along the bank to meet us had turned out to be a epic journey of nightmare proportions. It was the rainy season and every tributary they struck was in flood. Crossing them involved hiking back upstream until the gorge narrowed enough to effect a river crossing. In that respect they were better off than the army expedition. The Army had had to resort to swimming ropes across the flooded tributaries and during one these manoeuvres, crossing the Abaye, one of their team, Ian Mcleod, had drowned when he couldn't quite manage the swim with the weight of the rope hindering him. He had been swept downstream and held under when the rope went tight. The bank team released the rope whilst at the same time another of the team, Roger Chapman dived in to save him. Chapman managed to get Mcleod to the bank but the rope frustrated his efforts and the weight of it dragged Mcleod out of his hands and down the river. His body was never found.

At least our team were carrying their kayaks and Dave was able to ferry the river-crossing ropes across with little risk. But in other respects it was hard going. Dave and Steve weren't used to hiking 12 hours a day through rugged terrain between 6–10,000 ft. and apparently their porters and guards were all relatives of Abiba Bakila, (the Ethiopian Gold medalist in the Marathon), or so it seemed to Steve and Dave who were struggling to keep up. They needed help! Mike and I looked at each other in amazement. They were the bank support team with all the food and porters. We were the half-starved sharp end of the team sitting miles away at the bottom of the gorge. What could we do? Hence my cynicism about radios.

As it turned out Mike and I spent the next two days on the bridge waiting for the rest of the team to catch up. We got up at first light and joined the throng on the bridge rather than having dozens of curious locals visiting our tiny camp. By means of much pointing up and down the river we managed to communicate to the old guard what we were about and they took us under their wing. We were only once visited in our camp by a rather shifty looking individual who had the look of a hungry hyena. We whiled our time away watching the donkey trains negotiate the rickety bridge with much tugging and beating to get the poor beasts to cross the log section. There was a degree of pantomime as various people tried to evade the bridge tax with claims of poverty. Good-natured banter would be replaced by dark looks until finally the chief of the old ruffians would meaningfully start caressing his revolver and the money would miraculously be found. I had decided that there was a great deal of bluff in the whole business as the revolver only had 2 bullets in its chamber. He could only really afford to shoot one person per decade to maintain his authority. But he had a gap-toothed grin and enough charm and manner to make the revolver a last resort.

Word soon got out that we were there and people started to bring their ailing relatives to us. This was a hangover from the army expedition which had administered first aid freely. Mike's department! Not too many medical students got clinics like that. But with a first aid kit out of a kayak there wasn't a great deal we could do. One 5 year old boy had a serious compound fracture of his right arm. Mike smeared it with the last of our anti-septic cream and tried to persuade the father to make the 70 mile hike out to the nearest medical aid.

Thus we had two days' rest and it was rather ironic on the evening of the second day to see the support team struggle down the hill and limp across the bridge to meet us. Steve was limping and using a walking stick and Dave seemed tired but wired! They had walked for four days and covered between 90 and 100 miles of very rough terrain. Steve wanted to rest but their arrival had produced a not so subtle change in the mood of the crowd on the bridge. Steve was wearing his .38 in a shoulder holster and Dave was carrying our shotgun. We obviously weren't as poverty stricken as Mike and I appeared. So despite Steve's protests we loaded the kayaks, said goodbye to the porters and shoved off into the river. Easy grade 2 boating…

We adopted the tactic used by Arne Robin on his attempt on the river, stopping to light a fire and cook before it got dark and before the evening rain but moving on a mile or two to camp in the dark. We were acutely aware that the British Army Expedition, much larger than ours, had been attacked twice on the next section of the river.

The first meal went fairly well, an evening of shared experiences healing some of the wounds between the group. But the next day shattered all that. The day started well enough, easy kayaking through a spectacular gorge with sheer rock walls and pinnacles but our sense of being over the worst of it was spoiled by a series of splashes in the water behind us, followed by the sound of rifle fire! My initial reaction was to paddle furiously until it dawned on me that salvation was not in my hands. I couldn't paddle faster than a bullet and our fate depended entirely on the marksmanship of the riflemen hidden up on the crest of the canyon. I remembered having heard that ammunition cost a dollar a round in the bazaars of Addis Ababa and I was hoping that the sheer expense of trying to kill us would be too great for another volley. Whatever the reason no more shots came and we lived to tell the tale! But there were ramifications from the attack. I felt obliged to tell Glen on our 5 o'clock radio schedule that we had been fired upon but were OK and in fact were probably 20 miles downstream from the scene of the incident. Unfortunately my message coincided with the afternoon electrical storm and Glen only picked the "been fired upon" bit. This information he relayed dutifully to the authorities in Addis Ababa who promised to despatch a platoon of soldiers to our aid! Oh dear! Perhaps they are still looking for us. Radios!

The attack also produced an atmosphere of fear in our evening camp. People were trying to kill us! So as well as the Arne tactic we also decided on having sentries. We each took turns to stay awake for 3 hours to make sure that we weren't murdered in our sleep! Here events took on all the appearance of farce. Poor Dave was so wired by the whole business that he stayed awake to make sure that the sentry stayed awake! Consequently he was getting less and less sleep and more and more agitated. And the African bush is not a quiet place at night. Our attempts at sleep were punctuated by Dave's "What's that?" at the slightest rustle in the trees. I think Mike was close to shooting Dave on his sentry watch!

Things went from bad to worse as the rapids eased off and we got to see the crocodile population first hand! We had seen a croc on the first day but it was relatively small, under 3 metres, and very far away in an eddy whilst we were out in the middle of the big rapids moving at speed. Here on the lower stretch of the Nile the situation was reversed. The crocodiles were huge, up to 6 metres long and the river was slow. Remember this is 1972 and we were paddling fibreglass slalom kayaks built to ICF regulations. My Prijon "Isere" was exactly 4 metres long. I had done my homework on the subject of crocs...saurians...the last survivors of the age of the dinosaurs...highly efficient...impersonal killing machines designed to scavenge the rivers for offal but capable of pulling a 400 pound wildebeest into the river with jaws that could exert pressure of up to 4 tons. In all the reading I had done there were only two recorded instances of people surviving crocodile attacks in Africa. One was a tribeswoman, taken whilst filling her water pot at the river's edge. The crocodile took her quickly and dragged her underwater through a mud and sticks tunnel into its nest and then left her for dinner. The terrified woman regained consciousness in the crocs' absence and was able to break out through the roof of the nest to stagger back to her village, covered in blood and mud, in time to disrupt her own funeral service – much to the consternation of her fellow villagers. The other case was a South African game warden who was taken in shallow water and with the aid of his companions was able to fight off the croc before it dragged him into deeper water. The ranger needed hundreds of stitches and was extremely lucky not to die from septicaemia. Armed with this information and remembering the incredible display of raw power provided for us by the hippopotami on the first day I had already developed a policy of shoot first and ask questions later. The British Army expedition had navigated this section of the river in high-sided assault boats from which you could leisurely whack a croc on the nose to make it go away. We had our hands in the water!!

A pattern quickly developed. Round the bend, small riffle rapid followed by flat moving water with a long eddy against the river bank. The crocodiles' territory. Out they would cruise from the top of the eddy and follow us down stream. Our first such experience saw Mike going for his camera and me pulling out the Webley. Both exercises involved taking off the spray deck, leaving me feeling especially vulnerable. The Bolex was slightly more complex than the revolver and I managed to shoot the crocodile before Mike had filmed it. He was upset but I remember thinking at the time it was a very one sided game and that Mike had too little fear or not enough imagination for his own good. Firing a .45 from a kayak required a two handed shot down the length of the boat to hope for any degree of balance and accuracy and I soon found out that the advice of the London Zoo keeper was good – you had to hit a croc between the eyes to stop it!

Dave was in a hurry to get the trip over and had taken to setting the pace. Unfortunately this meant he ended up a long way in front of the rest of us! This was nearly his undoing. A particularly large crocodile started to follow him and Dave tried to outdistance it. We only had three handguns and a shotgun. The shotgun was far too cumbersome to pull out of the kayak and assemble in an emergency so Dave was unarmed. As he sprinted for the bank the crocodile naturally gave chase and was gaining on Dave as he hit the beach. He ripped the spray deck off and ran for a low bank. (We were on the river at the same time as the Augsburg Olympic slalom. Any of you who were there may have thought you were watching the fastest white-water paddlers in the world....I don't think so! For my money Dave was definitely the fastest paddler in the world for a brief time.) The crocodile was much more interested in the kayak and Dave got away. Meanwhile we were trying to give chase and pull out our revolvers. Steve was wearing his .38 in a shoulder holster and with considerable courage paddled up to the croc and fired five shots into it. The croc sank from sight.. alive or dead, we had no way of telling.

As you can imagine the day intensified somewhat and every big eddy had its resident crocodile. Tactics became the order of the day. They had theirs, we had ours! The crocodiles all followed a similar instinctual pattern. They would surge down the river towards the nearest kayak until they were about 20 ft. away, at which point they would silently submerge and come on underwater. This left us with two options. I always tried to shoot them just before they sank, but if they sank too soon then there was a brief respite as croc and kayak played at triangulation. As soon as they sank we would paddle away at right angles and the croc invariably popped up at the last place we had been. This gave a chance for a second much closer shot before the deadly game continued and the croc submerged for another much shorter charge!

This pattern continued all day and if we weren't avoiding crocodiles we were being terrified by bits of driftwood that crocs are very good at impersonating. Late in afternoon Mike came up with a plan. He was still keen to film an approaching croc - told you - no imagination! So after much argument we came up with the defensive phalanx, Mike out in front filming the croc, Dave sat directly behind him flanked by Steve on his right side and me on his left with our guns at the ready to shoot the croc as it reappeared after its short submerged run! We opted to try this with a small croc! So when a mere 4 metre one appeared we went into action. Unfortunately this one wasn't fully conversant with the crocodile attack manual, either that or it was lost. Whatever, it sailed towards us submerged and, whilst we were all straining to see it appear in front, it swam under our little flotilla and surfaced under MY LEFT

ELBOW. This necessitated a cross-boat shot at a range of no feet. I changed from the two handed down the boat pose, let go with my left hand and shot the croc between the eyes. Difficult to tell who was more surprised - myself, the team all straining forward or maybe the presumably dead crocodile. I resorted to the vernacular "Fuck this for a game of Soldiers", feeling very thankful that the revolver had performed first time! Whereupon I refused to partake in any more attempts at filming crocodiles!

Our evening camp was a crocodile-free zone and it was a major relief no longer to need eyes in the back of your head. But we were all too wired to relax and I slept but fitfully. The next morning saw a repeat of the croc syndrome but gradually they tailed away as the concrete structure of the Shafartak bridge came into view. It was with a degree of relief that we dragged our boats up to the edge of the road. But boy! were we wired. We had to wait for the support Team to appear and for a Reuter's reporter from Addis Ababa whom Mike had organised. Mike whiled away the time showing off our shot gun to the bridge guard and impressing him with the noisy boom it caused. I got my one and only shotgun lesson and failed dismally because I didn't know how to flick up the barrel quickly to engage the triggers. Fortunately I had never been in a position to fire it in anger.

A hiatus. Mike wanted to go to the Sudanese border, our original destination. Dave had definitely had enough and Steve and I were dubious. I had been mighty scared of the crocodiles and thought it only a matter of time before they got one of us. We adjourned to a local village for coffee and omelettes. Not quite fast food though! Unused to having large groups the woman hosting us had to pick the coffee beans and roast them under our noses and likewise chase the hens around the backyard!

A night's rest didn't resolve our differences. Mike had gone away from the idea of continuing and Steve and I were sort of keen to continue. Tempers were running hot - I think we were burnt out! I might even go as far as to suggest we were all stressed out. Argument raged backwards and forwards whilst Glen tried to intervene and the Reuter's reporter took notes whilst trying to buy our collection of guns! (When we left he bought them all except Steve's .38 which went to Mazengi who had coveted it from the moment he first saw it). In a moment of almost rational thinking I counted our store of remaining ammunition for the two Webleys. We had fired 47 rounds between Lake Tana and the Shafartak Bridge, distance of 220 or so miles. Most of these rounds had been fired in the last four days on the crocodile-infested lower reaches of the river. It was another four hundred miles to the Sudanese border and we only had 53 rounds left! In the end we chucked the boats on the Land Rover and drove back to Addis Ababa. We had done our dash as a not very together team and we didn't have the emotional energy for the bottom end of the river.. besides, we told ourselves, assuaging our egos, it was flat anyway and it had already been paddled!

We went home in a state of numbness! Mike retreated entirely from the group and hardly spoke to anyone. Steve and I shared a hotel room in Cairo on the way home and had a good old heart to heart about life, the universe and everything. And we never really got together as a group again, I am ashamed to say!

I arrived back at the Leeds/Bradford airport on a Thursday evening and caught a taxi to the pub in town where I wandered in with a pack and a pair of paddles and caught the ever reliable Stan at the bar (perhaps he'd been there ever since I left?) for a beer and ride home. I was back in school on Friday morning teaching kids, a mere four days after dicing with bandits and crocodiles on the Blue Nile!

Footnote.

17 years after the expedition, on a visit from New Zealand to speak at the Mike Jones Rally in North Wales, I finally bumped into Jim Hargreaves again. He told me a strange tale. Upset at missing our trip, he had applied for and been accepted on an Army expedition to the Mountains of the Moon in Uganda. On the way home their plane had had to stop in Addis Ababa for minor repairs. Jim had used his time to scrounge a vehicle and come and wait for us at the Shafartak Bridge. He had had to leave the day before we arrived. So much for "political clearances" I thought.

NOT MUCH EXCITE-
MENT ON THESE
RIVERS...

JAN KELNER

When I first met Jan Kelner he was living on the Ice Canal slalom course at Augsburg - there was a rumour of his having a house and wife but .... My other German friends spoke of Jan's addiction, the fact that he needed at least two fixes a day on the Ice Canal. This dedication led to a phenomenal skill level. Jan is a "thinking" paddler: you can watch Jan working on a move and you can see the thought process, you can watch the development as he masters the manoeuvre. This knowledge and understanding of kayaks and water have led to his designing kayaks, originally by making suggestions to Graham Mackereth at Pyranha and then later with Eskimo. The Kendo is Jan's design as is the Zwo.

It was always a good idea to call in on Jan when he was out; this way you avoided having to go out with him on the Ice Canal - and be shown up as he played on the more ridiculous holes and pulled off the most amazing moves. Jan was pulling rodeo moves in Rotobats and Mountain bats before they were invented or named. Jan is a teetotal vegetarian but I have my doubts about this being for health reasons when watching him demolish home-baked apple strudel - he has a phenomenal sweet tooth!

Squirt boats reached Europe late; they took two to three years to cross the Atlantic. Jan bought one and six months later headed out to America and came second at Chilli Bar rodeo, California, in the squirt class. He had to learn squirt technique from a pirated American video; there was no one to learn from, no one to show him the moves. (He won the float class).

People say "Take him off the Ice Canal and he returns to being a normal boater..." They're fooling themselves.

BANDIT RUN

translated by Nicky Manby

I certainly would not have heard of Imatra, a small village about 150 kms north-east of Helsinki, near the Russian border, had I not made the acquaintance of Mr. Kokula, a very energetic tourist officer with a 5 star attraction in his area. In his letter and a brief video, he described the characteristics of the Imatra gorge. What is special about this river is not only the enormous volume of water (about 600 m³/s) which storms through a narrow gorge, but also that this natural spectacle is limited to only half an hour a day.

The River Vonski was dammed in 1929 for electric power generation. Only because of the tourists (or the money they bring?) are the sluices opened and only for half an hour each day. Up until now, no one had paddled the gorge, yet according to the local kayaking club it was thought to be possible. Small wonder I wanted to be the first to paddle the Vonski at Imatra.

Well, how to put this? Of course I went to Imatra, accompanied by Werner, like me a veteran of the Fast-Water-Festival, but long-haired, and similarly obsessed by the idea of thundering through the Imatra gorge with 600 m³/s of water!

On the journey there, Werner and I had plenty of time to discuss our chances of a successful descent of the Vonski. All we knew was that for about half an hour the gorge would be flooded with 600m³/s, but because the video lacked any scale and had been shot from a great height, we had no idea whether the waves and holes were one metre or five metres high. The information from the local paddlers was no more helpful: "strictly speaking, it must be possible". If so, why hadn't they themselves run the gorge?

A fellow traveller on the plane seemed to be interested in our excited conversation. Although he spoke no German or English and our Finnish was limited to "thank you", "hello", and "goodbye", a richly informative exchange was conducted. What we were proposing to do in Finland, we showed him with gestures; his answers were easy to understand and when I showed him a picture of the Imatra gorge, his expression changed – he could hardly stop laughing! "Imatra? Imatra?" He could hardly restrain himself. He showed us, unmistakably, what he thought of our plan – his swimming motions were all too clear!

Once we arrived in Imatra we were taken under the wing of the ever energetic Mr. Kokula. He had brought along a TV. film crew and so together we surveyed the gorge. Finally we saw it for real. "For real" was actually the wrong expression: all we had before us was a bone-dry, 700 m. long, 30 m. deep, and about 15-20 m. wide gully in a cliff. We had to wait a further three hours before, thanks to the graciousness of Imatra Electricity Works, we were allowed to see the gorge in its real, "natural" state.

We used the time to study the dry riverbed thoroughly.

From the put-in, it dropped off very steeply, threading through many boulders; the middle section seemed more moderate to us, but it was the final stretch that was certain to be fast and furious. The exit from the gorge was barricaded with great boulders, but the worst headache for us was here: a huge rock overhung into the bottom third of the gorge. What the gorge would look like with water – lots of water, 600 cubic metres of water per second – we could not imagine. Would this overhang be way under the waterline or far above the surface and therefore constitute no danger to us? Or would the water level reach the exact height of the overhang where it would be the most dangerous?

We did not have to wait too much longer to find out. The loudspeakers on the bridge played music to signal to the tourists that the show was about to start: a natural spectacle to behold, provided thanks to Imatra Electricity Works. A taped message in Finnish and English provided the spectators with the basic information of the Imatra gorge's statistics: after all one did not want just to be thrilled, but also to have one's intellect stimulated!

Finally, it started! The sluices opened very slowly. Mr. Kokula explained to us that it would take ten minutes until they were fully open, and exactly the same time once they began to close until the river bed returned to its Sleeping Beauty slumber. We therefore had only ten minutes to scout the entire gorge at maximum flow and arrive at a verdict!

Much more slowly than we had imagined, the flood wave moved down the gorge, very slowly filling one hollow after another; it crashed over the boulders in the lower part of the gorge, building up into spine-chilling stoppers and insuperable recirculations. A run at this level was unthinkable! But this was far from 600 m³/s! With an increasingly loud thundering, the water rose further and further and flooded these un-paddleable stoppers and recirculations. Our feared overhang could no longer be seen; buried deep below the water level, no longer constituting any danger!

We were standing at the bottom end of the gorge, when we finally saw the full flow. On the right hand side of the river the water was boiling: giant mushrooms of water were shooting up and swirling back down again, it was as though the water itself did not know where to go. It seemed this was where the water came to vent its pent-up rage.

We jogged back to the beginning of the gorge. Monstrous breakers on the left and murderous stoppers on the right, and a crashing weight of water - it was just what we had been dreaming about for ages. Looked at objectively, it was not an insoluble problem: technically we could manage the 700 metre run, just as long as we avoided the biggest obstacles; we were tempted. We would, however, have to get through the monster breaking waves, but all that could happen here was that we would receive a watery slap in the face or be turned over a couple of times. Still, we trusted our Eskimo rolls!

From the bridge at the entrance to the gorge we clearly saw our put-in point. Although the water level was already going down, we did not think that we would encounter any great problems here, even when 600 m^3/s. was flowing.

So, no real reason why we shouldn't attempt the run! However, I already felt uneasy. Logic and gut feeling are not always in agreement and my heart had sunk quite low! Despite the safe, solid self-assessment, the 600 m^3/s. and its terrible thundering had made an impression on me. I had had the same weak feeling in my stomach as the first time I ran the Bockschlitz at Pegel. Meanwhile, the gorge lay dry again, and the spectators who had thronged the banks had left, looking elsewhere for entertainment. Werner and I agreed - we'd run it tomorrow; in exactly 24 hours it would be behind us! As we were fixing camera positions for the next day with the film crew, Mr. Kokula came towards us with a very official-looking man.

"May I introduce you to the Vice-president of the Imatra Electricity Works? He has something to say to us." Mr. Kokula had a very contrite impression. We guessed something was wrong.

"Sirs, my legal division has recommended me to forbid the run, for reasons of your safety."

"Can he do this?"

"He can", Mr. Kokula assured us.

"Why?"

Here follows a brief extract of the subsequent discussion.

"What do you mean 'dangerous'?"

"You could capsize."

"Of course we could capsize, we can't guarantee we won't, but we can also roll up again, if necessary, with our hands even our ears!"

"You could bang your heads if you capsize!" (The man had no idea.)

"Bump our heads? In that volume of water? How? Where?"

He stuck to his "expert opinion" and his decision.

"No! Too dangerous! It is our responsibility after all, it is we who flood the gorge!" He left us morose, Mr. Kokula deathly sad, and the film crew disappointed.

"We can do it. Let's do it. Let's run it anyway!" Mr. Kokula was not allowed to know anything about it, officially, and therefore left but with us in a better mood.

A local kayaker, who had followed the whole story, warned us: "When the sluices open, there are security guards with walkie-talkies all along the gorge. They are meant to prevent would-be suicides - I mean real suicides - plunging into the gorge. So watch out that they don't catch you. I won't tell anyone."

What a farce! One accepts travelling for hours, one overcomes one's inner cowardice and makes the positive decision and then something like this happens! If they have made wild-water paddling in this area impossible by building the dam, they should at least let us have the water for this one half hour! If the dam was not here we could paddle through the gorge with no complications, and nobody forbidding us! Now we had to plan how to get past the patrols.

That night sleep did not come easily. My heart kept pounding, whether in anger at our "expert" friend the Vice-president, or in excitement at the prospect of our first descent, I'm not sure, probably the latter. The tension would have been only half as bad, if the following day we could simply have packed our boats, warmed up with a gentle paddle and then set off down the gorge. But no - the water is only released at 7.00 p.m. - a whole day ruined! Werner did not seem troubled by this: he lay next to me, snoring. Or perhaps was it a deep unconsciousness because he could not quite handle the excitement either?

The next day did not begin that badly at all; the weather was certainly pleasant and we received an invitation from the Imatra Canoe Club. They would be delighted if we would join them for some training with the young talent on their home course "around the bridge pier". We were happy to oblige and were surprised what tricky and fantastic gate combinations were arranged under the bridge. At least the morning was saved.

The hour of truth was drawing ever nearer! We scouted the ground once more, this time paying particular attention to find secret get-in and escape paths.

6.30. p.m. For strategic reasons we parked the car with the boats immediately behind the police; from here it was only 150 metres to the put -in. We changed into our paddling gear so as not to waste any time later. Over this we put on our raincoats - to disguise our intentions. Then we mixed with the rest of the tourists.

Security guards really *were* posted along the bank, one of them only 30 metres from our proposed put-in. Our attention, however, was on the gorge which was slowly filling. My heart was in my throat! Not a pleasant sight greeted us: a gigantic compression was just below our put-in, and directly under the bridge a giant stopper was building that we had completely overlooked on our first inspection. We were uncertain what to do. In a few minutes 600 m3/s. of water would seethe down the gorge, and unless we acted immediately, it would seethe without us.

We decided at least to storm the put-in with our boats: once there we could still chicken out.

With innocent expressions we strolled back to the car, past the guards, and then everything went into overdrive; raincoats off, boats on shoulders and sheltered by a small slope, off to the put-in. We were immediately visible to the watchers. Although the river-guard must have seen us, he did not react. It was only when we were climbing over the railings that he realised what we were up to. When we ignored his shouts, he dashed after us. Werner only just avoided his grasp by a daring jump from the slope into nettles; a brave move when you realise that he only had his shorts on. I, too, barely escaped the guard's capture. With lightning speed we leapt into the boats and pushed off into the eddy. Now we were safe, at least from our pursuers, but only a few metres away from us huge volumes of water were barrelling through the sluices. Despite this, our nervousness had blown away. The compression which would have made entry into the current almost impossible a few minutes earlier had disappeared; problem No.1 had solved itself!

Problem No.2, the huge fat stopper under the bridge and out of sight – the gradient was too steep – could now be avoided. Anyway chickening out was no longer the issue!

Now it was each for himself – in the thrashing water in the gorge, neither of us could help the other. On the contrary, if we were both in the same stopper at the same time, it would be really dangerous. We had decided, therefore, to leave a couple of minutes between our departures.

I had to ferry across the main current far enough over to miss the "Overture Stopper". At first I thought I was not going to make it, then a surf on a lateral pushed me past it. I stayed on the left side of the river and missed the next, smaller – or more accurately – less big, stoppers. I was shot through the canyon at a colossal speed; it felt as if I was fired from a cannon. The first breakers crashed on to me and a giant wall of water built up in front of me. I plunged into it, held only for a fraction of a second, then this mountain of water exploded and I was catapulted into the next wave. Then my thighs felt cold and I realised that my spray deck had come undone in all this action, off for a little length – I hoped it would not come off completely in the next stopper. I still had two to go if my grey cells were still working! What had to happen, happened; the next wave broke over me, the spray deck burst off completely, my boat half-filled with water and with a hooray! I was into the grand finale. Actually nothing could have stopped me with all my speed and momentum and I passed through the last monster hole unharmed at a safe periscope depth. My relief was endless as I paddled out into flat water. Done it!!! In fact it had been straightforward, looked at objectively. Nonetheless, a gigantic weight had been lifted off my heart which lay, now much lighter, back where it belonged. Spellbound I looked for Werner. He too must, by now, be looking back upstream. But before I could glimpse him, applause and cries of jubilation from the tourists told me that he had been successful.

Together we let ourselves drift a couple of kilometres towards Russia, just to be safe – we had no idea what the mood of our river guards was. As we floated downstream Werner told me that his run had not been without incident. Right at the top, he had failed to miss the "Overture Stopper" and had been dumped upside down (despite all the earlier assertions to the contrary, he had not hit his head!) Because of the swirly eddy line it had taken him a long time to roll back upright. He had then to paddle the rest of the gorge out of breath. We agreed that another run through the canyon would be great now that we knew what was what but we had to dismiss the idea, firstly because of the river guards and secondly because the Imatra Electricity Works had let the river run dry again!

When we arrived in Munio, the venue for the Fast-Water-Festival, we were greeted with a hero's welcome. They had heard about our bandit run run and also had late news that the Imatra Electricity Works were refraining from prosecuting… They really were so-o-o kind!

"MAYBE THIS JUST ISN'T YOUR RIVER"

ARLENE BURNS

Arlene signs herself as "Freelance adventurer" at the end of her e-mails. She was the first person to ask me if I had an e-mail address, saying it had changed her life. It was the only way if you were always travelling - having freelance adventures - to keep in touch without a real address. The trouble for the recipient of these e-mails is that they arrive without exotic stamps which let you know where the sender was when they were posted. From Arlene's e-mail you always get the impression that she had stopped for just long enough to download her post and mail out replies before travelling on to who knows where. These missives from the ether would tell either of the trials of getting zoning to put up her yurt in Oregon, or of the trip to Mexico, or of commentating on the "Survival of the Fittest" TV show in British Columbia or of her upcoming trip to New York. I suppose knowing where she had stopped to log on is immaterial; it would be a fleeting visit.

I heard about Arlene from friends. Whit Deschner had done a river trip with her in Nepal; Dan Dixon "Greystoke" worked with me running trips down the Coruh; Slime talked about her; a photograph taken by my friend, Reg Lake, of her tying her kayak on a car was used to advertise Perception Kayaks. This was before e-mail; eventually her mother managed to forward her a letter inviting her to come and give the evening lecture at a Mike Jones Rally. She came and told this story of trying to paddle on the roof of the world. A slide show to a crowded audience wanting a few laughs before rushing off to the pubs before the beer ran out is not the easiest audience to address, let alone silence. She mesmerised it. Leaving aside the stunning slides, the tale is one of endurance and determination and at times just plain survival. I doubt whether many of the audience that night weren't affected by the lecture.

For those who caught her lecture, here is a welcome revision course. For those who have not heard the story, here it is - both the physical endurance of getting to the river along with the spiritual side of the journey.

TRESSPADDLERS

The Search for the Tsangpo's Source.

I was fourteen when I first studied a map of Asia. Having just taken up kayaking on a lazy South Carolina river, I was captivated by the vivid blue streak on the map that contrasted boldly against a pale yellow wash: the Tsangpo River as it flowed across the Tibetan Plateau. I dreamed of kayaking that blue streak, but for a girl who had barely set foot out of the Deep South, Tibet seemed as remote as Neptune.

Twelve years later, during a winter trek across Tibet, I encountered the Tsangpo as a reality. The frozen river carving through endless desert landscapes was even more dramatic than my childhood imaginings. My fascination returned, this time as a nagging curiosity. By now I knew that the Tsangpo (Brahmaputra in Hindi) was one of the few great rivers on earth so remote that it had not yet been fully explored. I also knew that the Chinese government demanded a $500,000 permit fee for its first descent.

As I journeyed back to Nepal, I could not shed the fantasy of exploring the river. It also seemed possible that distant border guards would know nothing about Beijing's marketing strategies, but the only way to find out was to show up at the border, acting on the premise that it would be easier to obtain forgiveness than permission.

Dan "Greystoke" Dixon was the only expert paddler I knew in Nepal at the time and I easily convinced him to join me. The first time I ever laid my eyes on Greystoke, he was falling through the air above a gravel driveway. I lunged forward to help him but he didn't need my help. He made a perfect barefoot landing and ambled off in his black Speedo swimsuit, not bothering to look back at the school bus from whose roof he had just leapt. Now, a few years later, Greystoke seemed as fit and crazy as ever. We talked for a few minutes, and I had a partner.

From Kathmandu we travelled to the border town of Kodari with 200 pounds of boats and gear. Warily, we approached the frontier; the moment of reckoning had arrived. We each filed out the obligatory forms: one Casio wristwatch, one Nikon camera, one kayak. When the officials queried us about this last strange word, I quickly clarified: "one PLASTIC" kayak. Yes, they had heard of plastic. They opened the gate to one of the wildest adventures of my life.

We begged our way onto a loaded lumber truck, which soon growled and seesawed up hairpin switch backs, climbing 7,000 ft in twelve miles before the radiator expired – just as a blizzard struck. When the storm finally abated at three a.m., we bundled

"GREYSTOKE"

up into our bed of lumber and snow and bumped ahead toward the high passes of the Himalaya. Stars filled the moonless sky, illuminating the vast white wilderness. Dawn's arrival coloured this with a radiant pink glow on the towering rock walls and ice faces that stretched as far as the eye could see.

After traversing the roof of the world for another full day, we crossed the Tsangpo, hundreds of miles downstream from its source. We were dropped off in the nearby village of Saka, which looked more Chinese than Tibetan. Bored soldiers played drinking games outside unadorned barracks. The Tibetans wrapped in furry skins seemed like refugees in their own land.

After three days of searching for a ride towards the Tsangpo's source, we learned that our road west had been closed for nine months. We had nearly resigned ourselves to putting in at Saka when a convoy of Chinese geologists arrived. They were heading toward sacred Mt. Kailas, close to the river's source, to search for gold. With four all-terrain army assault trucks, they felt omnipotent and decided to ignore the rumoured "non-road" conditions. They agreed to let us ride on top of their supply truck to a village near the source.

Also hitching a ride with the convoy was a penniless Austrian on his way home from Hong Kong. It so happened that he was carrying a letter he had promised to deliver to Kathmandu from some cyclists he had run into in Southern China. He felt bad, as he had never made it to Kathmandu, and still had the letter. Something was sounding strangely familiar and I asked to see the letter. Addressed to me, the letter was from my boyfriend, who was somewhere in China en route for Hong Kong, in the midst of a seven and a half year round the world cycling odyssey named the "Too Tyred Tour". He wanted me to meet them in Bangkok on my birthday in mid June and cycle with them to Singapore. He had no idea that I was in Tibet on a little adventure of my own.

Days passed as we headed west. Often the road dwindled to a faint track; sometimes it vanished altogether beneath shifting sands or into bridgeless rivers. Occasionally we sighted nomads following grazing herds of yaks and sheep through the barren desert. If we stopped to ask for directions, we received answers of dubious merit. At one point our truck broke through the ice and grounded on the river bed. We spent several hours hacking it out, only to move a few yards and break through again and again.

Westward we went. The blistering sun parched and devoured our skin.. For two days we had not seen any nomads. The road had vanished; the sobering truth of our situation revealed itself: we were lost.

Fuel and food had diminished to critical. Our convoy limped aimlessly through this vast wasteland. Incredibly, the geologist and the drivers had no maps of the area. I presented mine, drawn fifty years before by an Indian yogi, and my impressions of our position. The Chinese were not impressed by the ancient scribblings. Though I knew intuitively that we were now heading in the wrong direction, it seemed most reasonable to remain with the convoy.

One evening, as a sub-zero darkness fell on the desolate 18,000ft tundra, all four vehicles bottomed out simultaneously. We were lost; we were stuck; we had gone beyond the point of no return, meaning we didn't have enough fuel to get back the way we came or perhaps the courage to deal with the melting brittle ice across major tributaries again. These had already cost us several days of non-movement and nearly the loss of our supply truck, as its tyres dangled in open water while its belly straddled the ice.

Tensions surfaced and flared. Around midnight Dan and I woke to a chatter of Chinese voices and the revving of truck motors. We were being abandoned! We scrambled into the frigid blackness, sprinting in the thin lung-burning stratosphere after the departing convoy. On board were our kayaks and all our supplies and food. I ran haunted by the lingering image of the two naked, freeze-dried bodies we had passed in the desert, pilgrims who had not survived their sacred pilgrimage to Kailas. In the wild west of Tibet survival is a harsh reality and the odds are against it.

Predictably, our truck got stuck in the soft not so permafrost, and we were able to catch up. As we climbed aboard, the Chinese pretended their departure was some kind of grand farce. I encouraged my irate companions to quickly cool their jets and let it go... There were no courts or administrators of justice here. They needed one little excuse to eliminate us. Strange to witness the manifestations of desperation.

We continued climbing up the permafrost toward an obvious pass. Wild horses sprinted by as we cleared the top. Then instantly, we spotted Mt. Kailas among the distant peaks! Both Hindu and Buddhist traditions consider this 22,028ft peak to be the navel of the earth, the centre of the universe. Four of Asia's greatest rivers (the Tsangpo, the Indus, the Sutlej, and the Ganges) radiate from its near-perfect pyramid and flow in great sensuous curves to the far reaches of Asia.

As the convoy descended into the sacred drainage, we realised that our hellish reliance on the convoy would soon be over. They discarded us at the base of Mt. Kailas and motored off to the south.

Still separated from the source of the river by 100 miles of desert and two high mountain passes, we had little food and no means of transport. There was not a rent-a-yak for miles. But how could we be anxious? We were camped at the base of the most sacred mountain in the world, the dream destination for millions of devout Hindu and Buddhist disciples. My mind still held fresh the image of the two naked pilgrims, shrivelled and baked brown by the unforgiving sun. Not enough water to rot.

Our best option seemed to be to proceed to the sacred Lake Manasarovar. At least our boats could serve us there. If we paddled the sixteen miles directly across the lake to its south-eastern shore, we could ascend the Tag River Valley and climb over two 18,000 foot passes. After portaging our gear for over 100 miles, we would then be able to descend into the Tsangpo's glacial headwaters. Once this was more water than ice, we could commence paddling. It seemed a reasonable plan… But in retrospect, we must have been suffering from oxygen deprivation, hallucinating, to even think of setting off in that direction.

As we approached the shore of the sacred lake, my breath left my guts and climbed into my throat. It oozed a rare desolate precious beauty. I shivered as I felt its sacredness and started questioning the appropriateness of profaning the pristine waters with our kayaks. The Hindus believe that one immersion will cleanse you of all your sins: past, present, and future. I wondered if they would look upon two western paddlers as a source of spiritual pollution.

I truly did not know what was right to do, so I climbed the cliffs above a nearby monastery and sat for hours, lost in thought. Surrounded by this incomparable idyll of water, desert, and glacier peaks, I asked myself what "sacred" really meant. What are the sacred icons of our Western 'civilised' society? The one that popped to mind was green and had numbers in the corners and some president solemnly reminding us of his value. Here in Tibet, we had never even been allowed to purchase tsampa, the roasted barley flour that is the entirety of their staple diet. Food itself was sacred, and if someone needed it, it was given, not sold.

Greystoke climbed up and found me on my perch. Impatient, he informed me of his intentions to cross the lake, sacred or not. Was I with him? I decided to go to the shore and ask the first pilgrims that we saw what they thought. If they said good, I would go. If they said no good, I was staying put. It was now out of my hands.

The first pilgrims arrived shortly after we had dragged our kayaks to the water's edge. They were curious about these strange plastic wings and examined them thoroughly. When I queried them in my primitive Tibetan about kayaking in the lake, they looked at me with smiling eyes and gave an exuberant "thumbs up", the Tibetan gesture for "good". My decision was made!

I slipped into my kayak and launched into the turquoise water, feeling as though I had just entered a diamond crystal. The water was so clear that I could not tell if the bottom was 15 or 50 or 500 ft beneath me. A shiver of excitement pulsed through my veins as we keyed our sights onto the distant Tag La and paddled toward the centre of the lake. As the monastery faded in the distance, I casually noticed fluffy little clouds prancing across the heavens. By the time we had neared the midpoint of the lake, ominous black masses converged from the four directions, leaving a hole of blue sky directly above us. I felt a sinking dread as the hole was enveloped by a violent blizzard. Snow swirled into the tumultuous liquid abyss. Spray from huge waves coated us with ice, and I soon lost all feeling below my elbows and knees. I had no idea how my hands were maintaining a grip on the slippery paddle shaft.

I had been paddling substantial white water for more than a decade and had never felt so insignificant. Battling for balance amid the seething waves, I grew light-headed and extremely fatigued. The remnants of my conscious mind kept reminding my failing body to keep paddling to stay warm. Acutely aware that a flip at this point would be fatal, I knew that my survival lay within my own frozen hands – and within my will to not give up. Amazingly, our bodies' reaction to cold after the initial uncontrollable shivers was to want to just go to sleep. I could feel my body sliding in that direction. It was as if I was paddling within a dream, a hallucinatory state of warped reality, of unending undulation, of ice. Even though we paddled forward, it felt as if we were getting sucked backwards, as the winds were so strong that the waves outran us. When we could surf them, our gain was tremendous, and Greystoke was a marvel in the waves which carried us nearer and nearer to the far shore.

As we at last neared the shore, the winds shifted and began to blow us back into the lake! This sudden shift was utterly debilitating and again opened the door of demise even further. I paddled with all that was in me and barely inched forward. It seemed so close and insurmountable, but finally, numb, frozen, and exhausted after the seven hours crossing, we stumbled onto the rocky beach. Greystoke erected the tent and I collapsed inside it.

But the storm continued its assault. We huddled in our tent for nearly a week. The poles bent and broke; the fly shredded in the howling holocaust. We were under relentless siege. The winds must have been around 100 miles per hour, as movement was impossible. We ate tsampa and Indian baby food (the staple of Greystoke's larder). Greystoke counted the squares of ripstop that sheltered us. Interesting where the mind goes when the body is trapped in a cage of storm. I wrote a few letters in the tiniest print I could manage on the little bit of paper I had, and wondered how and if I would ever mail them, and what journey they would take... The mind plays games with the mind plays games with the...

I thought about my life, old friends, childhood traumas; what had formed me and plopped me on this path that maybe ended here in the sacred realms of western Tibet. What if I had taken that other fork in the road, and become a housewife and mother, living in American suburbia? Stripped of every imaginable security, I had ample time to contemplate the meaning of my life. Alas, the storm broke before I figured it out.

Wind and snows abated to a tolerable level, so we packed up and began our slog up the Tag River valley. It was impossible to carry our kayaks owing to the wind and their 100 lb. weight, so we set up a simple harness system and dragged them behind us. We definitely needed a beast of burden – just one yak – to help us with our load. We spotted wisps of smoke up in the distance and excitedly proceeded up the valley with visions of yaks, food and human beings dancing in our heads. After two days we reached the source of the smoke: smouldering sheep or yak dung that had combusted in a deserted encampment.

I was devastated.

Our food was running low and the weather was as foul as my mood. To reach the nearest source of provisions, we still had to drag our kayaks over two 18,000 ft passes and then descend back into an altitude that was habitable. We had stashed food in Saka, but that was a world away from here. If the weather allowed, we were looking at a minimum of fifteen days on foot, BEFORE we got in the river! It seemed to me that we only had five days of tsampa left. I mentioned my concerns to Greystoke. "I can go for fifteen days without food, no problem" he announced. Perhaps he could, but I knew my own limitations. Our little jaunt was beginning to feel like a death march, and I could not see the point of continuing with hopes that manna would fall from heaven. In order to survive, we had to stay together: we had one tent, one pot, one stove, and two inadequate sleeping bags. I offered it all to him, knowing that I had good chances of finding pilgrims along the lake shore. He headed on alone.

Maybe he missed my singing, but he did decide to turn around and met me as I was descending the Tag River, now frozen over with a thick to thin layer of ice. I was so relieved to see him, as I thought otherwise I would have been the last human that had. But each must make his own choices.

Again we attempted to enter the lake, opting for a shore-hugging route to the other side, but another storm's intensity froze water mid air and coated us with so much ice that it was nearly impossible to make any progress. Forced to retreat to shore, we set up our remnants of tent

and started counting the squares of ripstop again.

Greystoke and I opted for a plunge into the sacred water to appease the angry gods. When my head broke the surface, my hair was immediately frozen solid, and could have been broken off like an icicle! Then we waited....

Suddenly, the ferocious winds died. A sacred stillness enveloped the wind-scoured landscapes. The wild lake soon held no ripples. A mirror image of Kailas stood steady on its crystal surface. We packed up and launched into the essence of silence. There was absolutely no sound, of man or machine or wind or beast. It was as if we had gone deaf.

My very breathing seemed a harsh intrusion into the utter stillness. The waters enveloped me, empowering me with humility, awe and a deep deep peace. We had run the gauntlet and now nature was reaching out to guide us. Surely we would now be allowed safe passage.

As we approached a monastery on the southern shore at the base of the 25,000ft Gurla Mandhata massif, a large (relatively speaking) crowd of monks and pilgrims awaited. I was unsure whether we would be greeted or attacked for being in the lake, but we definitely needed some human contact and desperately needed food. As I scanned the shore, incredibly, one of the faces was familiar. Sonam! We had met this Tibetan weeks ago in Saka and spent a evening attempting to refuse cup after cup of his potent barley wine.

Sonam told us that the road we now intended to hitch-hike along was used about once every nine months to service a hermit's cave, and advised us to stay put at Thugolho Gompa until the Rinpoche (a recognised reincarnated lama) arrived. Perhaps he could arrange transport for us? But when would he arrive? THREE... was it three hours? days?? weeks??? months???? We were learning the patience game and slowing down to the time of fate.

We stayed at the monastery (for THREE) where Sonam spent many hours with us. Though we shared limited mutual language, we seemed to have no barriers in communication. He was on his way to the Nepalese Border, with plans to escape and seek refuge in Nepal or India. His companions were smuggling out ancient Buddhist treasures to deliver to the Dalai Lama. All they possessed they carried with them, and they generously gave us gifts of their precious belongings and food. I was astounded and deeply touched by their level of generosity. Their attitude of non-attachment manifested in a perpetual flow of what few material items they treasured. A bit different from going shopping for a friend's Christmas present.

The twenty-three year old Rinpoche finally arrived. He sported a "Shanghai" baseball cap and cradled a boom-box playing squeaky rock-'n-roll. My expectations were shattered by this anachronistic character. He smilingly summoned us into the inner sanctums of his monastery and showered us with gifts of dried cheese and coffee. He then clearly informed us of his wish to kayak in the lake!

A congregation of astounded expressions gathered on the shore and nervously chanted while rubbing the wood off their prayer beads... I held my breath with a similar anxiety while Greystoke interacted the Rinpoche on the fundamentals of the sport. Knowing that Tibetans have no experience in learning to swim, this was a grave situation. After the Rinpoche emerged a bit wet but unscathed, the monks and pilgrims all wanted a shot at it and more than one had their sins washed away with full-immersion dunkings. Sonam during his turn took off way out into the lake, way beyond the safety margin if he flipped, and all that I could do was watch the tiny figure fade into the mirage of desert and water and pray that he didn't tip over. We live on that knife edge between life and death, sometimes fully aware of it, and other times blissfully oblivious.

The Rinpoche offered us a ride (in what we had deemed the "rimp-mobile") to Purang, a village near the Nepalese border a full day's drive to the Southwest. We loaded out boats and ourselves into the back of a truck which already housed thirty-three Tibetan women! They had just completed a "cora" or circumambulation of the lake, and despite the bone jarring lurches through the boulder fields they laughed and sang and giggled and poked. We were so packed into that truck, that again I lost all feeling in my arms and legs, but this time it was due to the Vienna sausage phenomena instead of the cold. We topped Gurla pass and dropped into the spectacular terrain of the Purang area. Here, the Tibetans reside in exquisite cliff dwellings and caves. Mesa Verde was alive before my eyes.

We set up our camp in the corner of a courtyard that seemed to serve as the transport depot, and immediately became the centre of the town's attentions. My blue eyes and dirty blonde hair were features they had never seen, and they marvelled and giggled and poked. They exclaimed in Tibetan "Your eyes are like water, your hair like the sand". Maybe they were saying full of sand, which was certainly true as well. They pulled and stroked the strange phenomenon of hair on my arms, and pulled back my lips to check out my teeth as a horse trader might do. I don't know what they were expecting to find in there, but I certainly gained insight into the perspective of a caged zoo animal.

When not searching for supplies and transport, we explored the ruins of an old monastery above Purang. All that remained were fragments of windswept walls covered with faded Buddhist frescoes. All of the eyes had been gouged out by the Chinese soldiers. The Tibetans believe that the eyes are what give a painting its soul. The Chinese were clear in their intentions.

One night Sonam discreetly approached us, his eyes wide with a scare. He had overheard some Chinese soldiers that were drinking in a bar. They planned to arrest us in the morning, hoping to extract a huge ransom for our release. Sonam had already arranged transport for us with some of his new Tibetan brothers, who understood the torturous techniques used by the local soldiers.

Covering our kayaks with yak skins, we fled Purang at dawn. The truck headed north on the only road out of town, and our driver prepared us for soldiers' road blocks and gave us a signal that meant "run". After two days, we arrived at a town called Hali, or Sishwanga, which was a Chinese military outpost on the upper Indus River. Somehow we had managed to escape one problem and land in another. To make matters worse, we were now closer to Afghanistan than we were to the Tsangpo. We considered descending the Indus.

We decided to give it a few days, and if we couldn't find a ride east and south, then we could stock up on food and launch into the river going west and into the thick of Muslim culture. At the last minute, a truck full of Tibetan traders offered us a ride in back, so off we went!

For nearly a week we bounced through the wild deserts of central Tibet, enduring freezing nights, scorching sun, bone-jarring kidney-bruising jolts, and a piercing dust-spiked wind. We eventually arrived at the Tsangpo River at a ferry crossing somewhere downstream of Saka. We stumbled off the truck and collapsed at the water's edge. Since leaving Saka and our food stash, we had spent thirty-eight days wandering around Tibet, and now we were downstream from the place we had started!

But at last we stood before the river, ready to paddle down the long-lost river of my childhood dreams. We soon discovered that all of the bolts and nuts securing our foot braces, seats, and walls had vibrated loose and fallen out. Who cared! Drifting and paddling in states of weariness and bliss, we now moved within a smooth and gentle flow. Our boats were transformed from cumbersome cargo into precision "river Porsches".

The Tsangpo snakes its way through the arid deserts of south-central Tibet. Traditional villages colour the banks, and inquisitive people often followed us for miles, astonished at the strange sight. Days and villages soon passed in a blur of the sun's rising and setting. We were asked to search for lost yaks, warned of hazards ahead, asked to deliver supplies, and even asked to transport people. (But when they discovered the tippiness of our kayaks, the would-be passengers quickly found an excuse to remain on shore.)

Rounding a bend one day, we discerned the ruins of a fort with a beautiful monastery at its base. A sea of curious people surrounded us as we landed; as we had come from Mt. Kailas (although not by the most direct route!), many people touched our boats and bodies as a surrogate blessing.

Escorted by an amiable monk, I visited the monastery, feeling as though I'd journeyed into an ancient age. Intricate Buddhists paintings, framed in silk, draped the walls. An old monk sat cross-legged, chanting his mantras. Yak-butter candles emitted a soft glow in the darkened sanctuaries.

Whisked quietly into a special hidden chamber, I was shown ancient carvings that had survived the Cultural Revolution. I was witnessing first-hand, the art, spirit, and soul of the Tibetan people. I departed amid a symphony of chanting monks, their deep voices reverberating like rolling thunder and howling wind through the silken chambers.

Each day we paddled, often not missing a stroke for two or three hours. My body became a machine, my mind ran free. I sang every song I knew and drifted to the ends of the Universe and back again. Since I had left Nepal, nearly two months ago, I had been in a state of isolation and inadvertent meditation. I had been living on tsampa and water (with the odd bit of baby food), yet never had I felt so strong, so clear, so alive. The desert that once seemed so inhospitable now felt welcoming. My soul found home in the wind-sculpted mountains, with their subtle shadings of red-brown earth in tapestries of pattern and light; in the brilliant blue sky twirling into star-filled universe; in the dwellings and people of a land so unlike my own.

I began to understand the Tibetans' harmony with their environment and the peacefulness of their timeless world. Their strength and gentleness invigorated me, leading me into another dimension. This was the gift of the Tsangpo, of the hardships and isolation.

What one discovers is often altogether different from what one seeks. Our kayaks were a means, yet by no means an end. To let go of expectation and surf the wave of change is the essence of any adventure. To be open to constant change, the only constant. All we are is our response. All we can do is try to respond with clarity and integrity, to ride the wave with grace, to maintain a fine balance in motion.

After over 100 miles on the river, we reached Shigatse. A convoy of yak-skinned coracles (traditional Tibetan boats) drifted by us as we pulled our kayaks onto shore. These were the Tibetan equivalent of Grand Canyon boatmen. They would carry their boats upstream, load them with juniper or supplies, then float back downstream to market.

I had lost all track of time. When a bumbling biker nearly flattened me, I suddenly remembered my birthday date with my biker boyfriend in Bangkok, three days hence! The time had come for me to say goodbye to Greystoke and the river. I turned south with visions of Thai food dancing in my head.

I planted a prayer flag in the fierce wind atop the pass separating Tibet from Nepal. After a long and thoughtful gaze to the north, to the past, I bowed deeply and jumped onto a truck heading south. In a rainy fog with no windshield wipers or headlights, brakes sounding like a metal rasp, the truck shuddered down those same deadly switch backs we had ascended an eternity before. The lush green, the smells, the full force of monsoon season, the sounds all overwhelmed my senses. I was living in a dream

The end of one journey is merely the beginning of the next. Back in Kathmandu, I traded my battered kayak for a mountain bike and caught a flight to Bangkok. After a bout of Hepatitis (contracted in Tibet) I cycled to Singapore, then continued my wanderings to New Zealand and the South Pacific. Never a word did I hear from or about Greystoke… Did he get hepatitis too? Was he still alive? Did he make it through the notorious Tsangpo Gorge?

Ten months later, while skiing in Telluride, Colorado, I was wiped out by a crazed skier. Tumbling in a powdery tangle, I gripped my leg in searing pain as we ploughed into a snowdrift. I was about to utter stern words when a familiar voice rang in my ears.

"Ar, Ar, Ar".

Greystoke!! Licking me like a St. Bernard puppy, he told me his story. He had continued down the river from Shigatse, paddling alone through a steep gorge of treacherous white-water where portaging would have been even more dangerous. He slept in caves during the day and paddled at night, sure that the Chinese were still after him.

After his kayak was stolen from the river bank near Lhasa, he returned to Nepal and began making his way back to the States.

I have heard rumours that Greystoke's kayak is being used to ferry people across the river in Lhasa. Perhaps one day some curious Tibetan will journey downstream to explore the unknown lower gorges of the Tsangpo. Perhaps he or she already has…

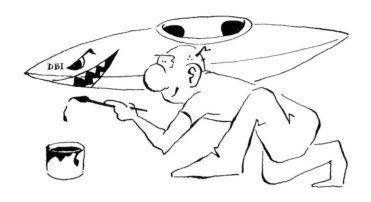

DONALD BEAN.

Where to start? For anyone who has met Donald, he needs no introduction – money changers in Katmandu recognise him four years on. He stands out in the world of canoeing. (Though he paddles a kayak he will have none of this Americanisation of the English language). I first met Donald way back when he must have been a mere youth, in 1979 at the first Mike Jones Rally I organised in North Wales. He was one of the 200 hardy souls who turned up on that cold January weekend to paddle the Dee. On the Saturday night we had a film show in the Town Hall and at the end of the show, after I had thanked everyone for coming and was packing up, this slightly built man came up to me and offered his thanks to me for running the event and hoped that I could make it an annual event. You remember people like that, dressed in a suit and tie with his trademark trilby hat on his head; he stood out from all the others' jeans jerseys and trainers. He was the one paddler who came and said "Thanks". Four years later, when Pete Knowles and I were running our first "Çoruh River Trips" in Turkey, Donald approached us saying that he could not take two weeks off work concurrently but would like to come for one week. This did not fit with our plans and so it had to wait until 1985 for Donald, now retired, to come on a trip down the Çoruh. I met the group at Erzurum airport, where Donald saw me in the waiting crowd, doffed his trilby at the guard – oblivious of the uzi machine gun he toted – walked over, and explained that he had to go back in (past the uzi) to collect his luggage. The guard – dressed in full combat gear, helmet and flak jacket and standing in the full heat of the sun when it must have been at least 35°C in the shade – shrugged his shoulders and allowed him back in. Twenty minutes later we were safely in my minibus driving down the tarmac airport road to Erzurum and Donald remarked,

"This is exciting!"

"Not really," I replied thinking of the road (if you could call it a road) alongside the river that we would drive later that week.

"Oh it is. You see I've never been out of Britain before, except in the army and that was not going abroad – that was just moving Britain

73

abroad. The tents were arranged the same as in Stafford and the food was the same. It was just hotter and more flies."

This was when Donald was 65. A few years later on another Çoruh River trip I saw Donald get swept into one of those micro eddies that form at the top of a headwall. Donald, never the most aggressive of paddlers, was never going to paddle out of this eddy. I was sitting in my kayak in an eddy on the opposite side of the river and watched the situation develop. Donald, true to form gave it a go; you could see all the patient coaching from Sammy Crymble and others come to the fore as Donald paddled up the eddy, leaned downstream on his paddle and was immediately swept back to where he had come from: he did not have the speed to exit the eddy. Not to worry, Donald repeated the manoeuvre with the same result. Several attempts later, Donald, tiring now, tried again; this time he capsized but was far enough out into the stream not to return to the eddy. Donald has much practice in swimming, an almost daily occurrence on the Çoruh in my experience. He has it down to a fine art: given the choice of two people to rescue I'd choose Donald every time. He is organised. He will exit his boat, after an attempt at a roll, allegedly 100% reliable in the pool but seldom seen in anger; then, holding on to his paddle, he will make it to the rear of his kayak and await assistance in the handbook-approved manner. This is what he did on this occasion. We watched as the bow of Donald's vertical boat bounced down the long head wall.

"Where's Donald?" asked one of the other customers, not au fait with Donald's habits.

"He's at the other end of his boat" I replied. Just then Donald's Boat lurched upwards about 3m as it/Donald hit a submerged obstacle and Donald appeared, just, still holding the kayak and paddle. Later, after he had been rescued, Donald came up with another of his gems.
"Gosh, that was exciting!"
"You had us worried there", was all I could reply. "No, sometimes I think swimming down the rapid is more exciting than paddling it - you should try it some time Dave," Donald, totally unfazed, commented.
"Weren't you scared at all down in there Donald?" asked one of the party. "Oh no! You see I do yoga every week and it is the Yogic philosophy of life that my mortal body may die but my Yogic soul is immortal and will live forever! So don't worry."

"It worries me! If you should die, Donald, think of the newspaper and media flak I would get, taking a 69 year old down a grade IV-V river."

Logical as ever, in his own way, Donald replied, " Oh don't worry about that, I want to carry on paddling as long as I can and I will write explaining this and exonerate you from all responsibility." (He duly did and I will continue taking him on trips.)

Donald, before he retired, was deputy Treasurer of Staffordshire County Council, an accountant from the Old School where his word is his bond. I am sure Donald cannot tell a lie. His accounts of events, particularly the size of rapids, may be economical with the veracity, but this is not deliberate; it will be the way he will have seen the event; that hole he went through was the biggest hole he went through though perhaps not the biggest on the rapid as reported. In 1992 he received a MBE from the Queen for "services to the community", and also accompanied some of the Duke of Edinburgh Award students, whose canoeing expedition in France he had assessed, to St James's Palace to receive their Gold awards. The same year, despite being 71, Donald was on the British Youth Expedition to the Grand Canyon (see below). Whilst waiting in Flagstaff we were in a cafe having breakfast and after serving Donald coffee the waitress remarked that she loved his accent.
"Where are you from?" "Great Britain," replied Donald, explaining at length and with great pride about the British Youth Expedition.
"Gee and I bet you've met the Queen!"
"Yes, I did earlier this year" was Donald's reply, oblivious of the waitress's mocking tone which quietened her attitude!

This inability to lie, no, that's the wrong word, this inability to tell you something that he is not sure of, means that I could not get Donald to tell me more about the three big trips he did in the 1930's. He cannot remember the detail and without his note books/diaries he cannot confirm what he thinks he remembers. A pity, since, from what I have pieced together from little anecdotes from around camp fires on river banks over the years, they seem to have been much more than just a long paddle. But then, what seems exceptional to me now was commonplace to Donald. He gives a unique view into the past. Donald has no prejudice. Either the status quo or change as it happens are accepted with Candide-like equanimity. His accounts of the past are told as they were; seldom with a judgement of the past or the present implied or stated. He seldom gives an editorial comment.

CANOEING: A LIFETIME'S INVOLVEMENT

1932-1999 and still going strong.

I commenced canoeing in 1932 aged 12 and have canoed ever since subject only to a few breaks, as when I was away in the army for six years (1940-1946). It was only after my retirement that at the age of 65 I was able to increase my canoeing activities and really "spread my wings" to encompass overseas touring on classic white water rivers.

Canoeing in the 1930s

It all started after the old Stafford Boat House under the former old brine baths closed down because the level of the nearby river Sow had been considerably lowered to reduce the risk of flooding in Stafford, with the result that the remaining few boats, which included one old open canoe were up for sale. My elder brother, a friend and myself bought this big old heavy wooden canoe built on the lines of a rowing boat. Obviously we enjoyed the fun of messing about on the river and soon replaced this canoe with a galvanised sheet steel open canoe, which was much lighter, easier to repair in the unlikely event of damage, and which had no seams to "weep" after being left off the water during periods when not in use. Very few of these galvanised canoes were produced as they did not prove popular and ceased being manufactured.

Younger people, and I include those born since the end of the war, can have little idea of changes since before the war, particularly in matters affecting travel, canoeing and other leisure activities. You now get out the car, or maybe use a minibus and trailer, and you are away, be it to some British river or even to the continent. Indeed you hardly think twice, unless there is concern as to travel costs or the family, about booking a trip to canoe in Nepal, India, the Americas, New Zealand or elsewhere in the world - you literally buy a ticket, jump on a plane and fly away, often knowing that a canoe can be hired at the destination.

Not so however in the 1930's. The early 30's were the age of horse and cart and railways, and to a lesser extent canals, some of which had started to become derelict and overgrown with weeds. There were few cars, and these were owned by a very limited number of top executives and the few wealthy members of society. Railway travel for our triumvirate was expensive, because our canoe needed a complete goods wagon! Canals too could be fairly expensive as there seemed a multiplicity of separate canal companies e.g. Trent and Mersey, Shropshire Union, Staffordshire and Worcestershire, Birmingham canal Navigation etc., all of which issued their own permits and charged tolls as they saw fit.

All our group's canoeing in the 1930's was in open canoes. There were however also kayaks which were either plywood type construction, or canvas on either fixed or folding frames. Normally, where transport by rail was involved for kayaks, whether plywood or canvas fix or folding, provided they could be transported in the guard's van of a passenger train, whether or not accompanied by passengers, they would be charged for by the weight. Canvas canoes on a folding frame packed into bags weighing not more than 60 pounds would normally be accepted without extra charge as part of a passenger's personal luggage.

Our group did not use kayaks for various reasons, partly because on our tours we camped out, and kayaks did not have the space to carry enough equipment etc., but also because local rivers were generally shallow and a bit rocky, with plenty of barbed wire fencing about, so kayaks could be easily damaged. Although kayaks had cockpits, there was no cockpit coaming and hence no spray decks. Eskimo rolling was introduced into Britain in about 1938 but only on a demonstration basis.

So in the 1930's our group paddled mainly on the local rivers and their tributaries, in our case the Sow, Penk and Trent and their various tributaries. Whilst still at school and enjoying our school holidays, we did a number of long canoe camping tours, for example:

(i) Stafford to Great Haywood (River Sow) and on to the Trent, paddling through Nottingham and Newark-on-Trent, and returning by the same route.

This was the first and longest of the trips, about 1934, undertaken in August, in the depth of the economic recession, when money was particularly scarce, particularly for schoolboys! We paddled for about four weeks, and commenced the return journey some distance after

Newark-on-Trent. We deliberately allocated more time for the return than the outward journey. It was a hard paddle back, not only because of the current, but also because in places, particularly in the upper reaches, the river was choked with weeds which had not started to be cut. It was heavy going, requiring a number of clothes lines to help tow the canoe back up some of the rapids and using a home made trolley for some of the overland portages. We looked enviously at the Trent and Mersey canal in those upper areas where the river and the canal were in the same valley, but the cost of using the canal was prohibitive to us. In those days most of the lock cottages were occupied by a canal employee, and we would not have gone far without a canoe permit, purchased in advance. We camped out at nights, and followed our set procedure of finding a farm house or similar, and asking if we could pitch a tent for the night. This gave us the opportunity of stocking up with water and often also food – eggs, milk and potatoes were often donated to us and were seldom refused: generally we were made very welcome and occasionally finished up with a free meal at the farmhouse. On occasions we gave short canoe trips to children and others of the host family and generated quite some interest. We carried a primus stove and paraffin, so except with specific approval we did not light fires or burn wood. We met very little other traffic. This was mainly downstream of Nottingham, and consisted of a few pleasure craft as well as barges. The weather was hot and fine and we did a lot of river swimming, notwithstanding the heavy pollution.

(ii)   Shrewsbury to Stourport by the River Severn and back to Stafford by the canal. Our canoe was wheeled to the former Stafford Railway Goods Depot, loaded onto a goods wagon and taken to Shrewsbury Station, which, conveniently, is almost above the River Severn. We paddled down the Severn to Stourport then back to the Stafford area using mainly the Stafford and Worcestershire and Shropshire Union canals. This was our most expensive trip, due to the high cost of rail transport for the canoe and paddlers and fees for the canal companies. The river trip was interesting though uneventful, and I do not recall seeing any other traffic on the river. We transferred to the Staffordshire and Worcestershire Canal at Stourport, where barges and other craft join, or leave, the River Severn a short distance above the first (top) weir on that river. On the canal it was relatively easy until Wolverhampton, with its "flight" of 21 locks, which we had to portage

- heavy work this was. How we would have welcomed an empty barge going in the Stafford direction on to which we could have loaded the canoe and its equipment as the easiest way of dealing with so many locks so close together. (Bargees were generally the most friendly and helpful of people, particularly to fellow boaters). Then followed the worst part of the journey - from Wolverhampton to Stafford area. This was semi-derelict, and choked with weeds, making the going very hard work. I do not recall any volume of traffic on this section, but seem to recall that the odd barge did go through. In all, we were probably away for a fortnight or maybe less.

(iii)Stafford to Llangollen and return. This was by canal using the Trent and Mersey, Shropshire Union, and Llangollen canals and also involved being towed through the Harcastle tunnel at the end of a "train" of barges. This journey saw us paddling across the Froncysylite aqueduct - a fantastic experience and not repeated for some 60 years by the author. The Trent and Mersey canals were very busy carrying a lot of heavy industrial traffic such as coal and clay for the pottery industry. Indeed, various locks were the double chamber type so that as the boats went through only half a lock of water was flushed downstream. But after turning off on to the Llangollen arm of the canal it was a different picture - the canal was almost derelict, choked with weeds and in places half-filled with tipped rubbish and other obstacles. I do not recall any traffic until the Llangollen area, and then this was all pleasure craft. The trip took about two weeks, including the return trip, the journey time being helped by the use of an outboard engine except where the matte weeds and obstacles made its use problematic, but there were still quite a number of locks to portage, each of which necessitated partial unloading and reloading of our considerable equipment and food. I recollect that it seemed to rain every day.

In the 1930's holidays for workers (other than top executives) were one week per annum, plus bank holidays, so from when I left school (one of the lucky ones to get a job), until I entered the army in 1940, no more trips over a week in duration were possible. Overseas journeys were just not an option then with the prohibitive cost of air travel which was not particularly developed before the war. We did however canoe most weekends for a large part of the year, as well as on summer evenings. Also in about 1938 my brother acquired a second-hand Ariel motor cycle, which provided a temporary distraction from canoeing activities. I was his normal pillion passenger.

Pre-war canoeing was mainly limited to Grade I and II rivers and capsizing, except at unloaded fun sessions, carried quite a stigma and was also to be avoided because of the risk to damage to the craft and loss of valuable equipment. It would be quite an eye-opener too for young canoeist to study the B.C.U. "Guide to the Waterways of the British Isles", first published in 1936 but now somewhat obsolete. For instance, (from the 1970 edition):

Page 64 "It (the river Sow) offers a convenient route to the Trent from Stafford Station, where many main line trains stop. The most con venient starting point would be the public tennis courts immediately across the bridge facing the station but the grounds-man may object and, unless permission has been obtained from the park's Superintendent in advance, it is best to turn R on leaving the station and start from the triangle of waste land immediately below the weir 300 yards away." (This triangle of land has been a petrol station from at least 10 years before the reprint!)

Page 189 " While the (Welsh) Dee has the reputation of being a difficult river, it is not until Glyndyfrdwy is reached that difficulties of any serious nature are encountered. The best stretch, from the sporting canoeist's point of view, is that from Glyndyfrdwy to the Horseshoe falls. From there to Llangollen is generally regarded as too difficult and is best avoided by transferring to the canal". (This "tail to Town" stretch is by far the most popular stretch these days, becoming seriously crowded on "open" weekends)

There were few canoes/kayaks, or canoeists in the 1930's and our group were probably the only ones in Stafford. We had no involvement with competitions, but then there were no local clubs, and slalom had not been developed. With the open canoes portages could be a problem and trolleys were popular - either bought or usually home made from old pram wheels and axles. There was little inherent buoy- ancy in these craft but capsizing was avoided. I cannot recall "luxury" items like wet suits, helmets, or even lifejackets or buoyancy vests until the 1950's.

In the 1930's although many of the rivers were heavily polluted, risk of the polluted water to all and sundry did not seem to be publicised, and no precautions were taken when swimming in the river, canals and lakes. This was quite a popular form of recreation in the summer time till the early war years, by which time levels of pollution had escalated, and such swimming was seriously discouraged.

Also at this time despite conditions of extreme poverty, one seldom thought about "poverty" - the chance of theft was so minimal.

Almost unbelievable now, on their marriage women employed by the public services (schools, local and central government etc.) had to cease their employment - a practice suspended during the war and rescinded following the cessation of hostilities. The rôle of family was paramount. Even so, few ladies seemed to become canoeists, though there certainly was no reason for this to be so.

People created their own leisure-time activities. Television had not come out yet and the wireless did not take off until about 1927, after which its development was rapid. I remember our first "crystal" set and headphones; then later wirelesses with valves using car type batteries, before they too were superseded by transistors.

Most of the street lamps were gas lit, electricity taking over later. Obviously calculators and computers were a post-war development. One cannot stop the march of progress, be it for better or worse.

Unfortunately due to my absence during the war, my relative youth before then and the wholesale destruction of documents, it is now a matter of some difficulty to recapture moments and reflections of my younger days. Memory over so many years is naturally neither complete nor infallible though in haste it can be highly creative!

My canoeing since the war until my retirement from work is best described as one of "steady progress", without however anything partic-ularly spectacular occurring.

My Canoeing Abroad since my retirement at age 65.

My retirement, at Easter 1985 from my job as an accountant gave me a chance to "spread my wings", not only in canoeing, but in other activities too. In fact I retired a few months before my 65th birthday to enable me to join an international expedition to north-eastern Turkey with Dave Manby and others, canoeing the Çoruh River from way up in the Pontiac Alps for some 200 miles to near the Russian border. It was fantastic, with enormous water, and in a part of the country remi-niscent of Biblical times. This area so close to Russia had been, until a few years before our expedition, a militarised zone, with no foreign tourists, and we were very much a tourist attraction wherever we went. This expedition certainly stimulated my appetite for overseas white-water expeditions.

1992 was my 60th canoeing anniversary year. I had decided before-hand that this was something special in the way of canoeing, perhaps unique, and the idea of "pushing the boat out" was a somewhat obvi-ous decision. Things started in a small way when I canoed French white-water with a group from Southampton. This was followed by an expedition, my fourth, to Turkey with Dave Manby, travelling overland with in an old Transit from Great Britain, picking up en route in Istanbul and Ankara other paddlers who had flown in from the USA, Nepal, and New Zealand, a truly international group. The trip was for seven weeks and we paddled on four rivers. After the heaviest snowfalls for sixty years, heavy thunderstorms and rain, rivers were in heavy spate and not unnaturally I along with others did some swimming.

Before leaving for Turkey I had a phone call late one evening asking if I was interested in canoeing the Colorado river through the Grand Canyon in the USA. Member No12 of the 1st British Youth Expedition had dropped out at a very late stage; they couldn't find a replacement youth with the necessary experience/cash, so would I like to fill his place? The answer was "Yes", thought this did mean cutting the trip to Turkey short. I first met the group at Manchester airport, feeling almost an interloper, particularly as the next oldest member was eighteen (mostly they were seventeen year olds). We canoed the Grand Canyon, all 225½ miles, in virtual wilderness conditions, with breathtaking scenery, terrifically high volume water, monster rapids, and high temperatures - 115° F one day. I tackled most of the rapids, swam in a few others - there was no shortage of rescuers. Everything was very successful and I shall long remember this expedition and the privilege of joining eleven highly motivated energetic youths and the experience of not knowing what might happen next!

This was followed by an expedition to Nepal with Chris Dickinson, commencing on the 4th October, just after the end of the monsoon season, when the water was huge with long wave trains. We canoed the 170 miles of the Sun Kosi and Sapta Kosi - both sacred rivers. I had only two swims throughout!

The final expedition of my jubilee year was to Costa Rica, canoeing through the rain forests some 10 ° north of the equator, and commencing in November. I was the only British canoeist on this expedition, organised by the Nantahala Outdoor Centre. How did I get on this expedition? Easy. I knew the two leaders, Dan Dixon and Diane Troje, having canoed with them in Turkey in 1989. We paddled the Rio Sarapiqui, and Rio General, one on the Caribbean side and the other on the Pacific side of the country. We had a lot of torrential rain and I now know why they call the forests "rain forests". Once again these were raft supported trips and we were looked after really well at the campsites.

Conclusion.

(Donald insists I include this. Ed)

Firstly I would like to thank Dave Manby for introducing me to overseas white-water canoeing expeditions. After Turkey in 1985 and other trips with him abroad, he has certainly changed for the better what my retirement, after a busy professional career, might have been, and widened the boundaries of my experience considerably.

Secondly, although I was awarded the B.C.U.'s Award of Merit and Award of Honour in appreciation of my contribution to the development of canoeing and of my services to the sport of canoeing, these services are still ongoing and canoeing is still my main continuing interest.

I've weathered well, but at my age I still cannot lightly miss opportunities where I can successfully participate and continue to enjoy the challenge, excitement and adventure which white-water kayaking provides, notwithstanding the possible dangers in the sport. I may be having one last fling, but haven't I been saying this for some thirty years? Each trip however is not only one trip more, it is also one trip less, unfortunately.

FRANCESCO SALVATO

This is not really an introduction to Francesco, it is more an explanation as to why the piece reads as it does. I have not corrected the English. I read this when it first came through the post and loved it just as it was. The original piece just made me stop reading and think of what was being said "..... the still very bounded Tibet" is far more powerful than ".... the closed borders of Tibet". I then took the piece and corrected the English and smoothed the awkward words that stop you when you are reading it and then reread the piece. I had ruined it. I had taken away its charm. I had removed its soul. This stopped me. Obviously my corrections were at fault. I worked at it again, I tried other alternative words, I used a thesaurus and dictionary, rephrased and re-ordered bits and still could not capture the feel.

I sent the article to Whit and gave it to my parents to read. They all agreed with me. Whit's reply sums it up beautifully in a round about way.

```
 "I went down to Boise to sign books at the spring sale and
didn't sell a one.  After that I went up to the S. Fork of
the Payette where everyone seems punched out of a mould:
fit, 30ish, driving sport utility vehicles and all doing
tail spins etc. ... It was cold and I had borrowed gear and
watching everyone get ready and talking was sort of like
watching a bunch of evangelical Jesus freaks.  So I sat out
instead.  I don't know Dave.  Watching this zoo wasn't what
the sport ever was to me.  I think it's Ali Baba and the
40 thieves where they discover all the jewels in the cave.
That's what boating's always been to me, remote and magi-
cal places: Seeing all these yahoos there was like being in
the cave with all those jewels and having them yelling out
for everyone and their illegitimate brother to come and get
'em.  Anyway, enough ranting and raving.  I was trying to
get to the Karnali piece you sent.  I agree with you: Don't
kill it with an editor's pen. He is describing exactly what
finding all those jewels is about.  If you are giving intro-
ductions to all these pieces introduce it as such: it's the
heart and soul of the sport."
```

This is just about what I have done. I have tidied bits of it and altered little bits for clarity but to large extent it is as written

Oh, by the way, Francesco is a hideous excellent paddler.

HUMLA KANARLI

translated by Carla Decker

The aeroplane jerks on the landing strip lifting a huge cloud of dust and then, buzzing like a big blow fly, leans right and becomes a small dot while it flies towards Nepalganj and the Indian plain.

We are in Simikot, a small village in North-Western Nepal, centre of the Jumla district in the heart of the Himalaya. This massive chain, 2500 kms. long, with its perpetual snows and heights standing out as far as the eye can see, is considered by its folks as the house of the gods.

For Hindus, it was the creating god Brahma who drew up the "great wall" of mountains and here he made the holy rivers flow. The spiritual centre is Mount Kailas which Vishnu settled in the middle of the universe as a pillar between the sky and the earth while Shiva chose it to raise his throne.

According to Buddhism, that made Tibet its reign, Mount Kailas represents the altar of the Buddha. Stuppas, Buddhist temples, with their shape, imitate the features of the mountain. From the four sides of Mount Kailas rise the holy rivers: Indus, Brahmaputra, Suttlej and Kanarli.

We remain in Simikot three days waiting for our kayaks which can be brought only one at a time by the small aeroplane. The village leans on the bare slope of the hill; the houses are on different floors linked with stairs carved in logs and on the roof stand yellow sheaves of straw ready for the forth upcoming winter. Walking in this maze of terraces and courtyards is like being in a timeless magical world.

Women have a proud glance and faces covered with ornaments that clash with their poverty while men, with an absent look, smoke "sulba" or spin wool using gestures centuries old.

The children look like elf, mysteriously appearing and disappearing with bodies naked or wrapped in rags and with faces covered with dust and dirt which has become part of their lives.

3rd December. We start to descend the 1000 metre gradient that will lead us from Simikot to the river, 50 kms from the source of the Kanarli in the still very bounded Tibet.

The copper-coloured sides of the mountains stand out on the crystal blue painted sky which is also a background for the tapering profiles of the cedars.

We leave Simikot with three porters who will take care of our kayaks and, while we walk out, the whole village stands on the side of the road to see us go away.

After a few hundred metres we get to a fork on a ridge, the porters stop and start to discuss. We understand that the subject is the direction to take so we wait for them to make a decision. The time runs but no agreement seems close so we intervene trying to make them understand where our destination is. Communicating is a hard job and with an Anglo-Italian-Nepalese conversation close to the grotesque, we get to the conclusion that the shortest way cuts down the slope on the right. The descent is so steep it seems it hangs over the river which meanders twinkling through the valley. At the beginning the track looks in good condition but it gets steeper and unstable as we walk down. We understand that we have gone the wrong way but it is now too late to go back.

Suddenly we hear a deafening sound breaking the Himalayan silence: Giorgio's kayak is bouncing down the slope like a tennis ball, the porter has slipped and has let the kayak go. Giorgio can't move and stares at the point where his kayak disappeared thinking, as we all did, that the boat must be destroyed after the 400m high drop.

The slope gets even steeper, I scream Giorgio to run down as far as he can to get the boat while Gianluca and I start to let our kayaks down using ropes. It is hard to stand, and so, not to slip, we are forced to get hold of some branches covered with resin that sticks everywhere. Our kayaks are filled with gear and supplies we need for the 10 days descent of the Kanarli and it is not easy to get them down in this situation. The porters look at us manoeuvring the ropes and carabinas, curious and fascinated, it is all so strange to them that they must be thinking that we must be using some kind of magical art.

On the steepest stretch of the track Gianluca and I are leaning on a big tree, the two kayaks are under our feet and the porters are holding on to our legs; this is when one of the two Nepalese boys asks "Sir, where is your country?" Gianluca and I share an astonished look and then start to laugh so hard we can't stop, thinking how lucky they are with their deep faith in destiny.

After a couple of hours we reach the bank of the river and find

Giorgio seated with his kayak that has a 30 cms. cut behind the cockpit and a broken dry bag.

After a few minutes of discouragement we inaugurate the repair kit but not long after I cut my hand deeply with the knife. We have to leave the repair kit and open the first aid kit and after having stitched both the kayak and the hand we feel self-satisfied thinking we have everything we need for a river trip!

We decide to put on, the shadows are already long on the sides of the mountains. It is late but our need of paddling the Kanarli is too strong, and the boats slide into the water moved by our first, shy strokes. We do not forget, anyway to ask the river god for his assent to paddle in his reign.

In 1987, with the help of the Nepalese Minister of Tourism interested in maybe using the river for commercial trips, an international expedition guided by Peter Knowles and Mick Hopkinson had run the river for the first time. Since then the lower part of the river has become a classic descent for the rafting companies while the Humla Kanarli has stayed untouched with a reputation of a hard descent. After 1987 only a couple of Americans have tried to run the upper Kanarli again with a cataraft but they ended up with a 20 days-long nightmare filled with long portages before getting to the confluence with the Tila.

Six years from Peter Knowles' descent we are the first kayak expedition to face the Humla Kanarli. We feel the load of this responsibility but in the meanwhile we are also impatient to get in touch with the river.

The description of the Humla Kanarli we find in "White Water Nepal" and Slime's accounts did scare us, but now we are so close to the water we are looking forward to live this trip fully.

The first night, we spend it in a hut of branches, caught us out with the severe cold and in the morning all our gear is frozen and covered with frost. But the worst surprise is the theft of my shoes and I cannot stop thinking about the portages and scouting I will have to do bare foot. I decide to transform my chancletas into sandals and start to cut the neoprene socks and sew them to the rubber sole; they will be handier than I thought!

The water is ice cold, around 4 degrees C., and our hands become stiff on the shaft of the paddle, I go back to when I was packing my gear in Italy thinking that the water of Nepalese rivers were never too cold!

After a few kilometres we get to the unrunnables, huge rock slides had fallen on the river creating confused piles of stone obstructing both the water and any kind of kayaking ambition. The reports of the first expedition described these rapids as V–VI but, according to my opinion, there is a lot to discuss about this subject. We portage, walking laboriously through the big rocks of the bank of the river, red granite with some grey striations. We have chosen not to have porters' support on the bank, opting for total autonomy and freedom. Our idea is to run as much of the river as we can, portaging each rapid we cannot paddle, keeping the closest possible contact to the water. Our boats weigh 50 kgs. each and portaging becomes exhausting; the second day of the trip we end up paddling about 40 minutes out of 8 hours of work.

The next day we leave the unrunnables and face the long rapids that move through the big rock gardens, with light green water that shades to blue and becomes bright white, wrapping us up in foam while we are paddling.

Downstream the hills we have seen bare and yellow in the first days, start to show few tall citrons here and there and the limestone's walls blend with the ochre of the grass in the autumn.

We live in a very introspective atmosphere. While we were all in the river, each of us is concentrated on oneself and on the big and little difficulties we find, but none of us relieves the tension on the group; this helps to create a positive vibe and great harmony.

Our trip on the Kanarli moves in a world with no time where the search for the line to follow is found slowly, stroke after stroke. On the water it is the river that becomes the conductor of our dreams and ambitions.

The swing bridges and tributaries that we sometime meet are useful landmarks for our orientation.

The small streams are usually synonymous with a complex of rapids formed by rubble brought down by these during the monsoon season while the confluence with bigger creeks means a radical change in the construction of the Kanarli. The biggest trouble we find after each relevant tributary of water, is to gauge the new hydrodynamic situation as quick as we can, for the water gets faster and more powerful forcing us to read the rapids with no room for mistakes.

The fourth day, after the confluence with the Lochi, we entered the Jair gorge. This is one of the crux stretches of the river, not only for the objective difficulties but also because the walls of the gorge itself do not allow the entrance of a rescue helicopter and the track runs 1000m above.

Giorgio mistakes the line on the first rapid and falls into a huge hole that makes him cartwheel for a while. After a few rolls he leaves the boat and reaches the left bank swimming. I go chasing his kayak into the pool at the end of the next rapid. When I turn around I can't believe my eyes: Giorgio is swimming at the beginning of the rapid. Later I will find out that he wanted to ferry the river swimming, but the power of the water has taken him and dragged him into the rapid. He disappears in a hole that seems eternal then emerges again in the middle of the river right before a heap of rocks. Absolutely NASTY! We remain still, unable to help him while he is dragged into such a terrible spot, but mysteriously he re-emerges from under a gigantic rock and swims to the eddy downstream where I get him with my kayak.

Giorgio recovers and we take up the paddles again with a certain tension, but not long after we realise we are paddling one of the most beautiful stretches we have ever run. The rapids are long and continuous, the river looks like a creek but everything is magnified, enlarged. A detailed description of the river and the rapids would be reducing its beauty and intensity; the Kanarli means days of extreme difficulties. The rapids are very dangerous and violent, the water breaks without precise lines through a garden of loose and huge blocks worked by the water which has made sculptures out of them and our fantasy is free to get lost finding faces and figures in them.

Behind these blocks are hidden very difficult rapids that force us into long scoutings. As days go by our skills in reading and interpreting the lines of the water get better, but often, we have to scout from both sides of the river and our alphabet of gestures gets more fluent everyday.

The river is very demanding and often we get to the end of the rapids tired of being pushed around by the water. We all are very concentrated and sometime worried but we always have the sense of pleasure and have the feeling we are living the "great moment".

My mind goes back to Mick Hopkinson saying "this is the most committing river I have ever done". It is 10 days during which we live in a nearly cathartic situation, completely given up to the rhythm of the descent. The camps come after entire days of white water and are the only moment during which we can go back in our minds and think about our sensations, either watching the chromatic changes of the sunset, or waiting for the dawn to wake us up and wrap us in its thick fog.

When we look at the gear spread out on the beach it seems impossible it can fit in the kayaks, but then, one at a time, everything finds its place and the beach is empty again.

We have never been really alone in the river, the locals have always followed us, running everywhere, as soon as they could see us floating on the water. They would run down the slopes to reach us and our "Namaste" was all we can reply to their smiles. Sometimes we could hear them whistling while they were watching our strange clothes and gear as if we were Martians who want to run down the river with some kind of unidentified object.

They have tried to dissuade us from running the river but when they have seen us determined they have blessed us their own way and rejoiced as we got to the end of the rapid unharmed.

After Benakot and the confluence with the Tila, the river gets wider and less steep. We are aware the Humla Karnali is finished. "It's the time to have a beer if you have one" said Slime. We cannot find any kind of fresh beer, but we have the best dudh chai, cookies and peanuts ever!

WHIT DESCHNER

Never expect a straight or quick answer from this man. His brain is seriously afflicted; waterlogged in its formative years either from kayaking, or from living in Seattle or from commercial fishing in Alaska with long time co-conspirator and antagonist, Frank Cranbourne. His move to arid Eastern Oregon and buying a fire truck do not seem to have provided a cure.

I first met Whit in Vancouver, Canada. He was giving a lecture entitled "Around the World in Eighty Delays" which was the screen version of his book "Does the Wet Suit You?" which was the prequel to "Does the wet suit you two/too?" also titled "Travels with a Kayak". Later, at my invitation he came and gave the evening lecture at a Mike Jones Rally. This was also the first time we paddled together. However I don't think that Whit had the same idea of paddling together as I did. My idea, involved the two of us fastening ether foam horse heads on our helmets, tying ourselves to a Ben Hur style chariot (mounted on two kayaks) and being driven down the "Serpent's Tail" rapid by a leather-clad whip-wielding Welshman. Not quite what Whit had in mind. Since then I have paddled in Turkey and Nepal and run the Grand Canyon with him, dangerous events for anyone else on the trip, as we try to out-ludicrous each other. The golden rules seem to be that guide books should be hidden from those who read them and lampooned mercilessly by those who don't; that some prank is never too much effort, and other people's reaction is what it is all about.

His articles appear with haphazard regularity in "Canoeist" and usually cause someone to write in complaining about his lack of respect for the Third World or the beautiful places he is describing. This gratifies Whit enormously, arguing that at least someone reads them. Occasionally his alter Ego, Semour Teton, from the foothills in Idaho, replies to the criticism.

Imagine a tall, skinny, long-faced, American hitching up his forever sliding-down pants looking at some incident from a detached point of view trying to find something in the situation that he can ridicule, and take it from there. As for me, he amuses me, maybe I have the same view of life. Everyone's sense of humour is peculiar to themselves, Whit's sense of humour is just more peculiar. Anyway I'm the editor of this book, so there, and if you don't like his humour skip the chapter and write to "Underpants 'R Us", PO box 169 HCR 88, Baker, OR 97814 complaining.

Whit is not married and has no daughters and lives happily with Carol when she is not there. A pot bellied Vietnamese pig and a second-hand fire tender with a "for Sale" sign on it, help him conduct very unusual "range wars" with his neighbours. His long-term political ambition is the overthrow of anarchy, whilst his short-term political ambition, I am informed by his attorney, is unprintable!

KARNALI KNOWLEDGE

The Journal of WHIT DESCHNER.

Compiled and edited by BILL HARZIA.

Recently, with the discovery of Whit Deschner's "journal" found in the trunk of a 62 lavender Cadillac Coup de Ville, new light has been shed on the "Gnarly Karnali" trip led by Peter Knowles. [1] As for the word "journal," this term here must be regarded in its broadest form for in actuality the journal was a wad of notes scribbled on the backs of old lottery tickets, unpaid bills, and traffic violations. Obviously at some point, Deschner intended to write an article on the trip. We can only surmise that he was struck with one of his many bouts of procrastination that he so often and tragically struggled against.

Although Deschner's notes in no way paint a complete flowing picture of the trip, we can easily imagine the flavour of events. Exactly why Peter Knowles invited the American Deschner on - with the exception of Rob Lesser - an all-British trip is unknown; for if Knowles was expecting Deschner to accurately document the descent he was grossly mistaken.

[Entry date probably sometime in late August]
Weighing the pros against the cons I suspect this proposed Karnali trip is a con job. Supposed to be a small excursion, ("...ideal group size is probably about 12"); old dog kayakers to be kicked around by nothing worse than the lower Karnali ("It cuts through and drains most of the Far West of Nepal - the wild west as it's known"). It's to be the tenth anniversary of the first length-long descent. [2] Suspiciously, besides Slime,

---

[1] Or as he was known in shady boating circles, GREEN SLIME.

[2] Here Deschner is mistaken since the dead have been descending the Kanarli for years, it being yet another feeder stream to the Ganges. Bodies are often buried along it and sometimes tossed into it. So technically the trip was the tenth anniversary of <u>live</u> people running the Kanarli. And to be spotlessly correct, this was the tenth anniversary of live people <u>voluntarily</u> running the Kanarli: Deschner admits later that he was out of control in some of the drops and therefore probably became the first living person to run parts of the Kanarli <u>involuntarily</u>. To be strictly accurate nobody ran anything except to the John.

none of the original party is signed up for this anniversary – Slime however is able to make it since not only is he organising it, the trip is also covering his expenses.

[Entry date sometime later in late August]
Don't know if I can take the three known members of trip [3] – and God knows, assuming others on trip are friends or even associated with these, then new definitive definition of trouble brews.

[Entry date sometime in September, late in the day]
Extortion began today. Carol [4] answered the phone and immediately I heard advanced stages of trouble..."Dave Manby?...Are you in the U.S.?" Frantically I began pantomiming in the background, lip-synching the words: "I'm not here. You don't know where I am. Gone away for an indefinite period." Carol however disregarded my pleas and covering the receiver said, "It's OK, he's in England."

I like Dave Manby. That isn't the problem. Some of my best friends are Dave Manbys, but...

Carol handed me the phone and Dave said, "Slime says you're coming to Nepal."

"Slime says wrong."

"That's funny, he says you are. I wasn't coming either until he promised me you were so I signed up too."

(This is worse than Gerry's presence on the trip. Hangovers go away; the anarchy I've seen Dave create is permanent...)

"I can't come," I explained, "I'm not in shape."

[Later]
Really, I'm not in shape for this trip. The last real river I've seen was six years ago running the Grand Canyon with Dave. Since then I've run a local creek in flood – a fifteen minute excursion. I've even ignored Idaho – just a few hours away! To fly to Nepal doesn't make a nickel's sense.

---

[3] Here Deschner is referring to Pete Knowles, Marcus Bailie, and Gerry Moffat. Marcus, in Pakistan on a previous trip with Deschner, constantly put the trip in peril by insisting on taking pictures of highly sensitive military structures (see "Travels with a Kayak" Eddie Tern Press, 1997). Gerry Moffat, at the time was considered the Typhiod Mary of Hangovers. Deschner suffered immensely from the unfortunate chance encounters with Gerry in five different countries. As it turned out Gerry could not make the Kanarli trip.

[4] Deschner's significant other girlfriend.

Probably the next day]

Turning on my tap I received a divine message: frog anatomies issued from my faucet. Deciding to evict all intruders from my cistern I got more than I bargained for. Floating in the water was a dead ground squirrel. I won't go into detail about what stage of dead it was, but after I was through being sick, I thought, "All this time I've been drinking this water and have lived, why, I can travel anywhere in the world!

Called Slime.

"Slime," I said, "Count me in! (Here, sounds of hands rubbing together could be heard.) You wouldn't believe the training I've been doing for this trip!"

[Later in the week but early in the day]

Phone rang again today, and a slice of the past began speaking on the other end. I'm not sure what extortion was used on him but it was Rob Lesser, and despite his severe character flaw,[5] he told me he was joining the trip also.

Rob suggested we travel together but quickly our opinions on how to get to Nepal differed. Rob - living in Boise - suggested flying out of Vancouver B.C. I - living three hours from Boise - wanted to know what was wrong with leaving from Boise.

"Two hundred dollars," Rob said.

"So let me get this straight." I said, "We drive fifteen hours to leave the U.S. just to get a flight that returns us to the U.S. so we can leave the U.S. once more thus saving us two hundred clams. It doesn't make sense."

"Exactly."

Which wasn't exactly at all. When I got to the bottom of this puzzle, it turned out the travel agent in Vancouver had an exceptionally sexy voice.

[If any other notes exist before Deschner travelled to Nepal they have yet to be found. Strangely, for reasons unknown, Deschner abruptly begins once more by describing the Annapurna Hotel. Most likely he was suffering with delusions from the twenty-six air hours travelled from Vancouver.]

Oct. 25th.

The Annapurna Hotel is as fine a luxury hotel as you can find any-where in the world! There are pressed linen sheets! Air conditioning!

---

[5] Deschner is referring to Lesser liking John Denver.

Clean hot and cold running water! And room service at the click of the fingers!

We didn't stay there. We didn't even stay in a flea-cursed, cold water flop-house.

Instead, we were given a four hour, three beer layover before departing, along with ten others, on a eighteen hour bus ride to the western never lands of Nepal. Gerry, as it turns out, can't make the trip, but wanting to make himself missed, has seen to it that half the trip's supplies carry the label, "RUM."

Oct. 26

Not a bad bus ride after all, despite the chicken that some idiot plucked in the back of the bus where a major portion of the trip's gear was stashed. Taking a flying leap in my sleeping bag I landed neatly in the middle of it where I nested for the night, almost comfortably if it hadn't been for the chicken feathers. All night long, just as I was slipping from consciousness, I'd inhale a feather, and gag back awake. Only at first light did I discover that it hadn't been a chicken that had been plucked after all. It was a goose, whose feathers had shortly before belonged to my spanking-new but currently-ripped sleeping bag.

Arrived at Surkhet, staging point of the trip and home of Nepal's recent typhoid outbreak. The bus-face our ride gave us to get here is nothing compared to that of the other members who have come from Delhi. Their faces are hideously contorted from the large quantities of alcohol that had to be swallowed just to endure their journey. At one point the trip was so bad one of the members leapt - or fell or was possibly pushed - from the moving bus. Fortunately the members were under the influence, otherwise they might have hurt themselves.[6]

There are eleven kayakers and twelve rafters - not counting the guides. Impression of kayakers' communal character: living on a farm, I'm used to talking to animals but never - as with this herd - have they ever talked back to me. There are Andy Middleton, Guy Baker, Ian Sherington, Andy Knight, Chris Nicole, Marcus Bailie, George Woods, Dave Manby, Slime and Rob Lesser.

Oct. 27

From Surkhet bussed to a ridge above the Karnali where Slime helped hiring porters: if his hands were tied behind his back he'd be illiterate in

---

[6] Here Deschner is just kidding. Actually the incident could have been far worse; they could have been in a plane.

Nepali. Several hours later arrived at the river. It was too late to put on, but thanks to the toilet that was erected so far downstream, we got a good preview of the next day's run.

This evening sipped a 1949 Krug champagne followed by a 1985 DRC Montrachet which washed down a lobster mousse dahl bat. After dinner we had five gallons of May 1997 Kukuri Rum cut ruthlessly with fruit juice - the effects of which were quickly evident, for no one could remember each other's name and when memories totally failed group began swearing in song that they'd play the wild rover no more. Other traditional British Isles ballads were sung like "American Pie" and "Ventura Highway."

Oct. 28

In the morning, major problem addressed; the kayaks. A majority of the boats looked like kayaks, only they were smaller. Obviously, they'd been shrunk going through airport x-ray machines. What bothered me though was no one else seemed to notice - nor did they care. Quickly, I snagged one of the larger-sized kayaks but, much to my astonishment, almost everyone else preferred the smaller boats! Nor did they give a stuff about the manufacturing defect of the paddles. Instead of being 90% feathered or no degrees unfeathered, these blades are twisted at arbitrary angles in between, giving the combined effects of catching wind and the user tendinitis.

After putting on the river I felt quite secure in my choice of a larger boat for everyone in the small kayaks was having trouble with their eddy turns. Water isn't huge but it is big and as hard as these small boaters try to make a normal turn, their kayaks rear onto their haunches and go spinning vertically out of control down the eddy line. Turning into eddies I felt pretty smug at my groomed control and ability to keep my boat on a flat plane. Then someone sidled up to me and in the manner of one regarding Rip Van Winkle waking, said, "Huh! The old Duffek stroke. I haven't seen one of those in years!"

OK! So I've never been in the mainstream of boating to watch its trends: but that doesn't explain the next puzzle: The average hang-dog age of these old dogs hung in the mid-forties. I reckoned that being communally older, this pack wouldn't be so foolish as to drop into large holes and surf pounding waves - and here they are doing it in tiny boats with smiles on their faces. I mean when I was younger I always used to think such behaviour was bravery - but really what I was suffering from was an overdose of hormones. Is someone slipping testosterone in the rum punch?

That night (after a salmon papillette dahl bat complemented with a bottle of Chateau D'Yquem) I made an effort to find out. After a gallant but losing struggle with the September 1997 Kukuri rum (it was a bit "young") and fruit punch melange, I conclude that this is not a river trip but a drinking excursion with a kayak problem.

Oct. 29

The punch has not affected my willingness to have my body subjected to mother nature's industrial-sized washing machines – as it has continued to do on the others. Why they insist on such foolery remains a mystery to me. Rob Lesser, possibly the oldest of the bunch, seems to be getting the wettest. Fortunately, his total wardrobe is made of Capaline and he dries out quickly.[7]

Tonight, for dinner, we had glazed shallots along with a drought-stricken chicken carefully diced in the dark by a dull machete. The pieces were then liberally seasoned with the national spice – sand – and dunked in dahl bat. This, alongside a bottle of 1961 Chateau Latour followed by 2 gallons of June 1997 Kukuri Rum exquisitely blended with fruit punch and iodine.

As I headed for my tent, Guy Baker warned me to bring all shoes into the tent at night.

"Thieves?" I asked pensively.

"No," he answered, "There're too many video cameras around."[8]

Oct. 30

Concerning this river: since I've flown all the way to Nepal to boat and in the meantime for years have ignored Idaho, I'll say this for the Karnali: it sure reminds me of Idaho.

Then again, Idaho is not lush green as this is at the end of October, nor does one boat in Idaho the first week of November without donning both heavy-duty cold, and bullet-proof gear thanks to all the enthusiastic but inbred hunters. Nor is Idaho known for fine food and alcohol – unlike what was enjoyed this evening: a bottle of 1945 Haute

---

[7] A common belief in its day. "Capaline" a supposed miracle fabric was made of recycled atomic waste. It didn't actually dry but rather made the wearers warm, thus thinking they were dry.

[8] Here Baker is alluding to a tragic incident on the Indus where his group had to bivouac with a shortage of tents and Baker was forced to share his tent with the expedition's lone female. Unfortunately, the woman's shoes were filmed outside the tent – a detail that did not go unnoticed by several girlfriends back in England.

Brion which absolutely flattered the navarin of lamb drenched in dahl bat which in turn was flushed down and out with a fresh five gallon jerry can of rackshee, locally born that very afternoon and delicately supersaturated into a quart of fruit juice.

Oct. 31

The other item worthy of mention and missing from Idaho's agenda are the Karnali's huge monsoon bred beaches. Nor standing on them this morning did the locals look like Idahoans. They look far smarter.[9] and in fact brilliant when Andy Knight dressed them in the river gear he manufactures and took pictures of them. However, confusion spread across their faces when he took his gear back again. Good thing he hasn't started selling bikinis.

Tonight had Oysters Rockefeller with a "Barbie" dahl bat followed by a baked Alaska along with Havana cigars and an Armagnac brandy perfectly thinned in Dettol soap water. Spoke this evening with George Woods but due to his accident it was hard understanding him.[10]

Oct. 32

Today encountered several rapids bigger than the rest. As I scouted the biggest of these bigs I was overcome with melancholy for suddenly I began to think of my wife and kids.[11] Meanwhile at these drops, I overheard Slime, father of Nepal white-water guidebooks, muttering such phrases as, "...vague recollection of this one but it seems to have changed location" or, "that couldn't be a new drop but I sure don't remember..." Then his voice would trail off into utter confusion. Diligently he jotted down descriptions to update his new edition. Once, his notebook fell open in front of me and I read several of the passages:

Look for beach with woman and three water buffalo on it; run drop centre.

Men will be chopping down tree on left just before this rapid.

---

[9] Here Deschner is making fun of the English usage of the word "smart" which he thought was really dumb.

[10] This most certainly os a mistake since Deschner was never a good speller. Most likely he meant "accent." George Woods was Scottish.

[11] An extremely strange comment for Deschner did not have a wife or kids. He hated kids. A founder member of "pro-compulsion".

This evening had a bottle of either 1974 Moet et Chandon or a recent vintage of Mad Dog 20/20 - I couldn't distinguish which because the label had washed off the bottle. Have to admit it didn't do much for the Boeuf Bourbonnais, however, this could have been due to the chefs' over-enthusiastic use of Nepali spice.[12] If they don't stop this practice we'll soon all develop gizzards.

[Several days later, probably November around 11 PM.]

River has slowed, rapids have diminished and the valley has widened. In the years that have intervened between Slime's first trip, Slime pointed out that, in many places, what used to be forest is now new housing developments and terraces - a trend Slime blames on the Internet. People can now move from the crime-ridden cities out into a rural setting and conduct all their business from a computer.

Still, the diminishing habitat has not answered for the lack of birds. I've seen more monkeys than birds - perhaps the monkeys ate them. So far I've noted exactly three species of birds and this in a country that boasts 500 species. Not a good batting average. Then again, there haven't been many insects either. Life, I suppose, is never easy. Either a riot of birds annoys you awake while you lie in your tent with the insect netting securely zipped, or you suffer through long silent periods of boredom while having nothing to itch. Fortunately the one insect that we have seen are walking sticks. These little arthropods have proved invaluable for lighting fires when kindling is not available.

Saving the best for last - had a bottle of 1985 Romanee Conti tonight. Served with omelettes dahl bat Rothschild, it was a marriage of tastes made in nirvana - a marriage however quickly destroyed by some fool who went and accidentally mixed rackshee in the dish water which they accidentally mistook for fruit punch. I've never smelled a more pleasant sewer gas. Naturally, the muse of this beverage was not surprising as everyone began surmising the conceiving of Slime's name.

[Here Deschner records many Irish, Nepali, Scottish, British versions of the story. Even Dave Manby who had actually been at the name's inception - but was too oiled to realise the importance of the occasion - tried conjuring up what he believed he might have heard that infamous night. The stories ranged from

---

[12] Or as they say in Nepal. "Too many Kooks spoil the Brothel"

an outer worldly illegal kryptonite-like substances to cockney slang to...[13] *The reader may get a flavour of the content from the following acronyms Deschner recorded:]*

Swamp **L**iving **I**nsidious **M**icroscopic **E**vangelist
Single **L**oner **I**nvites **M**emorable **E**xperience
Sexy **L**over **I**nvites **M**ating **E**lephants
Superb **L**eader **I**nspires **M**agnificent **E**xpeditions.

[sometime even later in 1997]

Entered the Terai (passing under a Japanese designed futuristic bridge that looked desperately in need of a modern city) and floated into Giardia National Park, staying in the Tiger Tops tent camp - and a woods where the tigers were. A tiger woods if you will. Here at last I saw some more birdies and a couple of eagles. Among the birdies - and I'm not making these names up - were: the rusty-cheeked scimitar babbler, the common babbler (not to be confused with the human ones), blue bearded bee-eater, red vented bulbul, orange-bellied chloropsis, red wattled lapwing, black-gorgetted laughing thrush, purple-rumped sunbird, flower pecker, brain fever bird, see see, did he do it, lesser racket tailed drongo, blossom-headed parakeet, and the stone and rock chats - although these last two require an ornithologist with background in geology to distinguish their differences.

In the evening a guide led us through the forest and kept telling us to be quiet but I couldn't figure out why we needed to be quiet to see animal tracks. But at last our silence paid off for we came across what he said was a dragon track.

"Dragon?!" I exclaimed.

"Yes Dragon. This one is where tiger was dragon its prey."

But we never did see any tigers; no one ever does because the grass is too damn long and even riding on elephants we couldn't rise above it. Basically, what the place could use is a good lawn mower - that or they should hire a person in a bullet-proof vest to carry a stick with a tiger's tail on it and walk through the grass.

The next day and beyond the tiger woods the guide escorted us to a village where we saw all sorts of developing dogs. Ironically, it wasn't

---

[13] Send $500.00 in a brown paper bag to Bill Harzia, HCR 88 Box 169, Baker, OR 97814, and I'll send you all the details in a brown unmarked and confidential envelope.

them that kept us up at night but the barking deer. And it was in this village where our guide explained to us how in the monsoons the villagers "go phishing."

"Go what?" we asked in shocked unison.

"Phish."

"Where?"

"They phish all over the place."

[This is the last "entry" of Deschner's journal. Other records indicate that shortly after - probably minutes - the trip quickly dissolved. Evidently, over the course of the float, the trip's toilet crew had become that efficient, that they kept habitually filling in the lodge's pre-dug toilet pits and the management quickly got fed up. As a result the group in its entirety was evicted. What happened to them afterwards is unknown.]

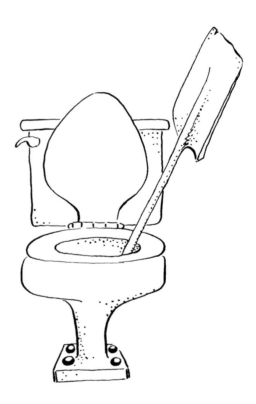

TAMUR OR NOT TAMUR

Originally, four of us were haphazardly planning for the Tamur; Rob Lesser, Guy Baker, Dave Manby and myself: leftovers from a Karnali descent. Yet on the Karnali I'd noted differences between these personalities. It was like three people going to watch a hockey game for their own various reasons: Guy to anticipate the fights, Dave to watch the hockey and, Rob to see a zamboni. Just the manner in which these three dressed pronounced the gulf between them: Guy styled himself with wrap around yellow sunglasses and had various parts of his body perforated with jewellery. He looked so much like a model fresh from a commercial that on his visa application he'd simply torn a look-alike picture from a magazine ad and pasted it on the photo blank. Dave bedecked himself in a multicoloured patched sports jacket I'd had tailored for him ten years before in Turkey. To complement this anti-complementary attire he'd found a likewise patchwork pair of shorts to match. Rob dressed himself in Patagonia chic right down to skivvies and socks. That was our line-up: two variously eccentric Englishmen, an all American boy, (and myself who wore a colour uncoordinated Goodwill outfit; yellow tag special; Oct. 21, 1997). If the descent of the Tamur proved inadequate entertainment, surely these paddling anomalies would fill the void.

The river itself drains Kanchenjunga - which is really the highest mountain in the world but since it is so hard to pronounce no one admits it. It would be a descent from vertical to horizontal geology; from mountain air to the stench of burning garbage; from Buddhist to Hindu influence; from frosty nights to baking temperatures; from yaks to water buffalo; from chickens to ducks. Word of mouth pegged it as "one of the best whitewater runs in the world," ad nauseam. Five days worth (not nausea but whitewater). On our descent, I planned on seeing the backs of all three of these better-than-me paddlers being trashed in holes that I hopefully, learning from their mistakes, could avoid. But it wasn't to be. During an ungodly wait in line at the permit office in Kathmandu, Dave and Guy wandered off only to learn from a mutated German rumour, that because of low water, the Tamur had been demoted to a class three. But what I think happened was, the two wiener schnitzels who had just come from the river couldn't count past three in any other language (like myself). In any case, on the spur of the second – and for the first time since being together – Rob, Dave and Guy all agreed on one thing: they hadn't travelled to Nepal to dawdle in class three. They changed their permits for the Marsyandi. Stoically, I stuck to my guns. My heart was set on the Tamur, and if the river really was class drei then I certainly didn't have to think zwei times about an eins-person descent.

With my hiking permit in hand, I headed back to my hotel and contemplated the obstacles: I had to learn some Nepali quickly; a written language that looks like something stuck and baked in a laser printer. Thus spoken, it was all stuck and baked gobbledegook to me, which wasn't going to help me shuttling my kayak between taxis and buses, and having to hire porters.

My second worry was that the trip wasn't exactly legal. Although the Tamur is slated to go commercial in '98 that didn't mean the door was open for private parties like myself to descend it. My rubber-stamped piece of paper allowed me to hike to the river – and back. It didn't say I could run the river, but it didn't say I couldn't run the river either. Or, if I really wanted to play by these arbitrary rules, what I needed was a costly expedition permit, yet on the other sleighting hand, no private party had been turned away from the river (or at least had been caught). As an American I never was good at interpreting legal grey matters such as this one – which probably explains why so many confused Americans own so many guns.

I imagined the conversation I might have with the police at check-points.

POLICE: So you are hiking from Basantapur to Dobhan.

ME: Yes.

POLICE: And back.

ME: Yes.

POLICE: With a boat?

ME: What boat? Oh that! Well, I'll be gosh darned. I hadn't noticed I accidentally packed it.

POLICE: Ha! You crazy westerners! Always kidding around. Hope you've also accidentally packed loads of baksheesh.

So as I got closer to my hotel, I began thinking it might be nice to share some of this misery with company. And, if someone did accompany me then there wouldn't be the mystery surrounding any accidental death I might encounter with headlines that would read:

ENIGMA OF LONE BOATER'S DEATH DEEPENS
Kayaker's Patagonia shorts found on water buffalo near Bay of Bengal.

...Which would really be a mystery because I don't wear anything Patagonia. I can't afford it. Not even factory seconds. Have you ever priced that stuff?

So on the off chance that I could find another pariah kayaker looking for a trip, I stepped into the Equator Expeditions office and told Pauline Sanderson, co-owner, that I was leaving the next day for the Tamur and if she heard of anyone who wanted to do it, they were welcome to join me.

Ten minutes later there was a knock on my hotel door. It was Pauline. She informed me she was joining me. I began to stammer.

"You did say anyone," she said.

"But..."

"That won't be an issue," she explained, "I'm married."

I began to stutter.

"I'm a class three boater but I can hang on in class four. Anyway, that won't be an issue either since it'll only be class three... Please let me come, I haven't had a break in two months.... I'll get us to and from the river if you can get me down it."

I began to splutter.

She continued: "I'm also an ex-lawyer. I'll can take care of any legal matters that arise, like reducing our death sentences to life in prison for doing a river that we aren't necessarily supposed to be on."

I began to think. "You'll be ready tomorrow?"

"By all means."

We shook hands and I began to pack.

Half an hour later I was ready.

With nothing to do but wait I began wandering around Thamel, one of Kathmandu's tumours and hitching post for budget travellers. My first time around Nepal on original tread was in 1979. I remembered a short conversation I had on a hotel roof with a not so fellow American from Brooklyn who had just arrived to both Nepal and the hotel roof. He was fresh out of Peace Corps training and quickly into our conversation I asked, "Let me get this straight; you're from Brooklyn and you've come to tell these people how to live?" For some reason he immediately stopped talking to me. In any case, seven years later I held him personally responsible for the change that had come to the country, so much so that I swore I'd never visit Nepal again...

What happened between '79 and '86 was profound change; the transpiration between '86 and the present was radical mutation – especially in Thamel. The district had gone vertical. Sun-drenched tea gardens were all but extinct and the few outdoor restaurants which hadn't been built on now lay in the multi-storey cold shadows of those which had. Another metamorphosis was the handicrafts. Not that Kathmandu was ever handicraft deficient, but the quality of crafts had vastly improved. For example, locally knitted sweaters no longer contained manure in the wool that if watered would sprout and grow the seeds that were also in the wool to maturity - seeds that you could get hanged for in Singapore.

Communication, too, had improved. Before, phoning out was like trying to connect with life on distant planets. But now, in every office I passed, I saw computer after computer. Today, the information age is levelling the playing field, making it possible for hormone-crazed eleven year-old Nepali boys to surf the web and ogle the same naked women that American boys lose their sight over.

However, of all the changes, the population increase snatched the cake. But wanting to be optimistic and letting all these people have opportunities in life (despite the traffic jams they will have to endure to get to their opportunities) I began noting job openings.

Population control expert. Job description: Must be able to feign population control but not actually control it as that would quickly eliminate job.

Dog Catcher. Job description: Catch and destroy all dogs. Benefits: Will be able to work from your home daily.

Trash collector. Job description: Must be able to identify trash. Translating language trash was written in is not necessary but will add hours of enjoyment to the job.

Heavy load shifter. Job description: Must be able to pick up large objects with penis in front of tourists. Females need not apply.

Proof reader. Job description: Must be able to spell correctly items on menus such as "frid igs."

Etiquette school for Israeli tourists. Job description: Must teach

Israelis notions of queues and politeness. Job comes with lifetime supply of alcohol.

Yet of all these opportunities, the latest fad was the one that Nepal hardly needed any more of: hucksters selling raft trips. You could hardly eat a meal or check into a hotel without being harassed. Even the free-lancers on the street sold them and in a whispering contraband tone of voice they asked: "You wish to buy rafting trip? I have good rafting trip for you. No? Change money? How about my sister? No? Marijuana? Tiger Balm?"

Because of its popularity, rafting now pumps more money into the local economy than tiger balm sales and due to its skyrocketing success Nepal is one of the few Asian economies whose currency did not recently collapse - a startling fact that I just made up. Yet because of this popularity, the Sun Kosi, the Marsyandi, the Kali Gandaki, and the Seti are now so overrun that their white sandy beaches have become what sandboxes are to cats. Fortunately, the monsoons cleanse the rivers each year, washing all garbage safely out of sight into the plains of India where it will hardly disturb the tourists in Nepal....OK, so you detect a tone of sarcasm but if something isn't said then what's to stop Disney World in ten more years coming in and purchasing the entire country?

★★★★★★

The next afternoon, after shuttling our kayaks to the bus station and lashing them aloft our bus, we boarded, and sitting in the two seats behind the driver's cage that Pauline had specifically reserved, I commented, "You call these the best seats?"

"Absolutely." She said, "Look at our leg room!"

"Do you sit in the front row at horror shows?"

Moments later our driver swaggered aboard, and slipping on a pair of thin leather Italian driving gloves, he gazed out over us mortal passengers as if he were Beelzebub observing a new batch of arrivals. After a condescending "huuuh!" he sat, shuffled into his seat, tested the steering wheel, started, raced and blew the clinkers from the exhaust, grabbed the shift knob and, as if entering a mortal combat with the engine, he jammed the shift forward, popped his foot off the clutch and from that moment on we never slowed, and Dharan, our interim destination, became like a distant planet, its gravitational pull speeding us forward at an ever-increasing pace. The only problem was that there were approximately two-thousand hair-pin corners and fifteen hours between us and Dharan.

Pauline, quick to notice my concern, said, "Don't worry, if he was a bad driver he wouldn't be here now. He'd be dead."

"What if it's his first time?"

"But just look at him!" She marvelled, "He seems to know exactly what he's doing."

"What, passing on blind corners?"

"Maybe he's psychic. Maybe he knows no one is com...Jes...Ahhh!...That was close! I, um, don't think he's psychic after all."

Worse still, that evening - thanks to El Nino - it grew dark. I thought night might help B'bub discern oncoming headlights around blind corners but even this didn't equate. I told Pauline, once a good Catholic, to dust off her saints while I went to work invoking every deity from every religion I could think of. "Please Gods," I prayed, "I don't care how hard the Tamur is, just get me to it alive, ANYTHING but this driver!"

In terrifying time, the divinities delivered us temporarily from evil onto the blessed flat terai, and there, we switched drivers. Of course I didn't identify the other driver until he sat in the driver's seat. Up until then he'd been a:

General bus go-for. Job description: Must occasionally boss conductor around to show superiority. Must be able to engage driver in interesting conversation to take his mind off on-coming vehicles. Also be able to climb out of moving bus up onto roof to pilfer passenger's bags without being swept off roof while bus passes under low tree branches. High count of hormones required.

B'bub fell quickly asleep on the engine cowling, leaving our new driver alone at the helm, merrily grinding gears. The road was cornerless and at first it appeared our new man seemed lacking in death wishes. I almost nodded off as I balanced on the edge of sleep for the next few hours. With our legroom I might even have slipped into real sleep if the seats hadn't felt as if they were chiselled out of granite. Once, shifting positions to let another part of my body take a turn at going numb, I cracked open an eye only to see the driver's head nod down then jerk up. I bolted upright, but I was quickly relieved when he woke himself thoroughly by opening the window, standing, and poking his head and shoulders into the rush of night air.

Concerned, I stayed awake and a short while later he sat back, raced the bus to a new land speed record, popped the engine into neutral and began coasting. As the bus slowed, so did the driver's consciousness. At about fifteen miles an hour, his head slumped once more; around five he twitched back awake. I contemplated waking Pauline, but she looked so peaceful asleep and I didn't want to disturb her. Besides, I thought, just like B'bub, this driver can't be all that bad as he too remains alive. Surely he knows what he's doing....

After three or so more bursts of speed and some quick catnaps he stood once more and thrust his head out the window. But this didn't last long and soon he reverted to his coasting nano-naps again. I thought: "Maybe I should go talk to him." But if I could navigate around the cage and lean over the more permanently sleeping B'bub, what would I say to the driver? If I tapped him on the shoulder maybe I'd scare the bejabbers out of him and cause us to wreck. Again I debated waking Pauline. Maybe he'd like her tapping him on the shoulder instead. Besides, she could at least say something to him in Nepali.

The driver raced the bus once more, this time almost heroically. Turning around I gazed at all the other passengers. No one was awake; no one was concerned, so, I thought, why should I worry? I turned around and my heart tried leaping out of its rib cage: I've never known such terror: In my forward-attention's absence I had become the last person awake on the bus: The driver was sagged over the wheel, fast asleep. I wished desperately to close my eyes too but there wasn't enough lid to stretch across the bulges of my eyeballs that now probably looked more like pickled onions. A tree we should have passed on the right swept in then out of our headlights and, as it brushed past on our left, we plunged off the shoulder down a ten-foot bank and, in the middle of a country that boasts the highest mountains on earth, we landed...in a swamp.

The impact threw Pauline into the driver's cage - which probably knocked him awake. As we jarred to a stop there were staccato screams from the woken and a burst of hissing steam from the engine.

The driver shook his head and when he at last turned and I could study his face I swear he looked content. His expression read; "I just beat my old record by twenty minutes!" I thought B'bub, who was extracting himself from the dashboard, would be livid but he said nothing, not even "Why'd you do that you knucklehead?" I turned to look at the passengers. Their faces were blank slates. Obviously here, bus drivers falling asleep is purely providence. In America though, this wreck would have been a gold mine. Besides Pauline's head which had started to bleed, there were miraculously, no other injuries. We could have all sued for severe emotional trauma and collected millions for the rest of our lives living happily ever after. But not in Nepal. We weren't even given refunds. And we were about to be knee-deep in a swamp just to get back to the road.

As I climbed onto the bus roof and untied our kayaks and gear, our driver joined me and undid a couple of benches. These he threw into the water placing them end to end for the passengers to walk on. Although the benches were oriented towards the road they were thirty feet short of dry land and were nothing but a gangplank into a swamp-- a swamp that made all others I'd been in impostors. This swamp was brown and soupy and had leeches and probably bred malaria and yellow fever mosquitoes and in general smelled like a pile of athletes' socks in need of a wash.

In the meantime other buses had stopped, both east and west bound, giving us a choice of continuing or returning. As we reached the road neither Pauline or I could decide if the wreck was a good or bad omen. Was her wound a small but necessary blood sacrifice? Or was it just a taste of bigger injuries to come?

After dressing the cut with iodine, I dug out her helmet and said, "Here, see if this still fits."

"Why didn't you suggest this a half an hour ago?" she asked.

"Because your head wasn't swollen then. Besides, I didn't want to wake you."

Pauline nursed the helmet over her cut.

Snuggled in place, she shrugged and said, "It'll work: shall we continue?"

We loaded our gear onto an eastbound bus and took residence, this time, in the very rear.

As it was, we arrived in Dharan at five a.m. - ahead of schedule. Despite the early hour, the street was a hive of activity. We carried our kayaks a block to the Basantapur bus. This bus was shorter and more beat-up than our crashed bus - before it crashed. On its side was painted, "Swastika Travels." A man sold us tickets from a booth that looked like a Punch and Judy theatre. We requested sanctuary in the rear.

It was still dark when we left. The engine struggled as we headed back into the mountains. The bus was jammed. Although I couldn't see our driver I did try monitoring his activity. But over the drone of passenger chatter, it was impossible to distinguish what he was up to. As far as I could tell, both the brake and throttle pedals were reneging on their responsibilities; at best their function seemed merely to change the whine of our forward momentum. As we inched uphill, gravity became this bus's worst enemy: downhill, I knew it would become ours. But I was gun-shy and needn't have worried. Whoever was up there behind the wheel kept us securely on the road.

Dawn came and I charted our progress on a map which Marco Polo must have transcribed in his feeble-minded old age. After four hours of jolting, both the road and our speed diminished. We went from about four miles per hour to four hours per mile. Although riding a bucking bronco would have been far more relaxing, I still wasn't complaining about the driver. Even though the road completely disappeared at times he at least kept the bus where the road was supposed to be. Good old Swastika Travels. They only hire the best.

After leaving Kathmandu -twenty-two hours, three bus rides and one bus crash later, we finally arrived in Basantapur. Porters swarmed our equipment. I was glad I had Pauline, for it was her difficult task to pick three competent porters for our three day walk to the river. I didn't envy her but a deal was a deal. My job, I gloated to myself, getting her down such an easy river, would be a cinch. Carefully I watched her, thinking she might conduct job interviews, but instead in her eye was the look of a woman on a shopping spree. Sweeping her gaze through the crowd she announced, "You, you and you."

I was stunned.

"What's was wrong with the guy already holding my boat?" I wanted to know.

"He's not very nice."

"And that one clutching our bag?"

"He'd rob us."

"And that one?"

"Lazy."

"Then why these three?"

"They're friendly."

"How can you tell?"

"I just can. Don't question me."

Their names were Dopasaan, Lockman, and Teg and if they were friendly, I couldn't tell. If fact Teg, a dead ringer for Peter Lorre, looked more qualified for serial killing than portering. But whether Pauline's snap judgement was sixth sense or pure luck it didn't matter. For our march to the river, we couldn't have had better companions.

The walk traversed along ridge tops through meadows and in and out of rhododendron forests. The first morning Lockman woke us at six-thirty and insisted we get up. We insisted on sleeping some more. Five minutes later he returned with a cup of tea. This time, grumpy but subservient, we complied with his wishes, rose, ate and stepped from our tea house. Awaiting us was a crystal clear panorama of Himalayas; Everest to the west, Kanchenjunga on the east – and a whole lot of malcontent geology in-between. An hour later, while we would have otherwise still been asleep, the mountains dissolved into the mists.

As we hiked I began brushing up on essential Nepali words that I'd learned each time I'd visited the country. These were: Hello, goodbye, dahl bat, fast, very, good, how much and boat – all the words a kayaker needs to know. With these you can fabricate such key phrases as:

Dahl bat fast goodbye. Meaning: Quick! Where the heck's the out-house?

Boat very fast goodbye? – Is the river hard?

How much hello goodbyes? – How many children do you have?

Once I tried constructing a question that included every Nepali word I knew, feeling that in doing so I would be regarded as an extremely learned and sophisticated person. Unable to understand the response I received I asked Pauline with her limited but-knew-more-than-me Nepali to translate. She said: "The old man says that it wouldn't be compromising your intelligence to call you a moron."

Often we were asked if we were married. Instead of letting this slide Pauline would thoroughly baffle anyone who was foolish enough to ask by trying to explain that, well, she was married but no, pointing to me, I wasn't her husband.

But her answer always failed to parry off the next question: "How many children do you have?"

And always when we told them, "none," they would offer us a child or two in consolation. I was hardly sure of what to do with all the kids if we did take them; however, with only three cans of tuna, our menu was lacking in protein.

On the third morning we at last saw the Tamur. We were still about

1,500 feet above it, yet even from our altitude the river looked white. Funny, I thought, all these years kayaking and this hasn't happened before: never has a class three looked this white from this high up! Incredible! The other thing that bothered me was that the valley seemed too steep to contain a runnable river.

As we dropped down I reckoned I'd at least see straight routes through the white, but the more we descended the frothier the river became. At Dhoban - and river level - I knew there had been a serious communication breakdown but I couldn't decide between a rusty German/English translation or if Pauline and I had mistakenly instructed our porters to take us to the wrong Dhoban.

At a teahouse we ordered dahl bat, and Pauline asked, "What's wrong with you?"

"Nothing" I lied.

"You sure have become awfully quiet."

A plate full of steaming dahl bat that challenged my lack of appetite quickly betrayed my apprehension. I wasn't alone though: Pauline's plate also went uneaten.

Still, we pretended nothing was wrong. Teg, Lockman and Dopasaan carried our gear and boats to the river's edge. They too felt our apprehension for after we had settled up with them, tipping them handsomely, they stuck around, hoping I'm sure for the opportunity to carry our boats back to Basantapur - which was what our permits were for anyway. As we pulled into the current I'll always remember the communal look on their faces: It must have been the same one friends and relatives wore as the Titanic pulled away from the wharf.

★★★★★★

As for the run, I'll say this: The Tamur is not, never was and never will be a class three. And it's especially not a class three the first day. Although the rating system has seriously eroded in the last few years, my personal ranking method, one that has never failed me, has not. It works on the simple principle of my legs going numb. In hard water, shoehorned into my boat, my legs are rendered into a pins and needles factory. Since my attention is elsewhere, the numbness is the least of my worries and rarely does it register. In water less than class four my legs are stretched out and fully awake whereas my upper body often falls asleep, not unlike what happens to certain bus drivers. Rarely, in my boat on the Tamur were my legs awake. Fortunately, my legs' circulation was restored by frequent scouting and an occasional portage. Not that the river ever rated over four plus, just that the consequences of screwing up and losing a boat or paddle were painfully obvious.

Often I would look up at the ridge tops and think, "It'll be a far longer walk out of here than it ever was getting here." And coming to yet another substantial rapid I would begin praying to the various deities: "I promise I'll never ever complain about suicidal or somnambulist bus drivers again, just get me out of here alive!"

In time the gods answered my prayer - and they even saw to it that Pauline never missed a roll, all eight of them. She paddled like a battery-advert bunny and all she needed to affix to her programming was a little steerage and she wouldn't have dropped into the various holes and turbulence that I specifically told her to stay away from.

When we did at last reach the safety of the Sun Kosi we felt like survivors of a natural disaster - something I'm not so sure the Tamur does not mean.

At Chatra, the take-out, we were quickly mobbed by several surly drivers, who due to their cornered market were demanding an outrageous rate to take us and our gear the handful of kilometers to Dharan. It was a repeat episode of trying to get off the Sun Kosi eleven years before. I was thankful for Pauline's level-headed dealings with this local mafioso: an old man with rheumy eyes who looked like a toad, a skinny twerp who wore an oversized suit and purple glasses and who kept spitting betel juice inches away from Pauline's feet and a dime-store thug who was yelling into her face. We were saved, though, by an ex-Gurka who calmly stepped forward, pointed to a distant parked bus and politely informed us that if we waited until tomorrow we could get a ride to Kathmandu for cheaper than these highway robbers' ransom to Dharan. I was so relieved that when I bought our tickets, I failed to check our seat numbers.

Although Chatra is just a one-lane bazaar, there was plenty to do. We parked ourselves in the Hamro Hotel and Sun Kosi Raft Cold Centre, and sipped beer in the sanctuary of its small garden. Then I got shaved.

Barber. Job description: must be able to steady straight edge razor on customer's throat while milling onlookers shake shack to Richter rating of 7.0.

That evening we attended a carnival. There were rides and shows and all sorts of job opportunities, such as:

Ferris wheel operator. Job description: Must power ferris wheel by running around inside it. Either gender OK but must be able to think like a gerbil.

Magician's assistant. Job description: Must be able to capture runaway rabbits and pigeons and return to their respective hats. Ability to levitate also required. Must be able to temporarily part with head and be handy at removing troublesome ketchup stains from around costume collars.

There was a contortionist also and I even thought I might see our sleeping bus driver featured as a somnambulist - but if he was double-shifting on this new job he must have slept through his alarm for we sure didn't see him.

The best show however, was Michael Jackson - well not the Michael Jackson but a five-year-old imposter who was dressed to the nines. Dancing and lip-syncing to the real Michael's music this midget-Michael had all the moves plus one Michael lacked: shoving his too-large of sunglasses back up his nose every time he looked down. If the little squirt had done an encore I would have been terminally ill from laughing.

The next day as our bus barrelled out of Chatra for Kathmandu, we sat reluctantly in our designated seats: shotgun.

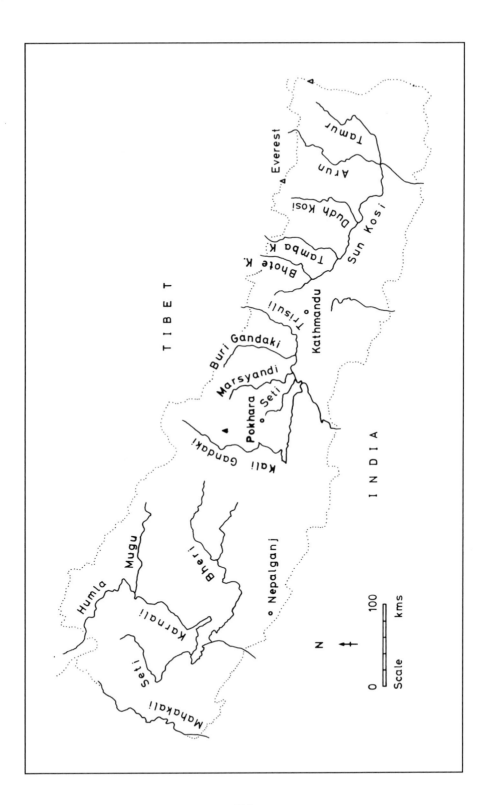

DAVE MANBY

How do you describe one of kayaking's most colourful and maverick characters?

Dave Manby was one of the team on the original Dudh Kosi 'Canoeing Down Everest' in 1976, so I thought that I would turn to Mike Jones' book and see what he had written: "Dave at twenty one would be the youngest member of the team – He invariably wore pullovers with holes in the elbows and oily, torn jeans. This sloppy dress was intentional – Dave deliberately cultivated a way-out external appearance that only masked his real qualities". Well, some people never change!

I first met Dave around the same time, in the mid seventies, in some low bar in Austria and a few years later we headed off together for a kayaking trip to British Columbia and to have a look at the Grand Canyon of the Stikine en route. I remember flying through the Canyon in a small 5 seater plane trying to read the map and take notes as we were buffeted about – and I felt an overwhelming urge to be sick. There were no sick bags and rather than spray vomit all over the plane I did the obvious, leant forward slightly and threw up in the hood of Dave's coat. This showed up one of Dave's qualities: you can rely on him to be cheerful in the stickiest of situations!

We did several trips together to British Columbia and Alaska, exploring these wild rivers and relishing the big water – rivers like the Liard, Thompson, Chilko, Taseko and the Fraser. On one trip we had bought our rations cheap and in bulk and were all stopped at lunch time, hunched around a fire in the rain, trying to look cheerful as we ate the same dismal lunch of nuts and raisins that we'd eaten for the last 5 days. Dave had landed upstream, lit his own fire, pulled out a cast iron frying pan, and started slicing up and frying an onion and 5lbs. potatoes. We all gathered round and salivated as this delicious smell wafted down the river and then Dave pulled out a huge Sirloin Steak and started frying that. Dave refused to give us any of the steak but shared the hash browns and sausages! We took the hint and the lunch menu improved from there on.

Dave is a communist in the non-political sense, someone who believes in sharing and not a great respector of individual property - I guess this sometimes makes him a hard guy to share your house with - you come back home to discover a van engine eviscerated on the iving room floor and your towels covered in black grease! - but his practical abilities make him a star team player and the first choice for many expeditions, trips and first descents around the world. He's been invited on numerous kayaking films, like "the Taming of the Lion" (The Indus gorges) but strange to say, rarely appears in the final film - Directors would take one look at his sartorial elegance and shout "Dave, get off the set"!

Whatever Dave lacks in sartorial elegance is made up for by a warm personality: wherever he goes in the world, he has the knack to relate with the local community and he has made many friends: particularly in Eastern Turkey where we went in 1982 to kayak the Çoruh. We were so impressed that we went back the following year and started running rafting and kayaking trips on a semi-commercial basis. Dave learnt Turkish, and most years since he has returned to sit in the tea houses and talk to the many Turkish friends he has made - also to run a few trips. Whatever the itinerary was supposed to be, and no trip with Dave ever goes quite to plan, so if you ask anyone how their trip with Dave went they start grinning, tell you some outrageous story and talk about the trip of a lifetime!

Underneath a gruff exterior is a soft heart and Dave has spent a lot of time furthering the sport: He founded and ran the Mike Jones Rally for many years and these became so successful and famous that they spawned a host of other recreational white water tours. No lover of organisational bureaucracy, Dave nevertheless has served on several Committees and is currently Chair of the BCU Expeditions Committee. If you asked him though, he'd probably say that some of his most satisfying experiences were the trip that he led to Turkey for disabled paddlers and the Youth expedition to the Grand Canyon of the Colorado.

Someone once said that you can tell a person by his friends; and it is a tribute to him that he has managed to persuade so many interesting characters to write in this book - a diverse collection of warm, exciting stories that illustrate the sport of white-water kayaking but also perhaps mirror Dave's own character.

Peter Knowles, (aka "Slime" to his kayaking friends) January 1999.

THE BRALDU

June 1990. Sitting in the sun leaning against the mud wall of one of the village houses in Tongle sharing a hookah of rough Pakistani tobacco. All the men of the village are there; the crops are sown, the

children are out looking after the sheep, goats, and dzo, the women are either in their houses or down in the orchard chattering together. No one speaks any English, I know only a dozen words of Urdu, far less of the local dialect, Balti, except to count to five (Chic, nis, sum, ghi, rha. There - I can still remember all these years later).

Contentment. The hurly-burly of the Indus is behind; the "Taming of the Lion". The cameras have left and that creation of an illusion has finished. The challenge and fun of the Gilgit river, just three of us on a high-water run, is over; an uncomplicated, four day bonus trip taken up by Dave Allardice, Cam Mcleay and myself after the rest of the Indus expedition members had returned home. Even the memory of the adrenalin surge from the more vividly scary moments has receded. The grief and desperate questioning of my responsibilities for Mike's death twelve years earlier has mellowed into history and a "fait accompli" acceptance; if you play the game you must accept the rules. My foolish (?) solo attempt to paddle the river (Noli illegentima te carburundum) five years later had failed, whilst succeeding in purging the river from my "hit list".

I stretch my legs, feeling a sad reminder as the knees click, damaged by the pinning that occurred during that solo trip. The hookah is empty. I offer round cigarettes: a few refuse, some light up and share with a friend who has saved his behind his ear. We grin. We talk about how many days it took to walk up to the village. Then they gossip and talk, possibly about an up-coming (Ibex?) hunt. I think I am following the conversation with the help of hand gestures, sound effects and drawings in the dust. After a while I give up listening to their talk.

Seven years earlier I had met these people when I had made a solo attempt to paddle the Braldu River. I had come to thank them all and especially the village headman, Hussain Bey (Mr Hussain), for all the help they had given to me then.

Back then, I checked into Mrs Davies Private Hotel in Rawalindi. Mrs Davies Private Hotel had been an old Officers' Club for the British army, and indeed some of the staff seemed old enough to have worked for the club. This remnant of the Raj maintained the atmosphere of that era. The attitude was that British Empire rule had not ended; rather that the Sahibs, eccentric as usual, had just taken a long holiday. Though the hotel ran for the benefit of the guests, it was to the "rules" of the original owners. The food was typical of this: you could order "English style" food cooked by the Pakistani cooks or "Indian food" (as it was called despite Rawalindi now being in Pakistan) cooked for the English palate. Neither cuisine made it. The corn flakes were a marvel in malleable papier-mâché. The slippered servants smiled down at meals and merely nodded at all comments, thank-yous, complaints, requests or questions. It made me think of the Cheshire cat from Alice in Wonderland: benign and ineffectual. It was a marvellous place to stay even if the roof leaked and the tea was cold by the time it arrived. I was not surprised to hear when I asked after it in 1990 that it had probably fallen down rather than been demolished. It was here that we had spent ten days waiting to catch the "daily" flight to Skardu in 1978. This flight, the "most dangerous commercially available flight in the world," flew up the Indus valley with the mountains of Nanga Parbat, Rakaposhi and others over 7,000m high on either side of the route. This meant that once the plane entered the Indus gorge it was committed because the plane did not have the ceiling to fly out over these mountains and that the valley was frequently too narrow to allow the plane to turn around and return to Islamabad/Rawlpindi airport. Since the plane had to fly on visual navigation, spotters were stationed along this route and only when the visibility was clear to fly all the way was the all clear given. After ten days of getting up at 4.00 a.m. driving down to the airport and waiting for the all clear before returning to the hotel with a mixture of relief and disappointment, we finally had flown to Skardu. In the mean time we got to like the "corn fakes, too eggs pooched/ scrammled/ boiled toast, tea or cofee." It reminded me of the menu at the Chain Bridge Hotel, on the banks of the river Dee in Llangollen, where you could order "Fresh poached salmon (when available)".

After checking in at Mrs. Davies I called in at the Pakistan Tourist Development Corporation office situated in "Flashman's," the more upmarket hotel across the street, to ask about plane and bus tickets to the Northern Areas. When I mentioned in general terms about going up to Concordia the officer had almost winked when telling me of the need for a registered guide, equivalent equipment, and $50 a day wages. The total bill to walk up to Concordia would have been around $1500. Even to go only as far as Paiu, the start of the river, the official cost was still over $500. Admittedly I wasn't actually going to Concordia - that amazing amphitheatre, all those mountains over seven thousand metres - much as I would have liked to; the cost would be out of my league and time was against me. The wink decided me; no official porters.

I had arrived in Rawalpindi not realising that it was the Eid festival and everything was closed down for a couple of days. The holiday also meant that all the flights to Skardu were full. The Karakorum Highway, however, though possibly more dangerous, was now open to independent travellers through to Gilgit and sometimes even on to Kashgar in China. "Inshallah," after an eighteen hour bus ride from Rawalindi to Gilgit followed by another eight hour ride, I would arrive at Skardu. I headed for the bus station to buy a bus ticket. The man in the tourist shop advised me to take two Suzukis rather than a taxi to the bus station at Pirudiae. The Suzukis are great. Like dolmus in Turkey they run a set route taking as many passengers as possible. There are usually two or three Suzukis competing for customers at the same stop. This means that, to maximise his income, the driver has to appear to always be on the point of leaving and his assistant has to give the appearance of urgency when gathering passengers. They will, however, leave only when he is full or there are at least ten aboard. The driving; it is hard to decide if it is good but appears dreadful, or dreadful and just permanently lucky. For example, a red light means stop - unless turning left or right in which case the traffic light will obviously be green for you once you have turned. Traffic islands are just that - islands and the traffic flows round either side. Municipal buses, long-distance coaches, taxis, Suzuki and Ford Transit minibuses, horses and carts, pedestrians, bicycles, motorcycles, all compete for the same space. Add to this animals: fifty sheep and goats calmly being herded to the bazaar by a far from calm herder, dogs dodging rocks thrown at them, cows wandering, seemingly independently, munching rubbish. Everyone stops anywhere to pick up anyone. Horns on almost all the time. One Morris 1000 taxi I rode in had a switch instead of a horn button so the driver could corner, change gear, and still have the horn blaring. I arrived safely at the bus station and I bought a bus ticket for five o'clock that evening then rushed off to finish the last minute supply shopping and check out of Mrs. Davies Private Hotel.

I caught the bus from Rawalpindi to Gilgit and then another from Gilgit to Skardu. I hired a porter in Skardu and a "cargo jeep" which took us to the road-head at the bottom of the Braldu valley. The first night we stayed at a government rest house and afterwards just camped out on any level piece of ground. The chokidar, the man who looked after the rest house recognised a kayak and then was surprised that I had failed to recognise him from when we had passed through on our first Braldu expedition five years earlier. That night I remember questioning my reasons for this solo expedition for the first time. My diary records of that first night on the trail.

"A bad night's sleep, waking up with my mind going overtime on why and also my future throughout the night. A prisoner of my wanderlust. One adventure is not enough but how many are sufficient? Escapism, adrenalin junkie. Law of decreasing returns: More travel = Less firm friendships. This need to escape the things I may secretly envy - a steady income, an address, a wife, 2.2 kids and a mortgage. 'Freedom is just another word for nothing left to lose' ....' Nail my shoes to the kitchen floor lace 'em up and bar the door.' "

Up till then I had just decided to go and run the river. It was what I did, run rivers. I dated years by where I was paddling: '75 Austria where I paddled up with Mike Jones for the first time and was given the invite to join the '76 Dudh Kosi expedition in Nepal; '77 the Orinoco in Venezuela; '78 the Braldu; '79 British Columbia for the first time and a 'recce' of the canyon of Stikine; '80 a bad year, only made it as far as France; '81 British Columbia and running Overlander falls on the Frasier river; '82 the Çoruh, Turkey. 1983 and I had already been to Idaho paddling for Channel 4 TV on the North and South forks of the Payette and the Snake river in May and then to Turkey for two months running commercial kayak trips on the Çoruh. After a half-hearted search for team members I had argued that I might as well attempt the Braldu on my own. If I got into trouble there was very little that anyone else could do to help me. The old team, the veterans of the Dudh Kosi, Orinoco and the fateful 1978 Braldu expedition when Mike Jones had drowned, had grown up and out of expedition paddling and I had yet to establish a new regular paddling coterie. But this was not a reason for running the river; just a justification for running it solo. I can't give a reason for the descent of any river, it is even more inexplicable than the reason for climbing mountains, and to give a reason why I personally wanted to have another attempt on the Braldu is almost impossible. All these years later I still have no real way of explaining why I wanted to run the river. My glib answer has always been "unfinished business" or "don't let the bastard grind you down". Other people have talked about a certain river or mountain or rock face "burning a hole in them". I didn't have that feeling but as I went on paddling trips and explored other rivers, I always felt that I was side-stepping an issue and unless I returned I would never be able to take other trips seriously. This is no answer, but it is the best I can do.

The next three days after leaving the government rest house were some of the hardest I have ever had. My budget for the expedition meant that I carried my own kayak with my paddling gear and the gallon of paraffin for the Primus inside while the porter carried the food, sleeping bags, spare clothes and cooking equipment, (one pot, one Primus, two plates, two spoons, one tin cup).

The walk-in is straight up the valley. At least the low water levels of September meant that I could follow the path at water level for more of the route than we had in 1978, but there were still several horrendous climbs and descents to make. In 1978, with higher water, we were frequently forced away from the valley bottom and up the steep slopes of the valley sides before side-creek ravines, three or four kilometres later, forced us back down to the bank beside the charging, churning river for a few more kilometres; only to be deflected back up to the high level by the incursive eroding river. These climbs and descents were up steep zig-zag paths precariously hanging on to the banks of rocks and pebbles cemented together by dried mud. Even without the altitude the walk would have been tough. Either Reinhold Messner or Peter Habler described the walk-in to Concordia as the hardest approach walk in he had made. On returning back to Britain from the 1978 expedition we discovered that Pat Fernioff, a British climber, had been

avalanched to his death down one of these valley sides a month before we had arrived. We also had avalanches to contend with on that trip. At one point our Sirdar (head porter) had set off up the river-level path to see if the water was low enough for us to carry on by the low-level path rather than having to climb the 400 metre bank and then walk along the high path before scrambling back down to the river. As we waited for him to return with the yea or nay, there was a landslide and he disappeared in the dust cloud. We dug around in the avalanche with sticks and our hands for a while, but the futility was apparent. The porters appointed a new Sirdar and we climbed. Life had to go on. Inshallah, If Allah wills it, guided the porters' philosophy. When we returned back down to river level after our four hour high-level detour we found the Sirdar waiting for us; he had been beyond the avalanche when it happened and, understandably, had decided not to return across its path. Nervously, and with a smiling remembrance of the episode, I passed the site.

I had no water bottle, a bad oversight, and so had to wait till I reached the river for something to drink after each dehydrating detour. The river water was heavily silt-laden and should have been filtered, but such was my thirst that I ignored this time-consuming palaver and drank the river water straight, allowing just enough time for the largest parts of the glacial debris to settle. Carrying my kayak up the river, up and down the sides of the valley, was where the damage to my knees started. It was impossible to carry the kayak vertically because of the steep slopes (3.5 metre kayaks in those days) and carrying it horizontally meant that my knees had to absorb all the rotational momentum as the kayak swayed while I walked crab wise across the steep slopes.

Eventually I made it up the Braldu river as far as Askole, where I stayed with the school teachers, friends of Ayub, my porter and interpreter. Any idea of continuing up the river to the glacier snout and the start of the river had evaporated on the walk in and so the following day, I walked a further half day upstream from Askole and paddled down past the village. The school was given a half day holiday and I could see them all watching me, silhouetted against the sky high up on the river banks. An easy grade II but a refreshing warm up and stretch. I paddled to just below the village of Tongle, where I stashed my kayak on the bank of the river and walked back to Askole and the school house. The following morning I returned to Tongle to continue my descent of the river. Hussain Bey, and a gaggle of children who weren't herding the flocks, came down with me to the river bank. Hussain, the village headman (and maybe their Imam), was old even then and he no longer had to help with the harvest that was being taken in. He saw the problem at the same time as I did: the kayak had gone.

The kayak, paddles, spray deck, lifejacket, helmet, wet suit had gone; all the equipment that I had left stuffed inside the kayak the day before had gone. There had to be an explanation; the river had come up and washed it all away. No, there were my foot prints in dry sand below the point where I had left my kayak. Then one of the children saw the helmet lying amongst the small boulders, rocks and pebbles that made up the river bank; this pointed us in the right direction and we found the kayak half-hidden under some bushes further up the river. The boat, however, was devoid of contents and the detective work started. Hussain Bey produced a stub of a pencil and piece of paper, drew a sketch of the shoe print left by the thief in the sand and measured it in "thumb inches." We then talked in gesticulation, sign language and sketches in the sand. I told him that I have to catch up with Ayub who was on his way downstream, and was unaware of what had happened but had the rest of my equipment and instructions to wait for me with lunch at a point where the river and path met. Hussain indicated for me to meet him back up in the village and then talked to the children and they set about playing "bashing the bushes" searching the rest of the scrub tamarisk for the gear – but there was nothing there. He then headed off up the scree slope back to the village. The children decided that since they were down by the river bank they might as well play there for the day; bashing the bushes had proved a popular pastime. I left them and set off jogging down river towards Chongo village until I caught up with Ayub.

Ayub was not a real porter. Portering was not his real "trade". He was an English student from "Down Country" who had been working, as part of his studies, as an English teacher up in Skardu. He was not a good porter when it came to carrying loads, and on the walk in from the road head I had ended up carrying considerably more in the kayak than he in my rucksack. But he spoke English, that strange dated, empire-influenced, subcontinent English. Now I needed him to trans-late. I explained what had happened. He wanted to know why we were heading back; after all, all my gear had gone and it could be anywhere. All I could say was that Hussain Bey had said to come back. Late in the afternoon we arrived back in Tongle and Hussain's house. While Ayub and I cooked some food, what can only be described as a council of war erupted around us with all the village elders arguing. After watching a while as the conversation move rapidly around the gathered company I asked Ayub what was going on as nothing was very apparent to me. "They are discussing what to do about your baggage." We finished our food and I asked what was going on now. "They are discussing what to do about your baggage." Some time later they were still "discussing what to do about your baggage." Finally the discussion ended and everyone left. Ayub proudly informed me that they had finished "discussing what to do about my baggage." I suddenly realised they had been discussing what to do about my baggage in Balti and Ayub's knowledge of Balti was limited to what he had picked up while working in Skardu. He knew almost as little as I did about what was happening.

About an hour later Hussain Bey and six others returned and explained, in Urdu this time, that they had searched the village and had found nothing and that it was now late and nothing more could be done about my baggage tonight. We retired to bed. In the morning there were more discussions about what to do about my baggage. Finally, despite it being the height of the harvest, it was decided to send two people down the valley to make enquires at Chongo; two more would go and search in Askole and a further two would cross the vine bridge at Askole and search the village of Sino on the opposite bank.

The theft had occurred in their village and Islam decreed that it was their responsibility to help the traveller in their midst. I was surplus to requirements. Ayub decided to take the opportunity to return to his friends, the school teachers in Askole, and make enquiries there. I went off, feeling guilty, to help in the fields but it soon became apparent that I was an embarrassment to the harvesters; I was male and not of the immediate family and for the women to work covered up, because of the presence of a non-family member, was difficult, so I left. I was also not as adept as they at tying up and carrying the sheaves of atcha being harvested: either I tied them too tight and the stems snapped or too loosely and the corn spilled out as I made my way up the fields to the threshing area. I wandered down to the river again and then worked my way back up the bank looking at the river; so very different at this time of year from what it had been back in August 1978 when the melt was at its height and the water was grey-brown and it was almost impossible to "read" the non–white water formations that guide a kayak paddler down a rapid.

In 1978, we were young, naive and inexperienced; we were the blunt axe at the cutting edge of white water expeditions. We went away in July and August, because that was when - still on student time - you did; to France, to Austria (the best time for Europe), to Nepal (despite it being the height of the monsoon when we arrived there) and now to the Northern Areas of Pakistan. The Karakorum contains the biggest collection of high mountains in the world: K2, Broad Peak, Golden Throne, Gasherbrum, Masherbrum, the Trango Towers, the Biafo Spires, names familiar to climbers and mountaineers the world over but new to kayakists and very new to us. We had come to paddle the Braldu River that drains these mountains down to the Indus.

We did not get to the start of the river, the snout of the Baltoro glacier, where the expedition was planned to begin. After four days of the wicked walk-in we stopped at Askole. Two years before for the walk up the path alongside the Dudh Kosi that leads to Everest Base Camp we had all gone out and bought new heavy sensible stout walking boots and found the locals walking in flip-flops or bare feet. Learning from experience we had dispensed with boots and come with trainers this time. A mistake. This walk was a horror show. As we walked in and we watched the river our youthful enthusiasm and confidence had been tempered by the sheer power and speed of this river. Unbounded for most of its course by rock or solid ground, the Braldu carved its way through the terminal moraine, with few bends to slow its path. Boulders fell from these banks into the river, forming the rapids. These boulders, loose in the river, lurched downstream moved by the force of the current. It was not unusual to see a rapid change formation as you stood planning a route through the obstacle course of waves, boils, holes, and just plain nasty water.

We had also learnt about the effects of altitude after tackling white water paddling at 4,300 metres. The perceived wisdom gained by mountaineering expeditions was to acclimatise for a couple of days at 3000m to prevent problems at altitudes above 5,500m. Though we were not going to go above around 4,000m we had learnt that for an explosive sport like kayaking it was necessary to spend time acclimatising. We decided to stop for a couple of nights at Askole and spend the following day "warming up" before heading on upstream and to the source of the river.

We also had a film to make for the BBC. The speed of the river was self-evidently so fast that once we set off down the river, filming would be very difficult. A day's rest was a good opportunity to get some footage in the can. Roger Huyton and Mike Jones were enjoying their roles as cameramen, using all the jargon when possible: cut aways, long shots, close ups and pans, had peppered the conversation during the walk in. These phrases were learnt from "How to shoot 16 mm film", a book borrowed from Birmingham City Library by Mike six years earlier because Chris Hawksworth, recruited as a cameraman and paddler for his Blue Nile expedition, had fallen foul of Mike's pre-expedition publicity. Chris had felt capable of handling the cataracts and rapids - he was a paddler and veteran of the Grand Canyon of the Colorado which was the benchmark of the time - and they had pistols for the crocodiles. But when Mike started mentioning to the press the possibility of armed bandits taking pot shots with rifles from the cliffs overlooking the river - that was a risk too many and he had pulled out at the last minute. Left with no cameraman Mike just went out and bought a second hand camera and borrowed the book. Somehow it never got returned.

A day's rest from walking was universally welcomed and a gentle paddle on the river below seemed like a sensible idea. We spent the following morning running a short stretch of the river - filming was left for the afternoon. It was fast and furious but not too difficult, just intimidating. The water was cold. Forty kilometres upstream, and probably three hours earlier at the speed it was flowing, it had been ice. On the other hand, portaging back upstream to re-run the half mile stretch of river in a wet suit was a sweaty business. The day was perfect: cloudless, brilliant sunshine, and blue blue sky, that high altitude blue sky. It was also hot, maybe 30°C. After lunch we ran the stretch again, this time filming. Mike had a helmet mounted camera to get some "POV" (point of view) footage. Roger and I were to lead the run with Mike following to film with us "in shot" to give some sense of scale to the river. We broke out of the eddy at the start of the run: the river had risen and increased in speed during the previous two hours while we had eaten lunch and rested. Our experience in Europe had taught us that the rivers rose over the day as the sun melted the glaciers. We used to while away the mornings in the campsites in Austria waiting for the river Oetz to come up. What we hadn't realised was that bigger mountains meant bigger melts which meant bigger rises in the water levels. I led off. I'm not sure what happened but suddenly I was in the middle of the river. We had planned to run the right side of a huge hole. I didn't and seeing the hole shot left of it. Roger, mindful maybe of his other responsibility as a film man, realised we were too far left and tried to get back right. He hit the hole, probably dead centre, but it would not have mattered where he hit the hole; it was a huge hungry hole, not one you could readily get out of. He swam. John Liddell on the left bank snapped some photos. Roger's boat was dwarfed by the hole, he was just a dot. I chased after him, came across his paddle, picked it up and Mike got the stern of his boat to Roger. I made it to the bank where Mick Hopkinson came running past, he had seen the whole episode from high up on the moraine and had a better idea of the seriousness of the situation. He yelled at me that the others were still in the water. I was scared. I got out of my boat and ran stumbling down the bank following Mick. We came across Roger just about on the bank. He was shocked, scared, and covered in rice; he had vomited. Mick asked him questions. "Where's Mike?" Roger pointed to the river. "Is he in his boat?" Roger didn't answer. "Is he swimming?" I think Roger nodded. "Shit" was Mick's comment and he was off down the river chasing Mike in a vain effort to catch up. Ignoring Roger in his shocked state I ran off after Mick and Mike. I caught up with Mick and sometime later we came across Mike's boat wrapped around a rock close to the right bank. We pulled it off but Mike wasn't in it. A local Balti on the other bank made ominous signs of a body floating down the river. We walked back to the campsite in silence.

A decision was made to stay the night and spend the following day looking for Mike. He just might have made it to the bank, he might have been taken in by the villagers on the other bank. It was a vain hope but it was an obvious decision. We spent the following day walking down the banks of the river looking. That evening, while we sat lost in our own thoughts, Rob Hastings cut the blade off a paddle and carved a simple note of remembrance to Mike which we nailed to a tree overlooking the river. We spent a subdued night and set off home the following day. Mike's body was never found.

Arriving back at Skardu we were a different group who checked into the government rest house from the one that had checked out ten days earlier. Then, while we were waiting for porters and jeeps to be arranged, a Japanese climbing expedition had checked in to share the rest house with us. Though their leader had died on Gasherbrum IV returning from the summit, they were in good spirits having climbed the mountain, and their attitude was that their leader had died doing what he lived for. They even recognised Mick Hopkinson "You on Evelest, You swim." "Eighteen years paddling without a swim and I get remembered for that", was Mick's muttered comment to this unwelcome TV fame. Now we were in the same situation but did not share their fatalistic attitude. Our liaison officer, assigned to us by the Pakistan government, pulled all the strings he could and got us onto the next flight out. A final quirk to the relief of getting on that flight was that after taxiing to the end of the runway we were told to get out of the plane. Standing there on the runway wondering what was happening, we were amazed to see a step ladder arrive and the co-pilot climb up this, remove a cover panel, reverse the screwdriver, and hit something with the handle. He then replaced the cover and calmly indicated that we should all re-board for this "most dangerous commercially available flight in the world" back to Islamabad. Inshallah.

In September 1983, five years later, I sat on the bank of the river waiting for the parties searching for my baggage to return. I could see the river was much lower. I could see the big head wall on the opposite

133

bank and I deduced that this was where Mike had drowned. I could see the huge, maybe three maybe five metre deep undercut running the length of the cliff. I could see that when Mike had met this head wall at higher water levels the undercut was probably just submerged and so with no guarding pressure wave, Mike would have been swept under for its 60 metre length. I could see that my getting out and running down the bank with Mick Hopkinson instead of remaining on the water would have made no difference.

I arrived back in the village just as a triumphant Ayub returned from Askole. Someone had been seen crossing the bridge at Askole carrying a pair of paddles. He was being fetched. Later that evening he appeared with my baggage. It turned out that he was one of Hussain's relatives; an added complication to the whole situation. Once again a council of war was convened. After some time a "solution" was found: the thief would be my porter, for no pay, for the rest of my descent of the river. This was the village decision. To me it was a little strange as a judgement. Now I had two porters, Ayub and one whom I did not trust, when one was sufficient, and not enough food to feed the three of us. I suspect Ayub had some input into the negotiations! I made a thank you speech that was trite and probably even worse after being translated.

The following day I put in on the river. No one came to watch me off; I had taken up enough of their time. A short distance downstream I came across the first big rapid. I got out and scouted. A large rock split the river, the right channel had the majority of the water, and, to the left, the water forced its way through a boulder garden. I opted for caution, thinking I might be pinned on the main drop on the right. I ferry glided across above the rapid, got out and scouted the left hand route. It looked simple enough. I made the initial slalom moves through the rocks at the top part of the rapid and then it all went wrong. I slid over a small drop, meaning to break out behind the rock forming it. As I went over the drop the boat pinned and the stern sank. Suddenly I was sat in my boat with the water flowing over my head. The boat was very stable. There was no sense of panic, there was only a very logical thought process. "Let's try one thing at a time, let's not make matters any worse by acting hasty, I'm all right at present, I can breathe". An air bubble formed around my head. I tried pulling with my paddle, knowing that it would probably make no difference. If the force of the river pushing against my back did not clear me from the pin the little extra force that I could exert with a paddle was not going to make any difference. It didn't. Next I thought I could capsize and maybe the water pushing against my body when I was sideways would swing the boat around and clear me. This meant capsizing and losing my bubble of air. I tried taking my spray deck off to change the buoyancy of the boat; it did, it sank further and the air bubble shrank. I decided to try and get out of the boat. As soon as I lifted myself up out of the cockpit seat I was slammed forward and my knees bent against the cockpit rim. I tried to get out, but the water pressure was just too much: I was wedged with my legs trapped, the cockpit rim acting as a fulcrum and my body the lever. The air bubble decided to leave. I vividly remember thinking "Come on knees, break. I have to get out. I need air." The strain on my knees was incredible. Yes, things do flash past your mind. I remember at one point thinking "Oh well, this is the end Dave", then a huge feeling of guilt and then "Don't be stupid. Don't give up. Water's a changing fluid not a solid. Regular laminar flow does not exist in the real world."[1] I fell sideways, the boat swung round and I was clear. I surfaced, grabbed air, and quickly realised that things were still far from "sweetness and light."[2] There were two rocks ahead of me and a narrow gap between them. Turning, head downstream, I tried to raise myself up to clear the gap that widened above water level. No joy. Luckily, my forearms hit the rocks on either side so my shoulders did not jam, but my legs swung under me and dammed the gap between the rocks, the water level quickly rose and water started pouring over my head. My air bubble came back! Slowly, an inch at a time, I levered myself up the rocks with my forearms until my head cleared the water and then, as I eased myself up further, my legs found enough space to squeeze through the gap and I was swept off down below. I made it into the eddy behind the left hand rock and managed to climb up onto it and collapsed. I sat on the rock, massaged my knees. I even took some photos of the couple of drops that had nearly drowned me. So much for taking the conservative route! I had to catch my breath before making any more decisions.

---

[1] A bizarre flash back to my Hydraulics lectures at university.

[2] Mick Hopkinson used this phrase in Leo Dickinson's film "Pushing the Limits: a breath of white-water" when complaining about the psycology of naming rapids - you would feel much happier paddling a rapid called "sweetness and light" than one called "widow maker" or "nut cracker".

SCENE OF MY PINNING: AN INNOCUOUS LOOKING DROP!

I sat recovering for some time. Quite how long this had all taken I don't know, as far as I was concerned time was not moving at a regular rate. Perceived time was compressed and stretched as my predicament changed. Time's speed depended on my emotions; relief, desperation, pain, cold, determination, acceptance, resignation. These emotions had flooded through me in quick and intense succession and masked any measure of the passage of time. Seconds and minutes, the quantifiers of time, seemed to expand or contract as emotions changed. Eventually, I stood up and fell down again. My knees were knackered. I tried again: they were just about all right so as long as I didn't straighten my legs. Then, just downstream, I saw my kayak washed up on the bank, the dayglo orange flashes of tape illuminating my black kayak against the black rocks. I thought, "When I get back to Britain I must thank Slime for that tape." This galvanised me into action. Real time returned and became important. It was time to move: if the kayak floated away I would be marooned on the wrong bank. It was a six mile walk - if I could walk - back upstream to the bridge at Askole followed by a long 42 mile walk back down the other side to the road head and the slim chance of a lift in a passing jeep back to Skardu.

I was still in mid-river, admittedly only about four metres from the left bank, but still I had to jump/dive/fall back into the river and swim to

136

the bank, and if I missed the top eddy, the swim would be a bad one. With no choice I flopped into the river, made it to the bank and crawled down to the kayak before the same fickle current that had saved me floated it away. It was stuck solid anyway. I hauled it up the bank but had to wait, exhausted, before I could empty the water out of it. Then, slowly, struggling with frozen thumbs that would not work, I unpacked the dry bag. The clothes were dry! I put my feet in the socks and wrapped my hands in the jersey. Feeling came back slowly. Inside the kayak was a pair of split paddles. I had to let go my others when I pulled my spray deck off, the power of the water was such that I could not hold them in one hand. Time to move, I was cold. Time to overcome the inertia of exhaustion. I must have been in the water for some time but only now did I feel the cold, my mind had been too busy with other matters.

I got into the kayak, gratified to find that the sitting position was the best, most tolerable, position for my knees. I broke out back into the current and made my way down through the tail end of the boulder garden and on downstream. I paddled the next rapid and pulled into the bank. My brain was on automatic, disconnected from the body; delayed shock. I was paddling on instinct / habit. I stopped, reassured myself, I talked myself through the rapid again. I told myself everything twice, I made my brain work. And off I went again. I paddled a length of flat that usually I would have drifted and felt warmer. I ran the next rapid on sight, jumping from eddy to eddy till I could see down the remaining run out. I bounced down the middle of that and was feeling better. The next rapid back-looped me, catching me by surprise, but an almost instantaneous roll back up increased my confidence and I began to enjoy things; that "necky" feeling of solo paddling, just you and the river, no one to help you, no one to give you support, out on your own. It heightens everything. Time is full. Everything is yours only. You don't share any of it.

I reached the place where the path meets the river and waited for my porters. Time for a brew. When Ayub and the thief arrived I got out and lit the Primus and we made a big pan of sweet tea the way that they make it in India and Pakistan; add the tea, sugar, and milk to the water and boil it up. Sometimes you wonder why, when they have some of the best teas in the world growing there, they muck it about so much, but not at times like this: sweet, milky, energy-giving, stewed tea is just the best. I massaged my knees and found that they would hold my weight. I could walk just. They hurt and I had to be careful as there seemed to be a lack of forward restraint. I had to be careful not to fully straighten my knees.

After a lengthy lunch break I paddled down the river for a further mile till the river got "silly" again. Time to portage. The portaging was slow work when all I could do was waddle. At about four o'clock we stopped for the night. We were in the middle of one of the scree slopes where a huge rock had a cave underneath. It was just what we needed as the weather had closed in. We crawled in and cooked dinner. That night sleep was hard as my knees could not take any weight and could not lie out straight. I slept with the aid of the painkillers. One every 3-4 hours. Also, during a period of wakefulness, I felt an earth tremor; not unusual for the region but very unnerving when camped under the rock and between two land slip areas.

Next morning Ayub and the thief carried the kayak, reluctantly, till the end of the "impossible" stretch and I could get back on the river rather than having to walk. My progress on the water was also slow work as I was apprehensive and lacked confidence after the day before and so scouted more than normal. Also I had to take care when inspecting on the banks to prevent a stumble and jerking my bad knees. I caught up with the porter and Ayub for some tea and then scouted the next rapid and decided to portage. It was tempting to try and run the rapid as it led into an amazing gorge.

The gorge was narrow and carved through solid rock, but if you entered the gorge the river was flat and it would have been an amazing place to paddle; it was so narrow that a couple of rough hewn planks only two metres long had been put across the top as a bridge some 20 metres above the water level. The walls, polished by the sand-laden river over the years, were carved into big smooth curved shapes which looked like Henry Moore sculptures.

Down below the valley opened out and, remembering from the walk in, I assumed the river would be much easier. I set off again, arranging to meet up with my porters at Chongo for the night. I had the feeling that I was in the clear, I was home free, and it was just a matter of a couple of days' paddle before I could drift down the end of the Braldu and into the Indus and on to Skardu. No need for any walking. A rapid of big surging waves on the next stretch put paid to the feeling of elation, as I was surfed sideways by a breaking wave into the boil line of an eddy. It was a nasty piece of water where two slabs of water collided and I was soon upside-down trying to roll, but the paddle kept catching the descending boiling water; there was no support to pull up on, and even when I switched sides my boat seemed to have spun round to put that side on the boil line. Time to swim again. I bailed out and was pulled down by the boil and washed downstream before surfacing a long time later, paddle and boat abandoned.

A long swim followed: every time I came close to the bank either I couldn't cross the eddy fence, or there was no eddy and the current too fast and the river too deep to get a footing. Fortunately the river eased and became flat, fast and cold, and so there was none of the desperate trying to suck air while being tumbled over rocks and dumped in stoppers. Finally, more by luck than skill I was washed into a partially submerged boulder and by swimming and clambering over it managed to get into the eddy behind. Then despair, as I was washed out into the current again. A couple more holes and some real mental effort and I made it to the bank where I hung on to a rock, gasping. Slowly the brain worked again: "Got - to - get - out - of - the - water". Slowly I pulled myself out. Legs - no pain; arms - no pain. I had no energy left to feel pain. Slowly I climbed onto the bank and sat there head on knees panting with the taste of sweet tea on my breath. Ah, that sweet tea, but now all that energy had been used up. The sun came out and I lay on the bank for some time slowly warming up enough to feel like walking.

There was no feeling of relief or elation or salvation; just exhaustion. I had been wearing thick socks but these had disappeared in the initial moments of the swim, sucked off by the current and my trainers, too big to wear when paddling, had also disappeared; I had stuffed them in the back of the kayak. I was faced with a barefoot walk across a field of stubble left from the recent harvest to get back onto the path, and then a couple of miles down the river bank on to Chongo to meet the porters and recover my second pair of trainers from my rucksack. My feet were so cold that I hardly noticed the stubble and it was only once I reached the path that they warmed up enough to feel the sharp stones which replaced the stubble.

Time to give up and go home.

From Chongo I walked to the road head and on down the road hoping for a jeep to pass and gave me a lift. No jeep passed and it took three days to walk to the village of Shigar where I caught a "service" cargo jeep. Ayub left me at Dassu, the hamlet of three to four houses at the road head; he had some friends there. I dismissed the thief/porter at Chapko between Chongo and Dassu. It had been a strange punishment. He was punished, he had to carry the boat or gear; Ayub got to supervise, which he enjoyed; and I, the wronged party, had to provide the food.

1990. I stayed for two days with Hussain Bey and his family. Two days of calm. Two days of unregulated routine, controlled by the sun. I spent the time wandering and watching their world go round. As far as the village was concerned their world was what they could see. Chongo and Chapko, one and two day's walk down the valley, were so similar that they offered nothing new and Askole, half a day's walk upstream, though bigger, offered nothing different. Skardu, with the trappings of "civilisation" - electricity, shops, roads and airport - was three day's walk down and four days back, along with an expensive jeep ride from and to the road head. When I left, I presented Hussain Bey with a carved wooden Koran stand for him and the village. It had been hard to know what to buy as a gift; what to give a village that has a way of life of which I had no real understanding. I could see how it worked, but I had no way of knowing the reality of their lives. I also gave his eldest son my Karrimat and was asked to bring an extra sleeping bag the next time I came to visit. I would have given him my bag but I needed it for the walk out. I think they realised that I had made a big effort to come and say "thanks" for their help; I am sure they had no idea what I had been doing the last time I had visited.

On the walk out I met a down country engineer with a level and theodolite. I asked him what he was surveying for; "A road" he replied; which confused me since no one up the valley could afford a jeep and no one from Skardu had any reason to head up the valley. His explanation was startling in its unexpectedness: "For you tourists!"

Now, I have heard, the road goes all the way to Askole.

NOTES

1.   Back in Britain after my solo attempt the diagnosis of my damaged knees was hyper-extended cruciate ligaments and several weeks off work. Also I had lost 16kgs. from hard work and insufficient food and a hookworm infestation. My parents were a little concerned!

2.   In April/ May 1984 six months after my solo attempt. Andrew Embick led an expedition of paddlers from the USA, including Rob Lesser, Kathy and Bo Shelby, and Bob McDougall that paddled "98% of the river from Paiu to the Indus confluence". Talking to Rob Lesser some time later I think they portaged the drop where I got pinned, which in a strange way made me feel better! See "First Descents" edited by Cameron O'Connor and John Lazenby.

3.   During the writing process of this account, Doug Ammons gave me great encouragement and also the shove to write more than just a narrative account of the three trips of mine. This I did, (so you can imagine how skinny the original was) but Doug still pushed. Here is an extract from one of my emails back to him, written late at night after returning from the pub. I have corrected some of the typos but left the rest as was written, in the drunken stream of consciousness form.

"To develop the story, you mention/suggest that I expand on Mike's death and my paddling history. This has crossed my mind but then I rejected the idea because I felt it would be hard to do without it becoming too much of a history/auto-biography of a period of my life and not enough of a story about the Braldu. Also I can see a point in expanding Mike's death but to do that in any way other than a straight "tell it as it happened" one event after another would be impossible - for me. The time is too long ago and memory is too dim to recall feelings/emotions. I have emotions of the event, I know what I feel about it, but now not then, now. I have been through this in my mind often 'cause I ran the Mike Jones Rally in Llangollen for ten years with over 15,000 people turning up over the ten events and that changes your emotions. Also the fact that Reg and Molly Jones came to all the events and they intervened and got me the Mike Jones award from the Winston Churchill scholarship so I could run the trip for people with disabilities to the Çoruh in Eastern Turkey which to date is the best trip I have done/put together. And Mick Hopkinson came and gave the lecture one year all the way from New Zealand and seemed impressed by the event. As a result I feel that writing this story is not cathartic. Maybe my solo trip was, but I never felt that it was - that was never my reason for attempting to run the river solo. But now we are into psychoanalysis! Your territory not mine I'm just … "a carpenter build houses stores and banks, chain smoke Camel cigarettes and hammer nails in planks" … as John Prine puts it. (I might just use this paragraph in the story to explain why I haven't tried to!)"

MIKE JONES RALLY

When we returned to Britain in 1978 Reg and Molly Jones, Mike's parents, decided to set up a charity, now part of the Winston Churchill Travel Scholarship, for "people doing expeditions, with preference given to kayaking and youth". Donations rolled in and we sold raffle tickets for donated prizes. I dreamed up the idea of the Mike Jones Rally. The River Dee at Llangollen is one of the best bits of reliable white water in Britain and I organised the necessary permission from the land owners and angling clubs to ensure there would be no confrontations with irate riparian owners. The following February some 200 people turned up and we raised a few hundred pounds. Then the next year I was informed that the dates the anglers had granted for that year's rally were in January. (I was not aware that I had asked for any dates!) 400 turned up - despite the snow - and I knew I had created a monster when one group forgot their tent poles but still managed to build an igloo despite discovering the error after leaving the pub. It became an annual event. By the time I retired from running the event after ten ral- lies, we had a committee, a turnover of £10,000 each weekend, free shuttle buses, free lectures on the Saturday night, divers on rescue duty, 2000 people paddling plus hangers on. We had flown Saturday night speakers from half way round the world. We had run cardboard canoe races, inflatables races, chariot races. We had taken on the bikers on the Dragon Run at rugby in the campsite. We had drunk two pubs dry one year and had Ted, landlord of the Bridge End, worried about whether his extra stock would last on a couple of occasions. Someone asked me, late and in a pub after I had announced my retirement from the committee, what I had learnt from running the event: never have ideas on the back of envelopes, (and how to spell Froncysyllte and other Welsh place names), that's what I learnt!

No, seriously. It was a good thing. A good memorial to a friend. Reg and Molly would come every year and lend moral support, and it would always make me smile overhearing people packing up at other kayaking weekends around Britain saying to friends "See you at the Jones week- end". Also, I could invite friends from around the world to come and give the lecture and drink beers on the Saturday night! Looking through the list of authors in this collection of stories, many veterans of those wet weekends in Llangollen will recognise some of the names.

MIKE JONES WEEKEND SPEAKERS

79 Mike Jones Films.

80 Mike Jones films and Chrisfilm Videos. 1st cardboard race

81 British Columbia. Pete Knowles, Jeff Gill and others 2ndcardboard race

82 Çoruh River Dave Manby 1st Inflatables
Iceland Breakthrough Paul Van De Mollen

83 Claude Castelain. Extreme gradient paddling in France
Chris Oliver. Zab river. Turkey (Mike Jones Award)
Jim Hargreaves. Bio-Bio 2nd Inflateables

84 Dave Manby Corsica Super 8mm Film Standing up Race

85 Wolfgang Haibach. Tamur, Nepal.
Guy Baker Zanskar. (Mike Jones award) 1st Chariot race

86 Whit Deschner. Around the world in 80 Delays 2nd Chariot Race

87 Arlene Burns. Tsangpo / Brahmaputra River. Tibet

88 Jochen Schweizer. Family Mad. 3rd Cardboard race.

89 Mick Hopkinson. Tales from an ex-pat living in New Zealand

90 Dave Simpson. Alternative uses of whitewater helmets!
91 Nolal Whitsell Whitewater open Boating
92 Alan Fox The Ganges.

ANDY MIDDLETON

I was wandering around the "International Canoe Exhibition" in Birmingham contemplating this a trade show: commercial sales, selling kayaks, selling equipment, selling paddling courses. Set in a huge grey overheated concrete bunker surrounded by a grey Birmingham on a grey February day, it was the antithesis of the sport; all so far removed from what kayaking is about; open air, fresh air, a challenge, a day out, a couple of hours relaxation. I bumped into Andy in this anathema of kayaking. I explained to Andy what I was attempting in collecting these stories and his eyes lit up. With his reply I knew I was on to a winner, "Keep me informed! I know just what I am going to write about. Look! the hairs on my forearms are standing on end just with the excitement of remembering the wave".

Andy was born in St. David's, Pembroke shire and after finishing college he set off around the world for a couple of years looking for the perfect wave. He failed to find it and did not really like what he saw and so returned to St. David's, Whitesands Bay, and the Bitches. He worked renting out surf boards and instructing novice wind surfers. A sudden realisation that this was not really the best career move led to his founding Twr-y-Felin Outdoor Centre. He then invented coasteering and started scaring management development personnel and thrilling children. Ten years later and his children are beginning to scare him by coasteering and the management personnel are being thrilled. Life changes, things progress. His message of the importance of play and risk is getting through. Even relaxing with him in the bar has a risk; Andy is still master of all known bar games and will take pints off you at any opportunity.

A DAY AT THE RACES

At the end of the land on the west coast of Wales lies an island.
An island named after Viking raiders, wild with birds, seals and porpoise.
Ramsey. Hrafn's Øy.
Off the coast of the island, volcanic and dangerous, lie the Bitches.
A line of knife-sharp rocks that cut the sea as it surges past this tip of land.

Every hour of every day, the tide runs here.
Sometimes gentle, inviting beginners to drift past the glassy movement of current.
Sometimes, often, harsh, unforgiving, fierce and ready to punish those who mis-tread their path.

The release of energy that happens on even a calm day with a flood tide running could be measured on the Richter Scale.
Plate tectonics like you've never seen before.
Huge slabs of green-blue water pour incessantly over the reef.
Waves are sculptures of cold glass as churning stoppers roll between the rocks.

Mist hangs in the air, oily with salt.
Seals hunt for fish in the forests of kelp.
When a spring tide runs on the Bitches, it's time to play...

It's good to play.
Children are good at it, able to amuse themselves for hours,
- experimenting, jousting, laughing.
Until they go to school.
There, it seems, play becomes something to be done at special time:
- for playtime, not lifetime.
Slowly, ever so slowly, play gently slips away, out of sight, out of reach.
It becomes something ephemeral, for weekends and holidays, detached from life in the real world.
It is time to take stock and get a grip on play and remember the pure buzz.
That's it.
It is still out there.
Remember risk and play with it.
Excitement.

Yesterday, I paddled out to the Bitches solo to meet some friends who were already there. Once again, in the early chill of a spring afternoon, the twenty five-minute paddle was a good warm up for body and mind. Time to wind-down, to think, and to play a few moves in my mind. The other two, Bill and Andy, were starting to get a few ends and fast spins as I arrived, with the tide building. We played, teased, laughed, performed, unthinking. Playing with friends, the best. A group of first-time visitors waited, cautiously around the eddies, ready to leave for home. A few of their more experienced paddlers occasionally played with monster and returned ravaged, ready to rest.

The monster on Ramsey is an eight metre wide hole that forms at the height of the flood tide. Playing with this beast is a strange experience when there's a swell running.

Timing.

Timing is the essence.

Water lifts and pushes, gently if you are lucky, past and upstream of the front face of a tiny stopper.

The rise of the swell peaks and a voice at your shoulder starts to murmur. Remember what it's like to hear voices?

Quietly, you'll start a drift backwards into a rolling, mauling, playful pile of water the size of a stretch limo but with more horsepower.

With truth in your heart, it can be hard to say that you are in control.

Are we ever though?

Does it matter?

Many of the best rodeo moves I've ever seen were invented here ten years ago by out of control paddlers in big volume playships.

James Joyce, in Ulysses, wrote: "a man of genius makes no mistakes. His "errors" are volitional and are the portals of discovery".

No risk, no reward. Nothing venture, nothing win.

I'd better not. What would they say? I don't want to look bad.

We played, we danced, we dared.

For fun.

It's easy though, isn't it, to not make that effort, to not drive the distance, to not put on wet kit on a wet, cold day.

Instead, stay in, work a bit more, save, unknowingly submit to the mediocrity of peer group pressure.

Time won't wait though, you know that.

If you don't make time to play today, it will be gone.

Jack knows, all work and no play.

Effort is what it takes to get a reward, like the apples at the wobbly ends of the branches in the old farmer's field. Hard to get, and sometimes risky, but sweet and tempting. Since when are the windfalls of life the best reward?

No matter how many times I've played at the races, I've come back elated, injected with adrenalin, salt water, and sunshine or wind. No two times are the same here - there are some big advantages to having a river that can get two metre groundswells and forty-five knot winds.

On a gentle day, the Bitches behave like a well-fed cat - languorous, rolling and predictable.

With a wind and swell, think of a caged panther, of raw undiluted power, of sudden moves and surprises.

Above all, the wind holds the power - Lord and Master of Ramsey Sound.

He can change the terrain from plains to mountains with a simple shift in direction. Wind or calm, sun or rain, there is fun to be had providing that you look for it, expecting smiles and laughter.

In my mind is an amazing day; a day maybe ten years ago, paddling the Bitches with Steve Q and a visitor, John, who reckoned himself competent on Grade IV. During our time at play on a medium size spring tide, the wind shifted, moving from south-west towards the north. Maybe north by north-west. There's spot in Ramsey Sound called Horse Rock that has a reputation for malice and, that day, it lived up to it. On a big tide, the Horse is a pour-over, seven and a half metres deep, with water piling in at twenty five kilometres an hour. Even with no wind, there's movement and some big whirlies. Mystery moves in old-school river boats. On a breezy day, with wind against tide, the place is something else. The waves on the edge of the madness can have five metre faces and upstream lies a field of haystacks exploding; moving pyramids to be surfed and survived. On this day, our visitor had his work cut out. The tide was piling up against the wind in Ramsey Sound like nothing I had seen before; Steve and I knew we would have to push hard before we even hit the main current.

Tired paddlers make tense companions.

Laughing at the size of the waves I shouted myself hoarse, cajoling John to paddle across an area of haystacks and exploding two metre waves at top speed. The haystacks in Ramsey Sound, like Horse Rock, slide up quickly. It's weird for newcomers to find themselves sliding sideways at ten kilometres an hour whilst surfing waves forwards. Halfway across the overfalls, a little test arrived, as they do, in the form of three enormous waves, travelling fast upstream, cresting at the top. I was paddling tail end and got cartwheeled backward and rolled up, relieved to see that John had squeezed by.

With a final drive of effort and encouragement, we made it over the next, critical hundred metres and skimmed the edge of the huge rolling overfalls of Horse Rock - the biggest waves on our Day had huge, wind-blown faces and demanded humility. We bowed and paddled past, buzzing, elated, wiser, and warm with excitement.
Years pass quickly and circumstances change
and my family is growing fast,
learning about fun.

Ten years of Tyr-Y-Felin Bitches Rodeos have been and gone,
Boat designs are focused on play and performance more than ever.
Younger paddlers will be performing more advanced moves at next year's events, and the year after that.
Yet there is still something missing for many people out there...
Thinking about play. Thinking about fun. Thinking about risk.
It is so easy to fall in with the devil of habit and stop noticing the challenge that might be just around the corner.

Just around the corner on Ramsey, not more than eight hundred metres from the Bitches, lies some of the best rock-hopping territory on the planet. Rock-hopping is a little-known dimension of sea kayaking; playing cat and mouse with big swells as they crash and flow around the cliffs. White water kayaking in salt water wine. Towering, intimidating, dangerous for twenty seconds, then gone - until the next wave makes a mark.
Few of the thousands of kayakers who visit this paradise on the west coast of Wales ever get to think about rock hopping.
"Sea kayaking is boring," they say. Not so. There is no other dimension of kayaking that exposes a paddler to so much power in relative safety.
On a day with a heavy groundswell before one of the rodeo finals in 1998, I took a couple of the Teva Tour paddlers out to play. They had never seen waves so big before and revelled in the power, testing boat control in a cauldron of kinetic energy off the south end of Ramsey. After an hour, the tide had changed and we moved offshore to the overfalls that lie one kilometre further west, in a turbulent passageway between Ramsey and the outlying islands of the Bishops and Clerks. Wave wheeling in bright sunlight over the back of three metre waves; we chased and surfed the biggest waves that we could find and returned home elated.
Elated and unable to describe the feeling to people who had never experienced it.

Play time,
Laughter remembered.
Take time to think.
Notice how you feel.
Remember the last time that you got wet and pumped adrenalin.
Remember the feeling.

I've got to go now...

WHAT 'TH HELL'S A
"SMALL CRAFT WARNING"
ANYWAY ?!!

ALLAN ELLARD

Allan's parents probably have mixed emotions about their son meeting me. This is because Allan's progress to University seems to have been delayed by a few more rivers to run. I must admit that some of these were my fault.

I first met Allan when he was sixteen and one of the "youths" on the First British Youth Expedition to the Grand Canyon and I was a "responsible adult". Two years later, after the trip down the Grand Canyon, Allan (along with Jon Pearson) were the first two names I put on my list of helpers for the New Horizons Trip for people with disabilities down the Çoruh. They had impressed me with their skills to such an extent that I had quickly discovered a new skill - miss the eddy so you did not have to play in the hole; (usually a hole I was proud and pleased to have missed): leave this sort of playing to Allan and his generation.

This was the first year that Allan did not go to University. The following year Allan did not go to University again - instead he helped me out with my Çoruh River Trips. This meant he had my family "Birthday Party" trip inflicted on him. At the end of this trip, having had enough of Manbys, he took the bus from Erzurum, Eastern Turkey, to Manali, Northern India where he started work for Equator Expeditions as a raft guide and safety kayak paddler. That was several years ago and University still has not happened but he has represented Britain at the World Rodeo Championships in Canada. His parents have, I think, forgiven me for leading him astray. His mother now makes made-to-measure "Canyon Gear" paddling clothing, but it has taken some time for them to work out quite what his job entailed. Allan once gave me a brilliant job-description of a Raft Guide: a cook and bottle washer who commutes 15 - 20 kms to work each day by raft.

On the youth expedition to the Grand Canyon, Allan met Jon Pearson and the White Water Warriors were born. (I think they had been conceived earlier but the expedition was the catalyst.) As they travelled they met Mike Abbott, another young paddler with a similar outlook on life, the rivers and everything. He was signed up as the third member of the WWW. Mikey brought another dimension to the group - fire breathing. Soon the three of them were semi-expert pyrotechnicians and entertaining clients on the banks of the rivers in Nepal. I received a length of Allan's dreadlocks through the post with a covering note saying that the weather was too hot for long dreads. I think that the real reason was that long dreads were too dangerous for fire breathing. Now Allan's fire breathing has improved and the dreads have grown back to their original length, but he still has not got to University.

ALLAN AND MIKES MOST EXCELLENT ADVENTURE

Mike and Al had an adventure. They were full of energy and the foolishness of youth. Back in Britain word reached me of Al and Mike's exploits but because of the way things are I never got to hear the full story in one chapter. Over the passage of time details emerged, some in letters or e-mails and some by word of mouth from mutual friends and also from telephone conversations with Al and meeting Al after many moons. The story below is gathered together from these varied sources and from Al and Mike's written account composed on river banks, in flop house hotels and on bar table tops.

Mike and Al believe that it began way back in August 1994, when all three White Water Warriors, venturing from three corners of the globe, found themselves hunting the lesser spotted cartwheel whilst safety kayaking for Equator Expeditions and chasing raft loads of manic Israelis down the adrenal flow of the mighty Beas River. This was exactly what the Warriors wanted from life: days on the river, waves to shred, holes to ride....

"On one day-off, the river gods decided to test us Warriors. We had cruised the morning, epic free, but then just before lunch....

"Wow! Hey man, wasn't there a huge rapid here yesterday?" Mike questioned as they drifted across the ominous depths of.... a lake??

"Yeah dude, must have been a flash flood! Hey check that out!" Al pointed to the frothing mist rising from the approaching, rather terminal-looking, horizon line!

Later that day Jonny philosophised, "Totally wild ride man, you just go in at the top, get worked, and pop out when toasted!"

155

From that day on the Warriors' description for any time you got worked became, 'Toasted', 'toasting' or just 'plain, no butter Toast'"

Unknown to the Warriors at the time, this coining of a new phrase this was to have a slight but lasting effect on a handful of Nepali River guides' perception of western culinary preparation. This was because after the Beas, the three White Water Warriors moved to Nepal and spent the Fall rafting season making Toast with 16 foot of rubber on raging, warm, sun-splashed, bug-free rivers, and it was small wonder that the Warriors vowed to return to Nepal for the following Spring season. Like most plans made on river beaches not all of the plan was accomplished; Mike and Al returned but Jonny was lost to fulfil his destiny with his beloved, (and much missed baked beans on toast). That spring they cruised the Kali Gandaki, guiding rafts and safety kayaking for groups. Their perception of river running became river play session and those nervous moments worrying about the next blind drop became but a flickering slide show from adventures past. Things had to change and it was whilst peering through churning mists of brewing rum punch, that they formulated plans and dreamt of the Toastage they might encounter in the next episode. The dreams had the same recurring refrain: "The Beas is pumping, and as usual toast is just waiting to be made."

"Yeah! The Nepali Spring rafting season was over and the monsoon impending, so a motley crew of us guides and girl-friends trudged with our kayaks, up to Manali. We all wanted to view the scene of the Warriors' encounter with toast. Also in this bizarre Himalayan region the rivers seem ridiculously fast! Now, this may have something to do with altitude, or maybe the influence of one of Kulu valley's 365 resident gods. But what-ever, the main flow is fast, the holes and waves are faster, even the eddies are fast. I mean you are left wondering just which eddy you can make - like which eddy you might actually catch. If you miss it, next thing you know you'll be trying to find a manual pop-up button in the middle of the next kayotic jumble sale of hell holes and pour-overs. It's just like the real thing..... but bigger! The speed, the gradient, everything, it's all there right to the last drop, and all the time the various

tributaries are dumping in, amplifying the proportions. Wild
times. Toast everywhere."

After a few weeks, and the loss of a boat and a paddle tip or two, the
rest of the motley crew departed, leaving the two Warriors momentarily
lost in space. New plans needed to be made. A change instead of a rest.
So for some inexplicable reason the two Warriors decided to trek over
a 4500m pass to the mystical valley and rivers beyond.

Dear Dave,

Expeditions. Huh! I suppose you have to suffer to be able to call a
river trip an expedition. Well Mikey and I have started on this stupid
idea of carrying over to some river on the other side of the pass at
the top of the Paravati River. The pass is 4500m high!! Our bodies
argued that gravity should be played with, not fought against; nevertheless we're trying!! During the first day of our anti-gravitational
mission up the valley we scouted the Parvati River, contemplating running the upper reaches of this wildly steep, voluminous river as a way
out, a reason for not having to carry on carrying up the valley.
Climbing up past cataract after cataract brought us back down to
reality and up to the spiritual hippie village and hot springs of
Kirganga. Cool – well hot – but you know what I mean. Mike was
heard uttering something like "wouldn't it be great to just stay here
and absorb some influence?" BUT NO, we are **Warriors**, we are heading on tomorrow!
Two Days Later......
Aaaah, yeahh, swee-e-e-t... just why didn't we just stay here on the
way up? Why didn't I listen to Mikey? I have just slid into the
sulphury hot spring water, and watched a thick scum dissolve off my
body. We've given up! Honest, it was the harsh elements and the
altitude (or the fact that the supplies of chocolate just weren't holding
out). Anyway we have abandoned our attempt on the pass and have
descended back to the hippie village, the hot spring, relaxation, and
vows to stick to gravity sports. New plan. We are headed for two
famous trout tributaries of the Beas, the Sainj and Tirthane. From the
top of the bus the Sainj, though hundreds of feet below, looked fine.
Like steep, but a pool drop creek. You've heard that one before!
More later. Time for some more relaxation now.

Later still......

This morning I sat on the bank sporting my Micro blades and Micro Bat, nervously searching for a line through the reality. Quivering in my wet suit shorts, I was wondering if the morning 'Toast' was about to appear! It's the first time in my life I have been shaking in my shorts. (Sounds like that Bonzo Dog Do Dah Band track you used to play in the truck in Turkey: "Shaking the Shirt")

The Sainj was deceptive but strangely consistent: the further we paddled, the higher we dropped. Side creeks kept adding more volume to the next recirculation we were trying to get though. Eventually we found ourselves frantically paddling the gnarly rapids between the gnarlier falls. We called it quits and extricated ourselves from the gorge. We got back on further downstream, to relax on a few kms of endless boofs and holes from heaven. Anyway the adrenalin rush from the bus ride back is wearing off. Hey here is a topical tip: if perched on a dubious roof rack, the best seat in the house by far is the padded Pyranha MICRO or the ACRO Lounger. Just remember that when the bus brakes hard to miss a Holy Cow, you will find yourself screaming forward about to boof the luggage box! Make sure you lean forward and keep the nose down or you will find yourself flying through the air about to get nailed by the bus you started from! We made it back to Aut, a strange-but-true truck stop cum bus stop village at the confluence of these steep creeks and the mighty Beas, and us Warriors have settled into a night of celebrating the day's adventures. Strange bus wallahs keep arriving and helping us devour numerous bottles of a seemingly innocent drink, Shimla No1.

Yours on a wave

AL

P.S. Shimla No.1. Warning, this stuff brings a whole new dimension to the word, 'volatile', and rather like really good chillies, you get to feel the effect three times, consumption, internal combustion and ejection!

The next morning despite their bodies' convulsions, the Warriors once again clambered atop a blessed and decorated TATA bus and headed for the Trithan river. The road up the Trithan river valley to the village of Banjar seemed to have more holes and bumps than an adolescent's face. After hours of jarring, with the remnants of the night before excesses determined to escape, the Warriors arrived at the village. Shortly afterwards, with slightly paler complexions but a more relieved stance, the Warriors found themselves and most of the village's inhabitants, on the banks of the Trithane. Everyone looked confused, except the river. It knew exactly where it was going........ down! And, as the Warriors were to find after about a kilometre, down like it meant it. Al, although not yet in full control of all his body's reactions, said he felt far more at home on this steep, low-volume water park.

"We were scouting section after section of mini gorges, bouncing from boof to boof, flying down bedrock slabs. I was having fun, then I suddenly found myself about to enter the wrong side of a fall that split, left to a sweet boof and right, straight into a smooth sided 'toaster'-shaped chasm!! No shit! I was heading, it seemed, into the toaster's jaws of death, when the little edgy thing on the bottom of my MICRO Bat strained, but found purchase on the slab of rock I was sliding along. Momentarily stationary with lightning reactions (yeah right!) I threw my body over the left side of this slab, put my hands down on the smooth grey granite and found myself in a press-up stance perched on top of the dividing rock! Like what to do! I'm there in this strange three point stance - right hand holding my blades, knuckles on the rock, left hand flat, fingers gripping the granite, and the nose of my Micro just resting on the smooth rock. All I can see is the 'Jaws of Death' on one side and 'a good beating down this side too!' on the other. Next, I caught a glimpse of a hysterical grin on Mike's face as he flew past cleanly boofing the hole on the left I knew I was about to throw myself into. No real option anyway. After a few cartwheels somewhere in the green room below, I was flushed out. Mikey started discussing the possibilities of this radical style of move. I didn't answer. I wasn't listening. I was still recovering from the emotional overload. I was reduced to spluttering wreck, all I could add was something about it being a better idea to get the right line to start with! We had a rest before going on 'cause the Trithane continued for miles and miles. When we got out we were really wave punch-drunk, dazed and confused, reduced to staggering around the dirt road waiting for a bus to return us to the temptations of Aut, chai and ABSOLUTELY NO Shimla No1 whisky..."

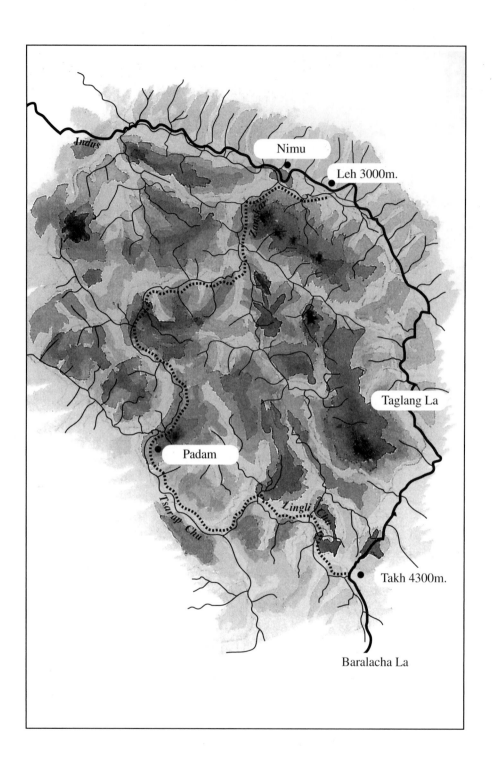

Nimu

Leh 3000m.

Taglang La

Padam

Tsarap Chu

Zingli

Takh 4300m.

Indus

Baralacha La

160

Kayaks dwarfed by the surroundings on the Indus.   *Dave Allardice*

Allan Ellard fire breathing.

Allan Ellard

Mike Abbot and all the gear for the trip down the Zanskar.

Allan Ellard

Papuan dressed for a *sing sing*. *Jonas Noker*

Trying to read the muddy water of the Strickland. *Jonas Noker*

Guy Baker hoping the line will work   *Joe McCarthy*

My father, mother, sister, sister-in-law, brother, nephews and niece rafting the Çoruh.

James Venimore

My nephew Kit, aged 5, and Horace Cliff on the Çoruh. *James Venimore*

Vietnamese girl. *Colin Hill*

Marcus on the Indus. *Dave Allardice*

Mike adopting stay dry tactics. *Allan Ellard*

Jon "You drop in and come out when toasted" Pearson   *Allan Ellard*

Porters carrying kayak through Simikot.   *Francesco Salvato*

Doug Ammons on the "Golf Course" below the upper ledge hole.   *Dave Russell*

Tony Brennen in "Pectoralis Major". *Dave Russell*

Donald Bean (74) being watched by Allan Ellard, Seti River Nepal. *Equator Expeditions*

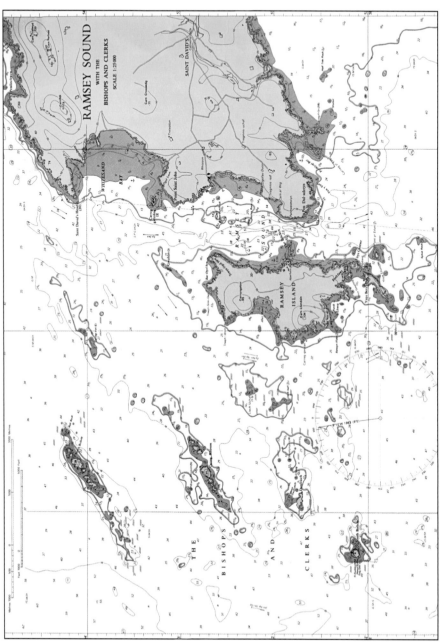

Reproduced from Admiralty Chart number 1482 by permission of the Controller of Her
Majesty's Stationary Office and the UK Hydrographic Office.

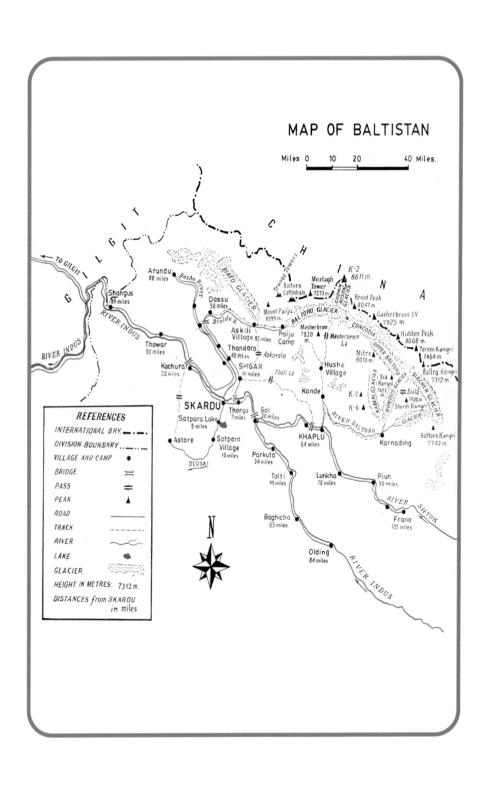

MAP OF BALTISTAN

Miles 0   10   20   40 Miles.

REFERENCES

INTERNATIONAL BRY.	—·—·—
DIVISION BOUNDARY	··········
VILLAGE AND CAMP	●
BRIDGE	⧓
PASS	⧧
PEAK	▲
ROAD	———
TRACK	– – –
RIVER	∿∿
LAKE	▓
GLACIER	▒▒▒
HEIGHT IN METRES:	7312 m.
DISTANCES from SKARDU	in miles

With monsoon rearing its saturated face, it was time for the Warriors to move. That afternoon, without a whiff of Shimla No.1, but in the hydrocarbonized air of the rush hour buses and trucks as they pulled through the main bazaar, the two of them planned their next move. Memories of tales of the Zanskar provided the two Warriors with a destination. From recollections of a drunken babble back in a Kathmandu bar with a Scottish doctor (Andy Watt), and a bazaar story of a nightmare three day portage by an Indian expedition, the Warriors concluded that the 300 km-ish journey (depending on which map they looked at) , would take something like 8 to 10 days. "Hmmmmm... that's a lot of rice to fit in my Acro!" was Mike's comment as he followed the wiggly canyon contours on the token map. (Jonny's stories from when he safety boated for a raft trip down the river a few years before were even more unreliable as a logistics guide - all he had ever mentioned was "great waves, man".)

So the Warriors headed north. Their route would take them over the Rhotang La, Baralacha La, Lachalang La and Tanglang La, down to Leh, (3000m) to re-supply and leave their dry clothes and catch the bus back over Tanglang La and Lachalang La, and down around the corner to a small river near Takh, or Sarchu, depending again on which map they looked at. Through moonscapesque Ladakhi valleys, the Tsarap Chu carves away through the Zanskar mountains to the trekking post of Padum, close to absolutely nowhere. From here the river becomes the Zanskar, and heads towards Leh, its chilled waters filling the canyons of the infamous Zanskar Gorge.

After surviving four of the world's highest road passes, and the two day epic bus ride from hell, (a long story in itself apparently) the Warriors reached Leh, the capital of Ladakh. Known to many as 'Little Tibet', Ladakh is an Indian state on the edge of the Tibetan plateau, with China (Tibet) to the north, Kashmir to the west, Nepal to the east and, at present, the rest of India to the south. Outside Leh and scattered around the arid moonscape are ancient Gompas (Buddhist monasteries), Stupas and Manis. Here, traditionally-dressed nomads still herd their goats and sheep in the plains between the 6000m peaks, and tar-covered characters, like extras from a Mad Max movie, keep the few roads usable after each frost-shattering winter. It is one of the coldest inhabited places on earth.

"Suffering some kind of altitude sickness, we experimented with load configurations. We still had to be convinced the boats would float as we tried to carry everything we would need. Billy, mugs, spoons, food, tea, sugar, chocolate, first aid, camera, water bottle, split paddle, thermorest, sleeping bag, bivvy bag, dry fleece layer, hat, sunny's, lippy, lighter, stove, fuel and pot.

To balance things up, we each had half the split blade wedged under our seat, shaft stuck in that little gap at the bottom of the footplate. This helped keep in place the thermorest, which was folded to line the floor in an attempt to fight off frostbite, as the water was cold enough to send a brass monkey packing, clinging to its family jewels, searching for sellotape!

That same afternoon, one of life's little coincidences occurred. I was relocating my hip pads after moving my seat position, when a weathered, agricultural-looking German chap set an interested eye on the little aqua-green boat.

"Vhere is you going in das boote?" asked the bearded one.

"Tsarap and Zanskar rivers and hopefully back here,"   I replied, thinking I would need to explain some more what that might entail.

"Yar yar, is das so? You know, ven I did this, for the first time, it took more than two months, unt we never knew ven it would end. Ve had no map, you zee!" The bearded one replied calmly.

It turned out that this guy had made the first descent of the Tsarap Zanskar river twenty years earlier in a small raft with a friend and an Indian mountain guide. He had documented the trip and made a film of his expedition and the communities he had encountered. His film had won an award in the European Alpine show, the same year in which Leo Dickinson also won one with his film of the first Dude (sic) Kosi Expedition!!

Our luck continued: the bearded one had an awesome memory and many a strange tale to tell. For a couple of hours we sat and absorbed teachings from our newly discovered guru, filling our map with village names and river notes.

Another bumpy bus ride later....

The next evening in what could meaningfully be described as the middle of nowhere, we pulled at the first of many mugs of sweet ginger chai.

"Well dude, we're here."

"No shit, brother, hope these boats float!" Mike replied in his 'intrepid' voice looking at a large pile of rice and dahl.

Takh, the put-in point, was at a breath and warmth-sapping 4,300 metres. Even the take-out was perched at around 3,000 metres, way north, in the supposed Himalayan rain shadow. With the air crisp and far more stars in the sky than there seemed to be space for, we fell asleep exaggerating Jonny's tales of godlike waves that lay in wait in the sheer-sided gorge of Zanskar.

As the morning rays intensified, we geared up and clambered down to the whisky-coloured river. With memories of Shimla No.1 whisky on the tip of our tongues we drifted down this brackish tributary towards the glacial water of the Tsarap, the cold Tsarap, whose water had probably melted that morning from the mighty Baralacha La Glacier. My Micro mother ship, carrying the heavy luxury items, floated surprisingly well, Mike was able to do Acrobatic whoopies along every crease, his stern dredging for gold in the Tsarap's silt. However, as the Tsarap surged and ebbed care was needed; the icy flow was so cold that anything which might have resulted in full immersion was not a option!

We were off!! Zooming away from the truck-infested Leh - Manali road, towards the surreal world of the Zanskar valley, a monument of erosion. Everything is eroding. Frost-shattered peaks rise around vertical canyon walls. Thousands of feet of scree slopes have huge boulders balanced on the lips of the flaking walls, defying physics. All this high above the mirroring water.

We had no gauge and the scale of the place makes it hard to assimilate, so we were unaware how massive the glacial melt happening all around was as we cruised winding canyons and gorges passing into increasingly surreal environments. At times the river spread wide and shallow, then gorge walls would squeeze it all into an unimaginably deep slot of only a handful of metres.

On the second day, we spotted two burgundy cloaks, complete with bizarre hats, scree-running towards the riverside. We paddled over to the eddy where these characters would probably land if they fell and awaited the yelping lunatics' descent.

"Sorry guys," Mike explained, in his best Nepali, "you can only fit one person in the things". After explaining the solitude-ness of a kayak to the excited monks, Mike shot a knowledgeable glance at me and pronounced, "I guess we must be near that monastery called Phuktal Gompa."

The Phuktal Gompa, perched perhaps 500 feet up a wall, spread on the lip and inside a huge echoing cavern, seemed to be a rather weird spot for a Buddhist Monastery. After scaling the heights by the countless steps, we discovered that at the heart of the cavity sprang a well. Life for trees, plants, animals and monks. The acoustic potential was revealed later that evening, as the earthy drones of the monks 'ohming' could be heard in all its amplified spiritualness.

The rice boiled over again, its extinguishing hisses distracting us from our map, which had just informed us that we shouldn't be where we were - yet. It should still take two more days to reach Padum which was the psychological halfway point. But before Padum, Reru Falls stood or rather fell in our path.

As we wrestled our food-loaded kayaks around the teeth of a fresh landslide, the jumbling chaos of Reru rapid roared past us. It was possibly runable, if you didn't goof up and end up toasted in the apocalyptic pour-over, stripped of all your worldly belongings, and dumped in the middle of a rather large cold rapid a few days downstream of the middle of almost nowhere.

Shreds of aqua-green polyethylene and a few stubbed toes later, we re-entered the gushing volume, to be sucked, thrown, flipped and flushed into yet another inspiring gorge. Somehow a section of the map was skipped and the we arrived at Padum a day early. From Reru, the river's iciness had rushed in a read-and-ride-runable, roller coaster, bringing the us out of the Tsarap's numerous narrows to the rather stark openness of the confluence. A valley of textbook perfection delivers the Doda river to the Tsarap, creating the Zanskar, whose flat vastness meanders towards the dark threatening peaks of the Zanskar mountains. Rain, snow or hail also threatened as we cruised towards the Zanskar Gorge. The imposing cold and stories of the gorge prevailed on us to call council from the increasingly inaccurate map. Finding a sheltered cove we settled down to an intense safety talk."

This gorge, the Grand Canyon of the Zanskar, is an isolated and incredibly harsh place to live. In the heart of winter the whole area is inaccessible by road, so the traders and monks travelling to Padam and all the scattered gompas do so by walking up on the frozen waters of the Zanskar. The journey can take many weeks as ice sheets split, forcing the trail on to the brittle ledges on the vertical canyon walls. In the depth of winter the night temperatures often plummet to around the 40° C mark. Many lives are claimed when the ice shatters and the traveller swept away to a swift icy ending under the frozen waves.

"Fortunately, the river was not frozen (and it was not quite 40ºC below,) but once we entered the gorge, we were in till we were out. It looked as if it should be a full day's paddle and being mid-day already, it would be unfortunate to get to the point of no return prematurely. Feeling far more relaxed about our situation, we set off and continued to drift towards the ever-nearing canyon.... The river was now pretty wide, murky boils and fold lines surged and gurgled, occasional whirlpools swallowed pockets of air and played with the intrepid wanderers like a pair of foamies. Surfs made in heaven beckoned, but we adopted stay dry tactics. Mike thought my lips were turning a shade closer to the blue of his Acrobat. Heads down we paddled on. Then suddenly it appeared that we had drifted into the mouth of the canyon. Passing beneath slabs of rock, thousands of metres high, there was a distinct lack of level ground or beach-

YOUR TROUBLE APPEARS TO BE HYPOTHERMIA.

T-T-THANK G-GOODNESS, I T-T-T-THOUGHT IT WAS TH' C-C-C-COLD!

es. Darkness crept over the mountains; we needed somewhere to escape the night. A solitary spot amidst the canyon walls was stumbled upon. Here a spring, spurting from the canyon wall, had built up over hundreds of years a travertine ledge. The one dry spot on this mound made an outrageous place to bivvy. The moonlight lit the towering walls and stars filled the gap between as   we settled down to more rice and a confused conversation about our whereabouts.

The next day began before the last finished as the worst weather in Ladakh for 20 years moved over the gorge and dumped on us. Warm sleeping bags turned to shrink wrap ice blocks. We waited for the sun to rise. Not a chance! With first light we emptied our sleeping bags and confirmed the facts - we had no food, no dry clothes and no idea of our exact location. So we ventured on, head down in the rain and soaked, down the grey shrouded canyon. A splash was heard as the extremities of yet another brass monkey plummeted into the icy boils in the depths of the frozen canyon.

Paddling with our goal: the Shrinagar - Leh Highway and Indus confluence, dry clothes, warmth and a bucket of hot Chai, our thoughts were, "I'm too young to become a popsicle!"

Frozen, we finally reached the village of Nimu. Here the volume of the Indus doubles as the Zanskar's icy discharge joins it. We would think about that later; our priorities lay elsewhere. We scrambled through paddy fields and along slippy, muddy tracks in search of a steaming pot of chai. Unfortunately, luck was lost somewhere back in the canyon; the chai stalls were all shut and the road closed because of a landslide. Standing beside the deserted road, we contemplated our fate; we could freeze to death in our rubber shorts and stripy purple thermals, or be taken in to the local community, be married or sold and never be heard of again. As it happened, our luck returned in the form of a Morris Oxford Taxi - with roof rack - trundling through the mud. We returned to Leh where our gear was securely locked away in our guest house. The landlord was out for the day!"

Ke Gar Ne!!

After recovering from hypothermia, and the celebratory hangover, the

Warriors made tracks back to monsoon–ridden Manali. Their eyes bulged at the Beas as it lapped the piles of rubble that used to be the roadside hotels. Even Mango Baba, a friendly holy man or Sadhu, known for providing some influence at the confluence of Doodie Nallah, showed some concern, as he stood in his Shiva temple, up to his knees in flood water.

For a few weeks the Warriors' veins strained with adrenalin as they played the newly formed roaring rapids of the Beas.

With all their accumulated adventures, they returned to Kathmandu, where in a drunken drivel, the result of Nepal's finest Kukhuri rum, they told tall stories. They knew a few people had been on their journey before, they had even met one of the first, but they still chuckled. Waves made in heaven had been shredded, thousand foot walls had been splat-ted. They had not "run" the Tsarap Zanskar, but played the river.

ROLLUP? WHO NEEDS IT?

DOUG AMMONS.

Doug arrived on my "List of Authors" to approach for chapters by reputation. Not the sort of reputation that is passed on in bars and cafes by sycophants, but a reputation that comes from conversations with mutual friends. Then later I was handed some of his writings by Slime to read (and return). I didn't have time to read them then and there and so I stole them and filed them in a box. My peripatetic life style meant that they were buried for a while, maybe months maybe even years. Along these years Doug's name would crop up in a pub, around a camp-fire or at some paddler's house around the world, "Did you hear about Doug Ammons ? he has just .....", "Do you know Doug Ammons he ...." Ka-boum! He was out there. It would be easy to have filed these stories with all those other bar room tales of exaggeration, except that these rumours/stories came from people with reputations that I respected.

Later, in a settled moment of my life when I could empty the boxes, I came across the writings again and this time I got round to reading the accounts of his trips. "The horizon line". "History of the Stikine". "Stikine solo". "First descent of Smith Creek". Here was someone who could write about paddling; what impressed me was the extremeness of the personal in them. Here was someone who, when describing the North Fork of the Payette, had me remembering back to my few runs on that awesome piece of water with vivid clarity.

By the time I had read the three or four articles I had nicked from Slime I felt that I knew the rivers he described, not only the character of the rapids, but also the emotions of this paddler. I began to feel that I knew him, but I had never met him. Suddenly someone was writing about rivers and kayaking and not a single washing machine in sight!

Doug describes the North Fork run as "the coming together of ten years of paddling in one perfect run run at an incredible level. I was so jacked, so elated... there was this bubbling pot of emotion that I had to make sense of. I did the best I could."

THE NORTH FORK OF THE PAYETTE RIVER

A Whimsical Intro.

Ahhh, the North Fork of the Payette! To my ears that name has a wonderful sound, a lilt and uplift, like poetry or good music. The name hints of great feats by illustrious rivermen in the Days of Yore. Of monstrous rapids, derring-do, Big Men bigger than life at the edge of the Do-able. It harkens back to when the Mirage was king, when Hydras were pink, when John Wasson had his beard, and a Dagger was only a canoe or a weapon of last resort.

But now, after suffering years of drought, paltry winters, and minuscule runoffs, entertain conjecture of a time when the snowpack returned and pouring spring rain filled the wide vessel of Idaho. Put 4000 cubic feet a second in the North Fork, no, put 5000, 6000, 7000. Add more and more until we have returned to The Edge. The Days of Yore arise again! Familiar rapids build beyond belief into unrun, exploding white-water. And we were there, grandson. Sit on my knee and let me tell you about the North Fork of the Payette, the best full-on river running in the world. Let me tell you the story of when the water returned.

Tony and the North Fork is dedicated to my friends Tony Brennen and Greg Moore.

Flows with the Bro's is dedicated to Rob Lesser, Bob McDougall, and John Wasson for opening their world to me all those years ago, and for everything we've shared since.

FLOWS WITH THE BRO'S

Long ago near the end of the Days of Yore, I paddled for the first time on the North Fork of the Payette. I ran the eight mile stretch from Swinging Bridge down to Banks with one of the masters, "Big Water" Bob McDougall. The river was at the medium level of 1500 cfs, but Bob led me down with caution suitable for a neophyte. I had a blast. Bitten by the bug, I returned the next weekend to join Rob Lesser and Big Bob on a full 'top to bottom' at 2000 cfs - 15 miles and 1700 vertical feet of class IV+ and V rapids from Smith's Ferry to Banks. There, I met the joys of the world beyond the horizon line.

Those two days were eye openers. I'd only been paddling a short time, but had managed to leapfrog from beginner to class V in that span. I glided past questions of experience with sheer enthusiasm for moving water. I had no idea what the limits were, didn't know enough to be cautious, and didn't really care.

After my first runs with Bob I became a regular on the river. This was a time when a small group of North Forkers was beginning to grow as the sport expanded. Early forays onto the river had proven that, although intimidating, it was not quite death defying. Stories of bruising, scary swims abounded, but those early paddlers had found the run was possible. Top to bottoms were possible, even fun, but only for a small group of devotees: Rob Lesser, Bob McDougall, John Wasson, Mark Fraas, Bruce Olson. I stepped into this world just as my paddling skills were developing. It immediately felt like the place I belonged and the people I belonged with.

For reasons of a shared world-view and paddling zeal, I gravitated naturally toward the Brotherhood of the North Fork. At that time the Brotherhood was comprised of the Big Boys in full stride. In my eyes, Rob, John and Bob were the living history of big water paddling and of expeditions to all corners of the globe. They defined what the North Fork was about - a staging ground, a proving ground, a place where one found Big Water experience and commitment.

To be accepted into this fraternal order was a mind-expanding experience. Here I was, working and in graduate school, married with beanhead kids popping out. But kayaking and my new-found friends sparked a joyful fanaticism. I couldn't paddle enough and the North Fork had everything, every challenge, and the aura of untamed territory. Both of my parallel lives were filled to the brim with seriousness and pleasure, growing skills and every challenge from parent to Ph.D. to class V. They all came together in that world. What more could one want from life?

More time, that's what I wanted. I had to squeeze every minute out of every day. During North Fork season, I'd get up at 5am on Saturday mornings and cram my gear into the Volkswagen Rabbit. Quickly tying my kayak down on top, by 5:30 I'd roar off in a cloud of diesel smoke. Over Lolo pass on Highway 12, down the Lochsa River, up the South Clearwater, over to Grangeville, down into the Salmon, up the Little Salmon, past McCall. Finally, after logging three mountain passes, six drainages, and all those thousands of curves, I'd rev past Cascade and down the North Fork.

If I put the pedal to the metal and controlled the shakes from all the coffee I'd drunk, avoided the highway patrol and early traffic in all the little towns I had to zoom through, I could make it the 300 miles to the put-in by 11:00 – just in time to meet with the Bro's. Then we'd put on for an epic day. A Top to Bottom full of scrambling ferries, hard moves, and sometimes desperate escapes from hole rides.

Surviving our adventures, we'd finally arrive at Banks. Celebrating our run with a beer was followed by dinner at John's house and discussions ranging from kayaking to politics to particle physics. By 10pm I'd tear myself away to the bemused looks of my friends and blast back toward Missoula, head zinging with thoughts. To my wife's dismay, I'd always arrive at 5am for some sleep and an exhausted family Sunday of dissertation writing and bouncing kids. For days afterward I relived memories of the North Fork, sitting hypnotised at my desk, washing through waves and over precipices.

My early top to bottom runs all had a special air for me. I was the junior member of the team, and felt like the younger brother who was able to tag along with the big guys I looked up to. It was still a time when a top to bottom was a big event, and people on the shore would follow us down the highway for the entire run. Each time we put on was a distinctive occasion – a celebration of life and growing friendship. Somehow, the seriousness of the rapids mixed with funny remarks to make a perfect blend and enthusiasm.

Rapid after rapid, running blind for much of the first year, I trusted to my reflexes what I couldn't read on the fly or remember from quick road scouts. *Which horizon line was this? Is this Bouncer-down-the-middle? Do I cut left or right here? Where the hell was that hole that got me last time?* It was ridiculous. No class five river should ever be run like that, and predictably, I had the only serious accident of my career during this time. In the lead-in to S-turn rapid, I got blasted upside-down and my paddle caught on a rock. I didn't let go, was smashed upright and stomped on by the next hole. Somewhere in the midst of that the weakest link was found. My shoulder popped. I rolled up and noticed I couldn't move my right arm, but somehow got to shore in the midst of the rapid with my humerus down in my armpit. Within two or three minutes Bryan Tooley and Big Bob performed a reduction there on the bank in the riprap. A foot in the side and a couple of yanks. The snap of the bone moving back more or less into its normal position was painful. I decided then and there to never let that happen again. Afterwards, the thought of washing through the entire long rapid stuck halfway in my boat, pummelled on the rocks, with my arm dangling loose from its socket gave me plenty to think about. But a few months of rehab later, back I came. Wiser for the experience, but still a dumb youth.

The years passed. Friendships became cemented within the Brotherhood. I found the North Fork was a place where we reached understandings different from those in normal life. The friendship pointed us toward other adventures. I made the step to expedition paddling, joining as a junior partner the longtime alliance of Rapid Rob and Big Water Bob. We went to impressive and occasionally frightening places. Sometimes these yielded experiences that changed our sense for each other into the psychic. There were also first descents, mongo play-paddling, and river silliness. Each bend in the river wove our lives closer together and became our bridges across time and whatever physical distance might come between us. Rob and Bob became friends I would do anything for and go any place with.

Because of its accessibility and difficulty, the North Fork was always a touchstone for us as our lives went in their different directions. It was the place that summed up what kayaking was all about - the centre of our universe, the measure of all things.

Top to bottoms multiplied, and I grew more and more comfortable on the river. One year Bob amazed us all by doing a vertical mile of white-water in a day. *Three* top to bottoms in a row! It was an audacious thought done in a controlled and careful manner - something just right for Bob. But it left us floored. *How did he do it?* But amazing as it was at first, several years later the idea had sunk in to the point where it seemed, well, reasonable and possibly fun, so some of us repeated it. Ideas were like dominoes and each step led to the next. And none of those steps was possible without the people going before.

Like some of the other Bro's before me, I began to run top to bottoms alone, revelling in the solitude, the focus and intimacy with the water. I enjoyed the river with the Clan; Tom Schibig came aboard. In addition, a small group of friends - Tony Brennen, Grant Amaral, Clint LaTerret, Mark White, Roy Piskadlo, Dan Givens - always made a trip to the Payette area a treat, with smiles, tasteless jokes and camaraderie.

Always one to pay attention to the big boys, I gradually distilled what I learned from paddling the North Fork with them. Pinball boating, I called it. This distinctive technique centred on controlling the subtleties of the dynamic rebound from holes and big diagonals and precisely angled hulls. At NF speed and gradient, this effect divides the river into myriad non-obvious lines. When fully zenned, you could ricochet serenely around the river at warp velocity, and apparent chaos turned into sharp certainty.

It was a time of innocence and fun. We read with raised eyebrows and a shrug of the shoulders articles that listed the North Fork as class six, or that recounted the efforts of outsiders getting thumped at low levels. We'd look at each other and say, "Well, I guess it takes all kinds." Groups of Eastern boaters would appear wanting to check the NF off their list of to-do's. We made scavenging runs to add to our equipment stores after each had left.

The cata-rafters appeared, led by a true character: Big Al Hamilton. Riding high on his double-pontooned raft like some Indian Rajah on his elephant, festooned with flip lines and radios, Al was a sight to see. No matter where he went, he always took big steps with big talk, but his grin and the tongue in his cheek told you he never took himself without a grain of salt. We stopped our runs to watch him lead his brethren down Jacob's Ladder, most of them careening completely out of control. Al was a competent riverman, but it was great entertainment to see his compadres clutching their seats with loose oars flailing wildly as the rafts lurched from drop to drop. We never could tell whether they'd actually run a *line* or not, because it didn't seem to matter, and we'd joke that a keg of beer strapped to the seat would run the same line. Their amazingly engineered craft would wash through Jacob's Ladder and down into Golf Course at any old angle. They'd blob through Taffy Puller and the Ocean Wave, disappear over the ledge holes in Golf Course - holes that would be life threatening for us in our kayaks. A run consisted of all this, with the occupant finally releasing his grip on his seat to grasp desperately at the flapping oars and give a whoop, "All right!!! Yeah!! What a ride!" to our collective cheers. "Hear hear!" we'd cry, and sitting on the boulders we'd raise a toast to these intrepid oarsmen and their ingenious technology. Such are the varieties of river running.

The days and the years went by sweetly. But throughout this time Idaho was in the throes of a drought, and the North Fork releases were our measure of that as much as the tinder dry land and sweeping forest fires of late summer. Spring water was greedily hoarded by the Keeper of the Reservoir and passed miserly into the riverbed.

On a few spring days scattered across the years the river perked up to 4000 or even 5000 cfs, but would be cut off quickly. During these times few paddlers ventured into the no-man's land above Hound's Tooth, a rapid that defined the lower 5 miles of the river and formed a psycho-logical barrier to 'the upper stretch'. The upper 10 miles of the run - the burliest rapids - never felt a paddle blade at such levels. There was scouting from the road, but far too much head shaking. I would hear of two days here, three days there of such great levels, and impatiently chomped the bit, waiting for the time when the old flows would return and give me a chance. I'd ask Rob what it was like to run various of the upper rapids at 3500, or 4000 - he'd even done some of the upper stuff at 5000. When asked, he'd get that faraway look in his eyes "Ah, young friend, let me tell you of the good old days...." I'd dream about when the runoff would return. Finally, one June, it did.

TONY AND THE
NORTH FORK

On June 11th, with me freshly back from a paddling and climbing trip to California, Rob Lesser called from Boise. "It's happening! It's 5000 or above. Come on down!" I was dead tired and my heart was skipping beats, but here was the chance I'd been waiting for all these years. There was no way in the world I'd miss this opportunity.

Saturday, June 13th, I made it over after a late start from Missoula. Coming down highway 55 along the river, I was hopping with excitement. Finally, *Finally!!!* 130% snowpack, it's been raining hard, Cascade reservoir is full and releasing 4000–plus cfs, there's lots of inflow. The North Fork is THUMPING!! I stopped to look at the rapids I knew so well, but which now were raging. Immense is a word that came to mind. Intimidating is another. Fast. Ripping. **Wild!** There were huge holes in the bigger rapids, long chaotic stretches of exploding waves 10 to 15 feet high. 50 foot logs jammed on the corners. But runnable - maybe. It required fully booting up the kayaking computer, paddling lasers on full, honing and serious. Between skips, my heart was pounding. Yah hoo! *It was time to go for it.*

I arrived at Hound's Tooth in late afternoon. Rob met me, and a few other Boise regulars were about. The North Fork was at an unheard-of level. Gage height, 11.9. Flow? No one knew. It was blasting! Off the conversion chart! The word was floating around that it was 6 to 7000cfs. People walked around and looked at the river, shaking their heads. Sheesh! Every muscle was jumping. *Let's get on the river and fly!*

For the last few days, a small number of people had been running the lower five miles as the levels shot up past 5000 cfs. As the water level rose the number of paddlers decreased. Tony Brennen, Jim Ciardelli, Greg Moore, Rob and I popped on and made a run on the lower five, from Hound's Tooth down. There were a few other people milling around, collecting themselves for a run.

Starting a hundred yards above Hound's Tooth was an interesting exercise in preposterousness. It took all of 5 seconds to be flushed into

176

the maw. Out of the eddy, Whoosh, sucked away downstream by the current. *Wham* into the gut of the rapid. *Outrageous!* Huge, irregular, crashing waves. Not many real holes, but everything hurtled along with unbelievable speed and power. A large Ponderosa log was wedged in an inopportune place on an island just below the main rapid in the midst of solid class V. I passed Rob getting thrashed in a big hole nestled between the Ponderosa on one side and a lesser, but bad log on the other side. The mound of white towered four or five feet above his head as it battered his boat around like an eggbeater. I scrambled to get left and miss its corner. As the current whisked me by, I caught a glimpse of Rob, struggling to maintain balance and work left out of the hole. *I hope he can get out of there.* There was no way to stop, and no way to help.

A quarter-mile below we found an eddy where we paused for breath. After a couple of minutes Rob caught up to us frowning and thoughtful. An exchange of glances, *whew!*

"Why didn't you guys wait for me?"

"Where? This is the first place we could find."

There wasn't much more anyone could say. We paddled back out into the current.

Waves four times higher than our heads broke every which direction, diagonals spiked us crossriver as we scrambled and hung on for a frantic ride. A bicyclist clocked us at over 25 mph in Juicer, just going with the flow. It was a hoot - a serious hoot. As I headed into Crunch and was cresting the first massive wave, I remembered Big Bob saying of an ancient run of his on the lower 5 miles at 5000 cfs, "As much fun as you can have in a boat."

Yes!

In an eyeblink it was over. At Banks, lots more head shaking went on. *Wow!* We poked at the air and gabbled, a consensus of gogglified amazement. Then, back up for another run and more of the same. Boats launched completely out of the water. Paddlers bounced all over, getting crushed by waves which opened up and snapped like the mouths of watery beasts. We'd pop out far to the side and way downstream to fend with the rest of the current. Riding with the flow was exhilarating, intense, rivetting. Incredulous smiles and frowns were on every face. Incoherent excitement reigned.

By the time the second run was over, it was getting along toward 8pm. The Boise guys headed home. Rob and I talked about the feasibility of going up top. We decided to drive up and scout the entire upper run.

The upper 10 miles raised the ante another grade of difficulty and then some. It had never been run at anything approaching this level. Rob was the only one who had run portions of it above 4000. And never Nutcracker or the long middle stretch, never Jacob's Ladder, Golf Course, or Screaming Left Turn. It was clear why.

Every rapid roared with wild, beautiful energy - several hideously so. Screaming Left Turn was one of the ugliest. After a long, scrambled fire-hose lead-in, the water piled straight into the island at the corner, splitting the current. On the front edge of the island four huge logs were jammed pointing upstream, like spears, ready to skewer any kayaker flotsam or wedge him underneath to be buried by the full force of the current. It was an interesting experience, looking sure death in the face from the safety of the bank. *But there was a line. Just don't make a mistake.* Not so at Jacob's Ladder.

"This is what makes hydropower people salivate," Rob said as we gazed in disbelief at the river. After a tremendously hard lead-in, the narrowed riverbed shot the water at 35 mph into the base of a river-wide mound of white at the Third Drop of Jacob's, 10 feet high and backed up 30 feet. *No. Clearly No.* The thought of heading into it in a boat was the stuff of our worst nightmares. Just below, Taffee Puller had transformed into what might be called a huge hole, but which at this level defied hydrological description. The water from the mound of white above shot down into the bottom of this hole, disappeared, and convulsingly geysered up in a huge *thing* that covered most of the river. We had no idea what would happen if you went in there. And it immediately led into Golf Course - a class six scramble for 400 yards, solid holes, logs and madness. Up higher, Bouncer-down-the-Middle was maniacal. Nutcracker had as a crux, amidst the rest of a huge rapid, two huge spilling heaps of holes like an Hawaiian North Shore break, into which the current funnelled. Rob looked at it for a second, then laughed and said, "You won't find *me* out there." The entire 10 upper miles was beautiful and very impressive. A different order of magnitude, a different world. I hopped about *inspired* by the river's frenetic energy.

It was nearly dark when Rob and I finished the scout. We drove back to the parking lot at the end of the run and talked about the possibility of doing the upper river the next day. He was noncommittal. Tired from paddling every day the last week, he was also annoyed at the bystanders who kept asking us if we were going to run the upper stuff. "I want to call my shots. I don't like the feeling of being in a circus and expected to perform for other people."

As twilight turned to night, we talked about a lot of things. Both of his parents had died a few months prior, and he was still putting the pieces into order. The kayaking company he was a sales rep for had just bumped him from his long time territory. A smell of rank commercialism was entering the sport, something he found deeply disturbing. Lots of emotions raised themselves to interfere with focusing on the run.

Life beyond the river always goes on. The river is our sanctuary - a place where time, youth, and friendship expand to fill us. But challenging runs demand more. They are more than just the refuge a beautiful river provides. In them, all life is encapsulated. Difficult decisions are made where you balance struggles and resolve conflicts. A top end run is an arena where your focus can not be deflected, your decisions must be careful and deliberate. And you need an edge, a push from within to accept the challenge. "Know thyself" a wise Greek once said. This Rob does.

Tying the boats on the van, Rob said, "I need a rest, then another day getting used to the boat and the water. I was shaky today. You saw my hole rides. They weren't fun. It's not that I was in danger, but that I wasn't on top of things like I should be." He looked at the river and said quietly, "You know, I also don't feel any need to do this run. At one time I would have, but right now the fires are burning lower."

Rob is a model of order arising from chaos. Of all the many qualities I love about him, none is more endearing than the transition I've seen in him time and again on the river. His homebody life sometimes becomes a self-created tangle as he deals with everyday trivial burdens. Rob's M.O. is Karl Marx's dialectic gone haywire: "Well, it is and it isn't...", "It might and it might not...", "Yes, but on the other hand..." Yet, when facing serious river decisions all the confusion vanishes. The bigger and weirder the river problem, the more luminously Rob shines. But when the fireworks have passed, he returns again to fend off the jungle.

He got into his van and said, "I might come around, but there's no way I'm going to commit to the run right now. I'll call you in the morning. Make your plans as if I'm not going to be there." I wanted Rob to join me, but he was also telling me that I was part of the pressure.

In contrast to his reticence, I was stoked. Through the window I told him, "I've waited for this since I began paddling the North Fork. I'm tired, but mentally tuned. I'm running tomorrow."

"Don't count me out, understand", he said as he started the car, "it's just that there are lots of loose pieces. The river is too unforgiving not to give it my full attention. I'm worried I can't."

"Rob, just so you know, I'm going to scout carefully and take it piece by piece. I'm going to treat it with the care it deserves. I'm not committing to any rapid I haven't thoroughly scouted. The pace will be deliberate and controlled."

Next morning Rob called me at John's to give me the answer I expected: no go. "Sorry Doug. I'm not feeling aggressive enough. I need time. There's a pile of little things I have to catch up on around the house. But good luck." I called Tony Brennen. He wasn't in so I left a message on his answering machine. *Damn.* I was starting to worry that I wouldn't be able to get anyone to go with me. *The level is finally here and I can't find a partner! Well, at least I'll try to get someone to drive along the road. But soloing is really pushing something that's already way out there. I'll decide when I get up on the river.*

I drove up to Hound's Tooth and found Greg Moore eating breakfast at the pullout. He immediately asked about the upper river. Ahh, I thought, a partner. "I'm planning to head up, Greg. Let's join forces." We talked for a minute about what we'd each seen in our separate scouts.

Greg got a little smile on his face, "I'll try some of the upper stuff. Maybe down to Slide, but not Nutcracker or the middle stretch. And not Screaming Left."

I told him, "If I'm feeling good the only thing I saw that I know I won't run is Jacob's Ladder. Those holes are ridiculous. I'm going to wait and see for particular rapids, but right now I'm up for a top to bottom." We agreed on doing a warm-up run on the lower five, then heading up to the top.

As we were getting ready, a few other people showed up. Then we put on. Tony Brennen, Dan Givins, Jim Ciardelli, Greg and I shoved off above Hound's tooth. Within seconds we were scattered across and down the river.

I was a little nonchalant heading into the rapid and paid for it. I went straight into a huge hole, got stopped dead and violently cartwheeled. I flushed out and rolled up, my glasses torn off and stuffed into my mouth. *Just a slap for my lapse of respect.*

Tony zipped through Hound's tooth perfectly, catching the surges and breaks just right, but in his incredulity at having scorched such a good line, he lost concentration and suddenly found himself wedged up against the big 50 foot log in the runout. The current pushed him against the two foot diameter hulk, but he kept his cool, his upstream edge cocked, and figured out where to go. He looked at both ends then decided to make a move around the river right side where he was pointed. Strong strokes, angle, and a fortuitous pillow action on the upstream face of the log got him to the end, but just as he made it there, the current splatted him into it and the boat began to slide underneath. *"Don't catch. Don't catch. Don't catch"*, he found himself saying to his lifejacket. The current levered him around the end of the log and out he popped. *"Stupid!"* he thought, *"Can't make mistakes like that."*

At the take-out, we talked things over again as we put the boats on Jim's truck. There were questions and answers as everyone tried to find his own balance.

"What did you think of the upper stuff when you scouted?"

"There's some hard moves, lots of scrambling, and must-make lines. It's bizarre."

"The big thing is to keep your shit together, be cool under fire."

"I think it's runnable. Jacob's Ladder isn't. There might be other portages. Take a look at it and decide."

"Man, there are places up there where it looks like you'll get ripped out of your boat, and you won't get a breath for a *long* time."

"If you're out of your boat up there, you're dead."

Dave Russell, a new Boise boater who had paddled the lower five with us asked Greg, "What would you rate this? Is the part below Hound's Tooth class V?"

Greg assumed a professorial stance, crossing his arms and rubbing his beard with one hand, "Yes. Without question. At 1500 or so, I believe I'd call it big water class IV+. It's continuous, you have to move around to miss things and run specific lines. But now? This is too big to call it anything but class V. Big V."

Greg's comment sparked an irregular conversation:

"Hey, give me a break! It's a grade harder now! *I say V plus!*"

"It seems like a big flush, where's the technical difficulty? I always thought of class V as rocky and steep..."

"This is steep! It's 100 feet per mile. In any of the real rapids it's probably at least twice that. Jacobs and Golf Course average 250 or more."

"Yeah but, ..."

"The rocks are *there,* man! It's just there's more water in this river right now than anyone's ever seen."

"Bracing, balance, dealing with the weirdness. *That's* what this is about."

"Yeah, and are you going to do a hand roll if your paddle gets torn out of your hands? What if you've taken a rock hit and sucked some water? What about dealing with logs at 30 mph?"

"I'm not touching that upper stuff."

"If parts are a flush, then what's the big deal?"

"Are you getting on?"

"What if I swam? Pretty scary. You can die out there and anyone who says differently is being stupid."

"That's the point, how you react to what you don't know. It's that feeling of doubt that hits your confidence."

Finally, Tim Shanahan waved his arms, "Guys, guys!" We quieted down and looked at him. He said, "Guys, I don't know what to say about the upper section, except it's out of my league. But this lower stuff - it's like plugging yourself into a circuit, with one end down at Banks and the other at Hound's Tooth." Arms outstretched, mouth open, Tim convulsed like a convict in an electric chair - "Baby, I *fee-e-e-l* the juice!"

We'd all tossed in our two cents - which left more questions unanswered than answered. The water brought out everyone's anxieties and excitement with no consensus - except it was *wild.*

The Hound's Tooth run was big and pushy, but it *looked* like you'd flush through nearly everything in this lower section. If you make a mistake, or were taken by surprise, it was hang on for dear life, keep your cool, and roll up. Usually class V means you've got to make specific moves to avoid something potentially terminal. The upper stuff was full of those moves, scattered down the gut of huge rapids that never seemed to end.

The danger seemed obvious. It sat there and leered at us. We didn't know how to make sense of it. The river was showing what water and rocks could do. And we were amazed.

The discussion wound down. To my pleasure, Tony was all for heading up top. His decision made for a good threesome - solid, experienced, and sensible. Definitely better than just Greg and me alone.

As we tied the boats down on Jim's truck and were getting ready to drive up, we overheard a guy talking in a confident tone about Steepness, the first big rapid of the upper stretch.

"It's a flush, big waves, fast, two really bad holes on the left below, but OK down the right-centre." The friend he was talking to asked, "Well, sounds good, are you going to try it?" "You've got to be kidding." came the answer. The two paddlers put their boats on their shoulders and headed in the other direction.

"It's always interesting to hear a paddler talk about a rapid he's not going to run. "I said to Greg. We've probably all done it. Once you're safe, it's easy to talk about all the things that someone could do." We both laughed and I added, "Problem is, you shouldn't say something is runnable unless you're going to run it."

Greg nodded and said quietly, "The proof is when you do it."

We headed up highway 55 to the put-in with the river just off the edge of the road, pounding downstream.

★★★

Something I love about paddling is that it allows you to see more about a person than they could ever tell you. Facing a difficult run sometimes brings out more than the person himself knows - much of which is otherwise hidden away inside. I call it the crystal ball effect. The magic mirror of the water. It comes from the bite of the paddle blade in the water. It originates where the power of the current hits the nether lands of the brain. It's easy to get to the real shit fast, and not as noisy as primal screaming. I'm sure that if Freud had known about it, he would have used a kayak instead of a couch.

Greg Moore is originally a transplant from Connecticut, but I should say moore. Since his cross-country exodus he has become a long time Idahoan, finding a niche paddling the clear flowing rivers of the state. He is a reticent man of uncertain Yankee puritan stock. I say uncertain, because some hint of primness in manner is still there if you look at the right time - in pursed lips or restrained hand gestures - even though most of the obvious properness has been scoured away by years of hanging around rivers and kayaking riff raff. This apparent conflict of qualities lives on in his style: obvious intelligence, his movements sharp and controlled, but with a curious little flap to it all. This appears in interesting ways, like the use of a very long, asymmetric downriver paddle in hard white-water, or the sense I sometimes get of his technique and strength flailing while he somehow runs a nice smooth line in a difficult rapid. There are other subtle incongruities. He is friendly, but aloof even with those of us he has known for many years. There is a personal barrier that I have never gotten past. Trained as a journalist, possessor of a logical mind, he is a very experienced paddler. Above all, I see him as someone with clear sense of what he wants to do and where he believes his lines should be drawn. A North Fork regular. To me, that says a lot.

Tony Brennen, Now here be a man. Playboater, river runner, all-round paddler and athlete. Teamed with Grant Amaral, he becomes a potent sniffer of first descents. He has the appearance of a strapping young warrior. He is thoughtful with a quiet intelligence, but you sometimes discern a certain amount of old bunkweed smoke wafting through his neurons. His speech and demeanour are mellow, kind, and even-keeled – I get the sense he'll make a great dad someday. I can see him years from now, laughing and bouncing kids on either knee as he tells them a bedtime story of running wild rivers. Inside, there is a strongly competitive core that provides more than a little horsepower. He is married to a lovely girl who knew exactly what she had found. Solid, dependable, he is a North Forker to the bone.

★★★

As we were driving up the river to the put in, Greg and I talked about the run.

"I love situations like this, the feeling of stepping beyond what you know. This river is so different, so powerful, you know you're entering new territory."

We were quiet for a minute, peering out the window as the truck passed several long rapids.

"It's not anxiousness, but fascination. Excitement. It's happiness with wariness mixed in. A chance to stretch skills, see if they can adapt, see where the boundaries really are."

The lure of a run like this is that it brings out questions that have to be asked and answered. These are questions most people find easy to avoid because modern amenities have all been invented to shield us from them. There is a certain counter-intuitiveness about it: not many people like to be cold, wet, and tired. Even fewer like to be all these plus have to deal with performing nearly flawlessly for hours in potentially fatal situations, thinking carefully and hard, analysing, focusing, committing to intuition and skill, exerting themselves under stress almost to exhaustion. In the abstract, that sounds outlandish! Choosing deliberately to be in places like that might just be the height of stupidity! But there are reasons.

It's not just that being in the river's current is so exciting. There are other sides, sides that are enticing and satisfying. And most of all, some of us want to see the real shit - we even enjoy it. It's just a simple fact that some things aren't available for half price. Some things you only learn if you ask the right questions. We're drawn to ask all these questions, and more. We aren't crazy. We aren't seeking thrills. *We just want the truth.* Confronting such things give the best answers you can look for in your life. If you're a serious paddler, your answers are your life.

There was a certain confusion among us as to how the North Fork should be approached. If it had just been a new river that we didn't know, then we wouldn't have had any problem. But it's a funny thing to have such a familiar place metamorphose and suddenly have to be treated so differently. Like a friend having a psychotic LSD trip, or your neighbour's pet grizzly bear gone rabid. Normal North Fork mode consists of jumping on and blasting down, hitting play spots in the middle of big rapids, avoiding known problems, making known lines, and weathering the storm where there aren't any lines. It's serious paddling with a high fun factor. After years of ingraining these habits on scores of runs it's hard to suddenly break them. But today, the river wasn't concerned about our habits.

We debated spending time scouting on the way up. But it seemed important to establish a rhythm with the river, just as on any hard run, and the best way to do that was to scout as we went. When you do that, a rapport is gained with the powers you're dealing with. You build your intuition in the give and take conversation with the river. It's a chance to pointedly discuss with the forces that be what they are planning for you when you venture into their realm. As the difficulty increases, the intuition you build this way becomes more and more important, far more so than mere skill or conscious analysis.

We piled out of Jim's truck and dragged our gear down to the put-in. Just like normal on an abnormal day.

"Hey, what happened to my regular launching spot?

"It's under five feet of water!"

"Sheesh, how do we get in?"

"Climb up and launch out of the tree!"

We slid in, warmed up, then headed downstream. As we came up to the first corner where the river narrows and begins the quarter mile class IV lead-in to Steepness, now class V+, it was time to take the step. The entire river was below us, all the suspense and explosiveness of a new love - and the door was open.

In the last 100 yards of flat water, I motioned Tony and Greg over to me and put my arms around them, "We know what we're getting into. Let's be deliberate. Scout carefully and make sure we're safe. Stay close enough so we each make sure where the others are, but not get in each other's way." I gave them a big grin. "I'm damn happy to be here with you." High fives all around, then we turned to the rapid.

It was the 33 rpm record at 78, the 25 mph curve at 75. Franticness squared. Down we flew through the long lead-in to Steepness, ripping into the waves. The river and its power were magnificent. Every few seconds we were blindsided or slammed by something huge and weird. Right through Steepness, sensing the line but unable to see, largely a flush with immense power, speed, and huge breaking waves. I was caught by a break from my right, suddenly the boat was mashed, then launched out of the water and spun sideways in the air. I went with the twist, pivoting in the air past vertical then setting it down on line into the next section. There was no time even to think about what was going on. The reactions were either there or they weren't.

After Steepness we tried to pull out of the current downstream in the run-out. It was impossible to get to shore. Huge waves broke in V-diagonals off the rip-rap. There weren't any eddies until a wide bend another 300 yards down. Finally finding a haven, rocking and bouncing in the eddy's boiling water, Tony hooted with an amazed look on his face. Greg's mouth was hanging open. *"MAN! That was WILD."* *he panted, "It's so FAST!"*

As powerful as the lower five miles had been, this was our first taste of the freight train the river was up here. As we came up to Nutcracker, we eddied out with plenty of room before the flush into the main rapid.

We got out of our boats and I said to Greg, "Well I've got to look closely to see where I need to go. It'll take me a bit to figure out the line."

"I know where I'm going to be. I'm getting out right here and walking."

Greg carried his boat up the bank, as did Tony. We walked together down to the corner where the first real difficulty was. Greg let out an astonished cry as we came upon the first of the true weirdities. The river broke through his Puritan decorum. "Shit! No way!" This was followed about fifty yards down by a second, worse hole in the midst of a very serious rapid.

Tony opted to walk around the main crux, putting in just below the second huge hole. Greg made a more conservative choice and portaged down well into the runout rapid.

I walked up and down the first big problem, sizing it up.

"This first hole is a bugger. But there's a chance for recovery before the big guy down below the Nut. The question is when to move to the right. Can't do it too soon because that next set of diagonals funnels everything left. Look at the speed, it must be 30 mph! A split second to make the cut. How quickly will I come up on this move, can I really see what I need to from the water? Can I keep my balance through this first section and break through? It's so irregular below, how to keep surges from blasting me back into the centre? Angle slightly left here, watch that diagonal there, sweeps on the left to punch it, if spin out even a little the next break will send me straight into the centre and I won't have time to miss the hole." The mental conversation wove in and out of the currents.

On a hard rapid it's common to see a sketch of potential lines first, centred around places where only certain moves are possible. As you analyse, major sections fall into place around these crux moves until a vector line appears within the chaos. The weirder the hydrology, the more exotic the line.

Once a course is plotted, the rub of running the rapid is staying on that line. If we could see life's hazards and quirks laid out before us in normal life! In class six water, these are exactly what are laid out before us.

I entered the rapid knifing down the centre through confused crossing diagonals, angling careful so not to challenge their power, fighting to keep my position as I rounded the first corner. They jumbled up onto each other in a wall of water towering a boat length over my head, swatting me every which way. At the first crux, I plunged into its midst along a seam between the breaking ridges of water - the one weakness it had. Blinded by spray and bubbles, I erupted out the backside seeing nothing but white. A dozen reactions: brace-wrist-counterbalance, then I'm upright, bodylean-kneepressure-hiproll-stroke!, all adjustments in a split second. Blindsided by a wave that surged out of nowhere, the entire boat pitched upward and out of the water onto the shoulder of the first hole.

My mind and body are automatic. A stream of commands: *arms in, watch shoulder, swivel to the right, sweep.* No words, just impressions and moves. I pop up oriented and heading back to the right. *Can see the monster hole coming. More angle, sweep,* I punch another diagonal to the right, three strokes, have room, another stroke... up the shoulder just two or three feet to the right of the spilling wash, *stroke, upUpUpUP so fast, so huge...* then whisked past and down into the huge rapid below. Tony's screaming as I flash by.

All right! The first truly big one is past. Now for Disneyland. We scouted. A wild one, all crashing back and forth laterally with one huge hole to miss directly in the flow. Tony had his brows furrowed, eyes burning a stare into the water.

GREG MOORE IN STEEPNESS   *Dave Russell*

Good runs through Disneyland and S-turn. We were in awe of the rapids, cautious as we rounded each corner. Bobbing in an eddy catching our breath, I remembered a comment Rob made last night, "I'm not worried about the biggest stuff, because it's obvious. I'm worried about the holes and weird things in places where there usually isn't anything. Something that turns out to be a bitch to get out of is going to be a potential killer. Something you didn't notice in all the big shit, and you end up fighting until you're exhausted and then have to contend with everything else. Keep your eyes open, and scout like your lives depend on it. Because they do."

We scouted everything carefully, taking lots of time to make sure we weren't heading into something stupid - although I kept having to fight the beguiling feeling that I really did know what was around the corner.

Below a rapid called Slide, after two hours, the river turned up a notch and became even more serious. Greg said, "I'm tired and have had enough. I think I'm getting out here." We eddied out above the little cable bridge, and he got out of his boat. "Yesterday, I scouted this centre section and it's more than I want to deal with." I looked at Tony with a question on my face - *you ready?* Tony was ready.

It was all a blur. 20 or 30 minutes of scouting, then committing to long, difficult big water lines that shot us through in a matter of seconds. Bad José, Know-where-to-run, Chaos, and Bouncer-down-the-Middle all blended together in the rhythm of scouting, analysing, then committing to decisions. Time and again, we gave up the water for dry land to get our bearings, then transformed back into watery creatures and descended into the storm.

We gave each rapid plenty of space, eddying out well above the lead-ins. In eddies the waves crashed us into the shore, making it hard to get out without swamping the boats. Up on the bank, we'd look down the rapids in disbelief. Rushing, exploding, solid white, pure power. We'd look at each other. That's where we're gonna be. Man! Then we'd smile at each other and shake our heads. Back at the boats after scouting, a high five, a nod, then carving out into the current. Even when nailing our lines we were flushed, smashed, and ricocheted around, flashing by the edges of ridiculous holes. Just dealing with huge stuff along the way was full-on reflexes even when we were on line. There was so much shit going on we were maxed. The autopilots were red-lining - but we were in control. Every big water trick we knew was pulled out to maintain the line.

At Bouncer, a small crowd of people lined the road as we scouted. It was a logical place to watch because the highway overlooked a roaring train of immense breaking waves and holes. There seemed one option: a hard move to the left in the midst of near absurdity, weaving among house-sized holes and logs wedged into the boulders, then straight down the centre of the lower section.

Tony was wound tight. I'd never seen him so intent. But he was paddling fantastically, right on top of things in the worst of it. As I put on my spray skirt, I said, "Good luck, Bro'."

"No", he corrected me, "we're not talking about luck here - just good skill."

I made the move left, was swatted around through the main straightaway, then glanced around, looking back upstream at Tony. Thirty yards behind, his silhouette was outlined by the explosions of the waves, sunlight glittered in a million droplets as he launched in perfect balance off the crest of a huge wave. As amped as I already was, a shiver shot through me, Yeah! The river ran through our veins and charged every stoke. We were completely in tune and revelling in the difficulties.

While scouting the next major rapid, Pectoralis Major, two older couples got out of their cars at the pull-out and looked at us curiously. One of the men walked over to us and asked, "You guys floating this river? Are you going to miss all those big gushers?"

"We've missed all the big ones so far."

He looked out at the river for a few seconds, then doubtfully regarded us again. "This looks crazier than bungie-jumping."

Now I've always been annoyed at the image our sport has - of adrenalin seekers without brains looking for cheap thrills. I figured it was time to scrub away some confusion.

"Kayaking is different." I said. "In bungie jumping you're just jumping off some high place for a thrill. You're a spectator and *that's* what's scary. Everything's left up to gravity and a big rubberband. If it breaks, you're dead.

"Out here, we have options because we have control. We can decide how we want to approach this rapid, where we want to go, how we'll get there. Then it's up to our skills. We can improvise depending upon what happens. In bungie-jumping, there's no skill in using the cord to control your fall. But in kayaking a river like this there's years of practice, understanding the water. Everything we do gives us control and a margin of safety. So you see, kayaking is totally different." I had been logical and persuasive, or so I believed. That should do it.

The guy, his friend, and their wives looked at me blankly for a few moments. The river roared in the background. Finally he said, "You're still crazy."

At any flow, Pectoralis Major is a *big* chunk of white-water to chew on. It consists of a long broken lead-in requiring you to zip quickly through a maze of several hundred boulders. A paddler can't let up or he'll find himself broached on a rock or stuck in a hole with nothing but more of the same for as far as the eye can see. The lead-in decides to get more serious when it presents one with three large and nasty off-set ledge holes that span most of the river. Without a break this turns into a hard left corner with ever more holes and boulders until the river is nothing but froth and rocks. But that's not the end. You're accelerated around a final turn back to the right down a very steep, boulder-strewn finale, then to confront another nearly half mile of continuous big rapids. This is what challenges us at a good flow of 2000 cfs - it's what the Bro's know and expect. It is also the kind of paddling that bewilders and shakes the confidence of excellent kayakers when they first come to the river. So it is, but now, at over 7000 cfs, the rapid had mythical proportions. For all the times Tony and I had run it at what we thought were high levels, we could only gaze in amazement at the transformation. Busy class IV became wild Class V, class V became ... well, we weren't quite sure what it had become. The river rose up like a giant's sweeping hand to explode and smash aside everything in its path - huge fists of white-water forcing their way down the riverbed.

DOUG IN DOUBLE 'S' TURN   *Dave Russell*

For a half hour we walked back and forth along the first quarter mile, mulling over different possibilities for the lead-in and first two corners.

A paddler's thoughts always start simple - it's natural. We're optimistic people so we hope for the best. A few dramatic moves and we're through. But sometimes that's not enough. Qualifications are added. The "if-then" sequences expand. At some point when the string of "ifs" gets long enough and the "thens" get too gruesome to contemplate, we give it up.

If we start left and work right, hmmm - then what?
If we stay left and... damn, look at that.
If we move centre-right, then back hard right, well... shit.
And anyway, how do we set up for the next section?
Just what the hell is the water doing out there, anyway?

Every potential route seemed a long, frantic scramble crashing into something horrendous - like a log covered with broken branches, or an 8 foot deep hole with no exit. Each left our lives extending only part-way through the rapid - and that was not even thinking about the final quarter mile below the second corner.

Maybe it's a portage.

No, take another look. It's so damn fast!! And the waves are so big. How can we see where we are? But wait a second! What if I enter on that left line and work centre there, but use the irregular breaking wave to move back right? If I'm angled correctly I'd be far enough over so then I could get past the second hole, and if I grazed the corner, spun back left and took two really hard strokes I could punch …

We hadn't spoken for 10 minutes, each immersed in his own thoughts. Finally, motioning a course along the river right bank Tony offered, "I think we should try the side here. There are still some big problems like those two holes, and what to do just above the second corner, but it's cleaner. I don't see any good options. The stuff in the middle looks really bad." His comment was reasonable, but it ran up against a personal quirk.

"No, this is a big water run - we can't sneak things. We've got to do the big water line. I see it, right out *there*." I said, pointing into the centre section. After I described what I saw as a possible line, Tony scanned the route for a few extra moments then smiled slightly. Of course.

We committed to a subtle line that required running right at some of the biggest things in the lead-in, twice spinning off the edges of huge holes and cutting around behind them to miss a third. If we could do it, this allowed us to set up for the second half of the rapid. If we couldn't…

There was no doubt.

To touch the water is to be engulfed in its energy. *We're off to the races!* Paddle blade to current, hull piercing and lifting, fingers of water grasping and releasing. As the water hurdled us into the crux it was hard to see where we were among the mountains of waves, but we nailed the line. Around the corners, down the straightaway. After 40 seconds of scrambling moves and gushing water, we found a boily eddy to escape for a rest. Both of us were breathing deeply and hard. Tony was ecstatic, "Great line! Man those holes were HUGE. They looked big from the bank, but when we went by the edge I just stared down and said, 'Shit, I'm glad I'm not in there!"

We both got out above Jacob's Ladder, already knowing it was a portage. As we walked down the road above the rapid I said to Tony,

"Nice to come up to something where the line is easy to draw."

Tony thought I was talking about running it and looked startled,

"I didn't catch that, what did you mean?"

"I'm talking about places where you know you don't want to go, ever. The edge is clear."

We got down to the main part of the drop and stopped to look at it. We'd been on the water for five hours and Tony had already made his decision. He gave me a huge bear hug. "Doug, thanks. This has been the greatest day of river running I've ever had. It's the hardest stuff I've ever done. Thanks a million." The stressed look on his face changed into a smile.

"I've got to get out here. I only had two hours sleep and haven't eaten anything since 9 last night. It's been a great run, but I don't want to push it any more." He gave me another hug. "You showed me today what real focus is. Thanks."

His face was beaming. I thought, *this is what river running is about*. I've known Tony for ten years, we've talked and paddled together, we've competed against each other.   But now there is a link, something simple but powerful. Friendship. Where you finally know just what is inside a person.

At Jacobs, we spent a few minutes looking at the ridiculous hole at the third drop. We joked with Adam Shandro, a young excellent paddler from Boise who had watched us run the last few rapids: "Here you go, pip-squeak. We're leaving this for you young guys. Just so the next generation has something to shoot for - Jacob's Ladder at 7000 cfs."

Shaking our hands, Adam laughed, "Well, thanks for leaving us something, you old farts."

Laughing with Adam, there was the funny feeling we were seeing the next generation - maybe like the older guys had done with Tony and me years ago in this very spot. When the time came, maybe Adam and the others would go places we never dreamed of.   Limits are like dominoes and the next step had already been set in motion. *Maybe they really will run Jacob's at this level.*

But not today. We headed downstream to look at Golf Course.

Along the bank we thrashed through the brush and climbed out on boulders to try and get a look. The water was roaring past up into the bushes and trees.

We talked as we looked. Tony was thoughtful, "Dana sometimes gets mad at me for boating by myself. I don't have anyone to go with because my schedule is so strange, but I also enjoy paddling alone. You know, marriage is so funny. You've each got to work hard to accept what the other needs. I think if I work on my kayaking, and test my skills, then I come back happier, knowing that I've accomplished something important to me. I think it makes for a better relationship when each person realises that and gives ground, allows the other to do those things they have a need to do."

We talked for a bit about the unlikely combination of strong marriage and commitment to paddling. The balancing of two lives and sets of concerns - trying to keep them from becoming contradictory. Smiling at the similarities of how we had managed to maintain both, and the places where the balance sometimes didn't work. Managing the frustrations that occasionally came from conflicting directions, and the great joys that appeared within each world. With each comment, I felt I could see exactly what he meant. It was a peaceful moment of understanding in the dappled light beneath the Ponderosas. We nodded to each other, shook hands, then turned back to the river.

★★★

With Tony helping in the assessment, I settled upon a line which was one of the wildest I've ever tried. At the top of Golf Course, he helped me launch off a sloping boulder directly into the fray. Punching holes, missing logs, slashing and muscling through diagonals. A thumb's up from a churning eddy. Then a suck-in-the-gut set of power moves, through the corner of the proverbial bus-sized hole, then slapped around through the lower section amidst mountains. Normally, I'm not sure I would have tried it, but my conversations with the river had convinced me the line was there. It went. I ran down to Screaming Left Turn and got out to scout, knowing this was the crux of the day.

Left Turn was a rapid where the moves were hard and clear - but for sheer intimidation outweighed everything else on the river. The line required keeping in control through a long difficult lead-in heading straight at the logs on the island, then making the critical cut. All the power of the current hurtled straight at death. The logs were terribly threatening - deathly ugly. But for all the power and inhospitality I was certain the move could be scalpeled. I considered, weighed, and committed.

Careening down the lead-in, my complete focus was on setting up the last move.

The water crashes all around, reflexes reach out, reactions without thought. I can't see but for an instant at the top of each wave. Riding out gusts and breaks, quick hard strokes, the boat and body and mind are all one entity, flowing with the power of the river. Forces rush me down the rapid tumbling and chaotic, but there is a place in my mind whose serenity is never breached, that focuses on the line and senses everything in the river. It is the centre of my being within which all is calm and ordered. Through it I see the rapid unfold and the crux appear -

Here it comes, <u>here it comes</u>, **here it comes** ... **NOW!**

Right in front of the log skewers, I cut through a funnel of water curling off the right bank and was catapulted into the air. The entire boat flew in a perfect arc six feet over the water, landed, then sliced into the right channel past the island. Down the technical class five channel near the shore, punching holes, missing a log, pulling an eddy at the bottom. A wave to Tony up on shore and down I went.

Greg got back in and we worked down another mile of big rapids to reach the Jaws sequence. He had scouted this half-mile rapid carefully while Tony and I were above, so I followed him as he wove a nice line between the worst of the towering breaking waves and holes. After what we'd been through this somehow felt manageable. From any objective point of view we were taking on a terribly menacing rapid. It was just as fast and powerful as ever - but now within our stride.

Coming down the long straightaway toward Hound's Tooth the tension began to dissipate, leaving a sense of lightness. The power was still crashing around but the roiling water seemed transparent, its currents obvious. And that was the wonder. Somehow, we had absorbed all the chaos and power, and all that was left was an effortless flow.

What are the limits? Where are they? I don't know. They expand and contract, melt away and reform - and they live in a world beyond what we see. But we felt we had reached into that world today and touched them.

We flew the last five miles from Hound's Tooth, slowing only to surf some beautifully smooth waves. Stopping below the old highway bridge, we looked at the gauge again. Waves slapping up against the gauge made it impossible to read accurately - maybe 11.9 feet, maybe more, maybe less. A top to bottom at something like 7000 cfs. It seemed fitting that we couldn't tell just how much water was there. Somehow, it was better not to be able to put a number on it.

At Banks, Tony came down to Greg and me as we got out of our kayaks at the cobble beach. I looked at both of them and said, "That was one of the best days of my life. Thanks."

We headed down to the Ponderosa cafe for a burger, and sat outside overlooking the Main Payette as it flowed below us, eating and talking. Fatigue set in, muscles started to ache. It became clear just how keyed up we'd been all day. Tony finished and leaned back in his chair with a blissful look on his face. Greg's aloofness had softened into an easy smile. Some back slapping and hand shaking, then it's back on the road. All things come to an end. The river was already starting to drop.

What is this spell the water casts upon us? It defies description. My words reach after it, but it slips away. I feel it filling me though, clean and pure like the light of the dawn, and I know it holds the truth. A man once said that the best things can't be told. He was right. But we still have to try.

It was late when I stopped at Jacob's Ladder on the way back up Highway 55. I hopped from rock to rock down to river level and sat on a boulder as twilight deepened. I was quiet for a while, looking at the water and listening to its roar. Then I talked with the North Fork.

I thanked the river for its power and its beauty. I thanked it for what it had given me through all these years, and what it had given me today. I know rivers are just water, gravity, and some rocks. But they are also beautiful. Their power and challenges inspire. My best friendships have arisen from their waters. It's only honest to treat them as respected friends.

I climbed back up the bank, shivering from the cold spray. I gave one last look at the exploding rapid below me. A few short hours ago, that was my world. Now, it was 10pm. I was tired and had a hard seven hour drive ahead of me. But inside, I had all of life.

★★★

GUY BAKER

I first heard of Guy when he led a youth expedition to the Zanskar river, and then met him when he came and gave a short lecture at the Mike Jones Rally about the trip. The next time I met him he was making his presence felt asking awkward questions at a London River Rats slide show. Fortunately I wasn't giving the lecture. It was Christina Dodwell talking about the BBC/SOBEK trip down the Wagi river in Papua New Guinea. His embarrassing questions turned out to be more pertinent than the audience realised as the full story came out over the years. A few years later he joined us to paddle some of the rivers of the High and Middle Atlas mountains in Morocco. Six of us drove overland with the kayaks while three others, including Guy, flew out. Guy gave us three bags to take in the minibus. Sensible idea we thought. When we collected Guy and the others from the airport, he had three more bags. Bringing lemons to bleach his hair, now that's extracting the Michael; but six bags all in all?! Since then Guy still t avels with loads of luggage but then it tends to be more toys than toiletries these days. Guy is the favourite to win the "He who dies with the most toys, wins" competition. For a kayaking trip to Nepal you obviously need a paraglider and I think we were lucky he did not take his wind surfer just in case there was a windy day on Pokhara Lake! On trips to Val Siesia in Italy you require, apart from the kayak and paddles etc., in-line skates, a unicycle, juggling clubs and balls, and other such things. Guy is very proud of his "style car", a Karmann Ghia, but has had to go out and by a Renault Traffic van just to carry everything he needs for a wet windy weekend walking in Wales.

Guy started kayaking when his parents, who worked abroad, sent him to school at Dartington Hall. Dartington Hall school is a very progressive school - my grandmother used to tell a tale of a Schools Inspector who, dressed in a pin-striped suit, tie and bowler hat, (this was between the wars), knocked at the doors to this pioneering school. The door was opened by a stark-naked girl. The inspector exclaimed "Good God" to which the girl replied "We don't believe in that here" and slammed the door. Dartington Hall is famed for its liberal and pioneering attitudes which obviously rubbed off on Guy and are reflected in his outlook on life and paddling and his self-confidence. He freely admits that his interest in paddling is driven by exploration; dangle the carrot of a first descent in front of Guy and he will sign up as soon as he can get his gold credit card out! Guy led his first expedition when he was 21 - everyone on the trip was under 21. Feeling that the expedition paddlers of the time were an aloof group and impossible to break into, he went and stuck his neck out and organised his own expedition to the Zanskar. When he was working for a management training company he felt he could do a better job and so went out and set up his own company, Catalyst Event Management. It now turns over in excess of a million pounds a year so I guess he was right.

Whether naked girls slam doors in Guy's face I don't know.

SERIOUS SATURDAY

Ambitions in kayaking are less well defined than in mountaineering. Getting to the top of a mountain is both obvious and definitive. Kayaking a river, unless it is from the source to sea, is much more subjective: river levels rise and fall, the put-in and take-out are (sometimes carefully) selected, short stretches are carried, and a descent claimed. Definitions are blurred. All this leads to a lack of real objectives and the feeling that "It has all been done". It seemed like all the rivers had been run.

Then the invite arrived.

How often do you get the chance to close a window on history? How likely is it that in the mid-1990's that the longest river in the world still has an un-navigated section containing some of the most sustained white water in the world? Why hadn't this stretch been run?

In July 1996 the last 85 kms. of un-paddled water on the Victoria Nile, part of the upper White Nile, in Uganda was our objective. Previously attempted by two other expeditions, both in the last year, one South African and one American; neither was successful. Crocodile attacks forced the South African expedition from the water after 5 kms. and the American expedition was abandoned, after seeing the water levels, without paddling any of the river (except to take some all-important photographs for the sponsors around Murchinson falls). This had made getting the appropriate permits from Murchinson Falls Parks Authority and the army particularly difficult for our expedition.

This stretch of the river runs near to the border with Sudan and the ongoing civil war is perilously close. Border skirmishes with Kony's rebels 100 kms. to the north are frequent, and these Sudanese rebels raid the Ugandan villages to kidnap children for conscription as soldiers to their cause. Also our proposed put-on point had been a favourite location for one of Idi Amin's less savoury activities; here political prisoners were thrown from the bridge to nourish the crocodiles of the Nile. Idi Amin may have gone but the crocodiles' taste for human flesh remains. These political problems have kept the river's secrets hidden from the world of river runners.

Against the advice of all the Ugandan residents we met our expedition, hand-picked by Cam McCleay and mounted by Adrift, intended to tackle some of the largest and most powerful rapids in the world. The ten-man team, many veterans of the Zambezi, the Grand Canyon and the Indus, chattered nervously before the descent as if convinced, to a man, that the river would claim someone during the attempt – as it happened, it was just a kayak that was sacrificed to the relentless surge of the river.

Saturday 20th July.

I could have been at the Phoenix Festival with The Prodigy headlining!

Andy Copestick, the New Zealand kayak paddler on the team, hit a crucial window between a crashing lateral and a large hole, pumped high on the surge he smashed his way downstream. My run was less proficient. Missing the window at the top – I blame the lateral for crashing on me – I was rotated on several axes, inverted through a series of planes, horizontal and vertical becoming indistinguishable. Imagine being a hamster running on its wheel when the wheel breaks loose from its mountings and falls spinning down a huge plug hole. I think this image may get close to what being subjected to big water turmoil is like.

Not one to panic, I timed my roll and surfaced with enough time to get a breath of air before I was hit by another crashing lateral, knocked over and rolled up again. This was not the line I had carefully worked out from the bank and now to compound the confusion, my deck popped – honest, you can see it all in the video – leaving me with just my head and shoulders above water going over the next pour-over. The swim started with me already breathless. My kayak was wrenched from my grip. I held my paddle vertically to act as a luminous yellow distress beacon amongst the turmoil, so that Andy could see it to rescue me.

I was shaken and still breathless from fear when I managed to make it to the edge of an eddy. Crocodile country. If a crocodile was going to attack this was the moment. I had no alternative; I had to swim through the pool to the bank. I made it and slumped on a riverside rock, Andy, seeing me safe, returned upstream for the video camera – refusing to go down alone to chase my kayak. I didn't blame him; the eddies upstream had already proved to harbour hippos and crocodiles. The two raft crews were unaware of the situation – they were preoccupied with trying to line the rafts down the drop on the far bank of the river. They were some 200 metres across and 500 metres upstream. Andy returned to help but just as he crossed into the pool a hippo surfaced – ten feet from Andy – and decided it was time to show us who lived there. Andy turned and sprinted back to the main current without a glance behind, leaving me once again abandoned, alone in the middle of Africa.

The hippo, now awake and not content with having frightened off Andy, lunged through the water towards me. Whilst I knew that hippos are vegetarian I also knew how territorial they are and it seemed that this one had not read the same script as me; he was showing all the characteristics of a carnivore. All I had was my rock to stand on and my paddle to fend off the one tonne invader. Feeling like a character from a Boys' Own cartoon strip, I stood eye to eye with my adversary. I didn't win, I just didn't lose! I stood with my paddle shouting at the hippo as it stomped at the water with his front leg, like a bull preparing to charge and showing me a fine pair of huge tonsils at the back of his one and a half metre mouth span. Not the time or place to fall off the rock and now this rock no longer felt such a safe haven as it had when I had initially embraced it as a life buoy.

After a prolonged stand off I gained the main bank and made my way through the dense undergrowth in search of anyone. Having lost my kayak, been deserted by Andy and separated from the two rafts by the full width of the White Nile, Africa seemed to be a much bigger place especially when alone and surrounded by nature in the raw. This was not a David Attenborough documentary. Piles of bones indicated some-thing very large had had a meal recently. The African bush takes on an all together different perspective from the familiar TV images once you find yourself alone in it. Suddenly you start to listen to every sound. Each footstep is carefully placed to avoid whatever might lurk in the undergrowth. You constantly check your "escape routes" – trees to climb in case you are charged, places to hide should rebels suddenly appear. All your senses go on "Alert".

A small plane suddenly appeared overhead and buzzed down the rapid. He had a bird's eye view of the chaos and dropped me a message to say my kayak was 2 kms. downstream on the North bank. Unfortunately the North bank was the bank we had been advised to avoid as it was the domain of the Kony's terrorists. Enemy territory. It wasn't my day; but at least I had the consolation of knowing I was not alone any more, someone was watching over me – from the sky.

Eventually Cam McCleay retrieved me in the oar raft, and we watched incredulously as the paddle raft flipped again. The fourth flip so far on the river, this time on what normally would just have been a simple run-out wave train, but on this river even the run out waves are twelve feet high.

Lunch. No sign of my kayak; the river had now entered a series of island and drops. As a kayak paddler, changing to the paddle raft felt like being demoted to a lower league only to watch on helpless as Cam flipped again. We rescued him above what we named "Waimia on a bad day", a reference to the big surf wave in Hawaii. A lucky escape for both Cam and the rest of us; the raft would have been stripped of its contents by the sheer size and volume of the hole and Cam would have taken a beating.

The light aircraft returned again this time pointing - yes, this pilot was so good he could make his plane point - at a spot on the opposite bank. I realised my kayak is resting somewhere over there. But with rapids upstream and down, the far bank might just as well be in Kathmandu as we just could not get there. We abandoned it.

We camped early. Tomorrow looked like a long portage of up to two kms. past the only un-paddleable section of this part of the river. The emphasis on the danger seems to have changed today from the hippos and crocodiles, now it was the water. Five flips by two of the world's most experienced rafters in these waters and one missing kayak, with 35 kms to go emphasised this fact. As Dave Tofler, the Australian rafter, said every river has karma, some are karma than others - not this one.

(Guy's kayak was found by a fisherman and returned to Adrift, complete with the new decoration of a perfect set of crocodile teeth marks. Adrift hung it in their Ugandan office to entice other tourist to join them on a raft trip down the river. Now that is ambitious marketing. Ed.)

MIKE HEWLETT

One year I was stuck at Grantully looking for a lift south - Dave Higson's car had broken down yet again. Mike was in the minibus that gave me a lift down from Scotland and he along with others in the minibus started asking me about the holidays that Slime and I were organising to the Çoruh that summer. Unbeknown to me, he, along with a group of his friends had checked onto the first of our trips down the Çoruh. This was when I first met Mike.

Both Mike and I were at the stage when our group of paddling friends were "retiring" from paddling and we were casting around for new paddling partners. After the trip to Turkey we put together paddling trips to Corsica, Morocco, the USA, the Grand Canyon, British Columbia and other destinations. These trips were great trips of friendship and fun, sometimes exploratory verging on expeditionary, sometimes just for the fun of paddling always with a group of friends. Sometimes we got into trouble. For instances include getting on at the wrong put-ins all over the place (because someone else was supposed to be listening to the instructions), ending up above the serious drop on Cayoosh Creek, British Columbia, (because we paddled into "Hourglass Canyon" and had to volunteer Ross to lead the very dodgy and very loose rock climb out), having to climb and walk out from half way down the N'Fiss gorge in Morocco after we had decided to run the gorge as the guide in a French magazine said don't. (We walked back in and ran it all once we had seen the other side of the last blind corner.)

His often said, "Oh my good God, you know what this will mean", summation of some proposed plan or action is usually followed by his (and my) acceptance of an inevitable adventure either in some bar or down some river. This gives the impression of an irresponsible and cavalier attitude to paddling; cavalier maybe but irresponsible no. Mike would always have the strength of character to turn around and say "No, this is not on" when proposed plans were a little too, shall we say, ill-conceived. On other occasions when we arrived in some predicament and the realisation that we were in trouble dawned, he would have the maturity to keep quiet rather than start an argument about how to extricate us from the problem. He would hold his counsel rather than exacerbate the problem by proposing an alternative to someone else's feasible plan; don't rock the boat, especially at times of stress.

Mike is also a keen proponent of Shotokan Karate (second dan) and his tales from the dojo have kept us amused in many a bar. Most of the others who train in his dojo are night club bouncers and security staff whereas Mike is a computer programmer. At the first training session of each week the others always have tales of the weekend's action to be swapped, tales of blood and guts, fights, bruises and broken bones. Mike has no input to this side of the club's social life. So when Mike arrived at the dojo one Tuesday evening, after a weekend away kayaking, with a stunning black eye, there was much barracking and even more hilarity at Mike's expense when he explained that the black eye was not the result of some altercation with "local yuff" but, that whilst walking from the pub to the curry house, he had been so engrossed talking to an old university friend, not seen for eight to ten years, that he had walked straight into a lamppost!

THE INDUS

When the Lion roars

"OK. Great. Cut out behind the rock, cross above the two holes on the right and catch the eddy on the far side". Despite years of living in Asia and the States, Gerry Moffat retained his Scottish accent. I just wished he retained some sense of reality as well.

We were perched on top of a boulder, necks strained skyward trying to inspect the monster rapid in front of us; two hundred yards of mountainous waves, deep holes and evil-looking pour-overs with a rock the size of a house in the middle. Like most rapids on the River Indus there wasn't a straightforward run down anywhere, hence the need for some devious route-finding.

Trying to match Gerry's calmness I gibbered back that the crossover, the crux of the route, was tight to say the least. It involved at least one rather large collapsing wave and the consequences of messing up didn't bear thinking about. I wasn't happy.

Mick Hopkinson, a Yorkshireman currently living in New Zealand, suggested an alternative to the left. Clip the edge of the biggest hole on the rapid and thread a delicate route between the rock and a series of pour-overs and paddle for one's life in between. Any chance of success required being right on line, through waves that would limit your vision at every crest with facefuls of water and in every trough by the next mountainous wave. I definitely wasn't happy with that route either and started to wonder about the effects of living abroad on the British brain. I didn't mention either worry to Mick …. One doesn't!

Marcus Schmid, a German friend from the AKC, just looked, glassy-eyed somewhere down the middle. That was one route I wasn't even going to contemplate.

Like all these discussions, we'd been through every permutation before, twice in fact. The same ideas rolled around; the same ideas got rejected. Of course it might have helped to have started from the opposite bank where Guy Baker, sensible person, was sitting.

Just when it was safe to talk about walking around, Ross Purdy threw in his considered opinion. "Well, let's get it done; the cameras are

ready." Before my mouth could hit the floor he'd starting walking back to his boat. With the slow realisation that if one person ran it we all had to, people started to follow. Then it became a race to set off; who in his right mind wants to be left at the back on a rapid like that? Even while putting on my spraydeck I had no real idea as to a route. My only inspiration was to follow the person in front ... and hope it wasn't Marcus.

Dave Manby, injured and watching from above, likened the scene to firing off a blunderbuss loaded with kayaks with the resulting explosion of boats scattering off in all directions. Surprisingly, most got down their intended routes. Even I managed to follow Gerry halfway across, rolled, lost him and found myself at the end in one piece, much as I'd intended.

Cam McLeay, our Kiwi rafter, and Helen, nurse and raft passenger must have known that it wasn't going to be a good day when the raft dropped sideways into a monster hole. Several minutes later, safely restored to their newly righted raft, whiteness showed on their faces. They had just been told that every second of the drama had been recorded by the TV cameras. What a bad place to flip a raft!

Starting high up on the Tibetan plateau, the Indus passes through Kashmir and then Pakistan and on into the Arabian Sea. Draining the Western Himalaya at the start of its journey and then the Karakorum, the river is often known as "the gutter of the roof of the world". Set within such a mountainous backdrop, it's a wildly spectacular and challenging place. Nowhere is this more so than in the deep gorges of Pakistan's Northern territories. Starting at the town of Skardu, base for many climbing expeditions, the gorge carries on for 100 miles before opening out at the confluence of the Gilgit River. Totally inhospitable terrain combines with the fury of the water to form one of the few remaining accessible white water runs to defy a river descent.

Here seemed the ideal place for Mick Coyne and John Taylor to plan their follow up expedition to their Kites and Kayaks expedition to Nepal and the Dudh Kosi. Whilst most kayakers limit their planning to one drunken night in the pub and consider themselves over-organised when they get both green card insurance and AA 5★ insurance for a single trip, Mick and John took a full year setting up the trip. They still forgot to get the official permission required to be on the river but did remember the budget to make a full length TV documentary. From the early days the expedition was named "The Taming of the Lion" (Buddhist mythology says the Indus flows out of the mouth of a lion). Either Marcus didn't follow Buddhist mythology or he had a more realistic understanding of the river when he questioned which paddler was being referred to as the Lion which was going to be tamed.

My first sight of the gorge was as impressive as I had been led to believe. Huge bare rock walls rose straight out of the river, carrying on seemingly forever before running out into mountain peaks. Boulder-choked tributaries fell out of the clouds, cutting deep V-shaped notches into the side walls. Vast scree slopes lay at the base of each ice-shattered crag. Everywhere were ugly scars of landslides above massive tips of precariously balanced boulders. Here and there, small plateaux left high above the gorge floor marked ancient river levels. Down one side a single-track dirt road was the only concession to the 20th century. As though to confirm the obvious nature of the gorge, the architects had decided on the colour scheme of grey. The rock walls were grey, the boulder fields below the cliffs were grey, and the river itself was grey. Like an attempt to brighten up an old room, the upper slopes had been whitewashed with a fresh coat of snow. Only occasional small settlements working the land on the flat plateaux gave any hint of colour with their fields of green crops. Outside the gorge on the not too distant skylines lay the snow-capped peaks of the Karakorum, including Rakoposhi, and Nanga Parbat.

Without the road the gorge would be impenetrable. Built originally by the Pakistani army, it links the Karakorum Highway with Skardu, capital of Baltistan and now a military outpost near the disputed Pakistan/India border. Monuments on the roadside pay tribute to the hundreds of workmen who died building it. Keeping the road free of landslides is a continual battle and still claims many lives. Driving on the road is not to be taken lightly either: carved out of the rock halfway up the gorge, on one side long near-vertical drops into the river, whilst on the other side of the road large delicately-poised boulders seem to defy gravity, hanging from rock faces above. Although it is possible to inspect the river from the road, access is possible only in a handful of places where the road drops down to meet the river.

It was the power and size of the river that continually threw us. With the eye subconsciously trying to reduce the scenery down to manageable proportions it was easy to be tricked into likewise reducing the size of the river. In order to make use of low water levels we had arrived at the Indus in April, before the main snow melt begins. Low for this river is 15,000cfs, equivalent to average flows of the Grand Canyon of the Colorado or translated into technical British terminology, "huge!" By July the river level would peak at just below 100,000cfs. Having spent four days with Ross doing an inspection of the river from the safety of a jeep, we were cautiously ready for some boating. For our first warm-up we optimistically picked a section Ross had marked as "Play" on our newly made schematic map.

It was Mick who was the first real victim of our false perspectives of the river. Dropping sideways into an innocent-looking hole, he disappeared from sight until only the top of his quivering paddles could be seen from my position in the breakout below. If he had been hoping for some playful sport then the river was one step ahead. Watching his boat perform some rather spectacular cartwheels, Dave, Ross and I sat and discussed whether we were in the company of one of the world's most hair-ball hot-dog boaters or someone whose glasses mist up at all the wrong times. Not knowing him well enough to wish for a very embarrassing swim (we'd only been paddling together for five minutes) we sat excitedly awaiting the outcome. All too soon the river tired of entertaining us and, with a final loop, let Mick go. His glasses certainly weren't misted up when he rolled up. That was by no means the last laugh the Indus had that day. For a section that we had been hoping to play, the river had the most fun.

With the warm-up safely over, we started the descent of the gorge.

Making a mockery of the 35 foot per mile average gradient the river, the river is the sort that likes to flow for nearly a mile then drop all its height in one or two thunderous chaotic rapids. Having had an ample demonstration of the power of the river by the way in which it nonchalantly sent Cam's 500 lb. raft spinning skyward before slamming it down on the former occupants, we treated the river with utmost respect. For fifteen days my nervous system suffered a succession of highs and lows as the excitement and relief of getting down the last rapid safely was drowned out by the fear and anticipation of the next.

To a paddler this never-ending supply of huge rapids could be either a paradise or a nightmare; it just depended on what kind of day it was.

Stopping to inspect rapids made us instant celebrities. In contrast to our nervous faces fixed on the water we would often be surrounded by crowds of smiling faces. From hidden villages and fields out of sight of the river, locals ran down impossibly steep rocky slopes to greet us. The spectacle of brightly coloured kayaks, a large inflatable raft, and weirdly clad aliens brought out a carnival atmosphere. Friendly but reserved towards us, they stood laughing and joking amongst themselves, waiting for some form of entertainment to begin. First runs down the rapid were cause for much clapping and cheering. Trips in the raft and lifts across the river also proved popular attractions. Amongst such tightly knit communities, word would spread that we were on our way. As we drove down the road on a rest day we passed a group of people waiting for us by the river; we had to tell them our circus would be one day late arriving.

We completed approximately sixty miles of the gorge before we decided it was time to leave. So far the river gods had looked after us. Now the river had started to rise at a dangerous rate: the flow was increasing by 10,000 cfs per week. The next section of gorge the rapids were harder and more dangerous, portages more numerous and commitment 100 per cent. From the road above it was possible to see rapids with no provision for scouting or portaging. That was a lot to ask even the most benevolent river god.

It was difficult to feel too much disappointment in leaving the gorge without a complete descent. The Lion contained within it had only just started to growl after hibernation. I'd paddled down rapids more challenging than any I'd paddled before among a group of rafters and paddlers stronger than any I'd previously paddled with and in the company of good friends. I knew it was a wise idea to leave before the roar got too loud. It had been a great trip and there was a certain amount of satisfaction in leaving something as wild as the Indus untamed.

A previous SOBEK raft expedition to the Lion gorges, which likewise pulled out halfway down, concluded their report saying "the Lion River had proved that its purpose was to take water from the centre of the universe down to the sea, and men of reason were not necessarily invited along for the ride". I'd go along with that.

THE INDUS BELOW SKARDU.

JONAS NOKER

I first I met Jonas at the International Canoe Exhibition at Crystal Palace in London. We were each giving lectures on our own expeditions. I was introduced to this tall, smart but casually dressed German carrying an impressive brief case. He just did not seem to fit into the mould of the expedition paddlers I knew. The group of scruffy seemingly disorganised paddlers I paddled expeditions with at the time would have mocked me incessantly if I had appeared with a brief case (smart or not). On our expeditions we had developed management techniques to their holistic limit: we had reduced the decision making process, utilising Chaos theory and the dither factor, to a fine art. Jonas did not strike me as someone who would fit into expedition paddling as I saw it. Then I saw Jonas's lecture and I began to doubt whether our "expeditions" were expeditions. Calling a bunch of friends travelling around paddling rivers in a foreign country an expedition does not make the grade when compared to Jonas's exploits. While we would be travelling around in an old minibus or local bus Jonas was having to organise helicopters; we could always walk out to the road in half a day max., Jonas and his group would need days to walk out; we were travelling in areas covered by tourist guide books, Jonas was paddling where the word tourist probably did not exist in the local language. The preparation and research for his trips was way beyond ours. Our research and preparation was usually limited to buying AA five star insurance for the minibus or air tickets if flying, and the correct map for the area we were heading to and remembering the credit card and passport. His involved negotiations with government offices, obtaining clearances and visa applications and chartering local transport Suddenly the briefcase did not seem so incongruous (and no doubt this has now been updated to a laptop computer linked to a mobile phone!).

His CV of rivers and countries makes impressive reading, not just the number of rivers but also how many he has managed to fit them all into such a short time. Between 1989 and 1997 he has managed to paddle in 23 countries (leaving out European countries) including Malawi, Madagascar, Uzbekistan, Kazakhstan, Nicaragua, Sikim, (and the rest of the countries are just as outlandish.) It is no wonder his letter heading reads "RIVER EXPEDITIONS, AUDIO VISUALS & LOGISTICS"

This story of Jonas will give you some idea of the meticulous planning and detail to the logistics that his numerous expeditions require, the photographs confirm the standard of audio visuals and the descriptions of the country confirm the exploratory nature of the trip and its expeditionary nature.

OBSCURED BY CLOUDS

Translated by Nicky Stephens

Papua New Guinea is the second largest island in the world. The official maps are strewn with the famous "blanks on the map": it has never been possible to survey these areas either by land or by satellite. The River Strickland which thunders through the mountains is mapped only incompletely. This was our objective; a first descent of the Strickland river, but first Wolfgang, Dirk, Lucas and myself had to check to see if the river was navigable. It was to be the most extreme expedition of our lives.

COURSE 323° - After a few minutes flying along the coral reef the plane altered course and headed towards the Highlands. The island loomed like a colossal monster rising from the Pacific. In the interior bizarrely fissured mountains and tropical jungle extended as far as the eye could see. A fantastic land relief; jagged like the spine of a dragon with vertebrae towering up to 5000 metres. Just below the Equator glaciers and volcanoes stand in solitary splendour above the omnipresent jungle, unexplored massive rivers and streams carve their way through deep ravines and canyons. Something of the country's prehistoric eerieness stayed with its inhabitants too. There are Papuans apparently still living here and there as cannibals and head-hunters as if in the Stone Age.

It was only yesterday, so to speak, that the highland natives were discovered. The British gold-digger Mick Leahy had the first contact with these inhabitants in 1933. Leahy - as a pale European - was considered an evil spirit by the original inhabitants, and spoke of the "last open-air museum of the Stone Age". The Papuans were familiar with neither pots nor metal, stone axes were their tools; nor could they write to record the vocabulary of their languages. Within half a century Britons, Germans and Australians had "civilised" most of these "Stone Age people". This civilisation of the foreign mining companies extracts gold and copper and also thoughtlessly contaminates the rivers of a land which does not belong to them. Further environmental problems are caused by large-scale tree felling. Those who are not involved

213

in this development do not understand what is happening to their world. Whilst in the fast-growing towns where shops are selling hi-fi equipment, there are still Papuans in the market who have little idea what to do with the Kina, their national currency. When they have sold their vegetables and tuber-fruits to the developers, they take the proceeds to money-changing shops, where, at a fixed rate of exchange, they get "Kauri cheques". These are the traditional currency and are the only accepted method of payment in remote villages. The enforced transition to the modern age has happened in only fifty years - all in the fast lane.

We were on the way to the highlands to kayak the Lagaip and Strickland rivers. Below us was the tropical rain forest with the tree tops looking like broccoli spears; ahead was the town of Mount Hagen, the metropolis of the highlands with 40,000 inhabitants. The pilot of the Twin Otter prepared to land and started the descent.

We arrived in Mount Hagen in time for the large Sing-Sing, a spectacular feast where thousands of Highland inhabitants meet anually. Ritual dances are fundamental elements of a Sing-Sing, which functions simultaneously as a bartering market, a country feast of freshly slaughtered pigs and a marriage marketplace. The most diverse highland clans and tribes meet up adorned as jungle gladiators. For the Papuans this is a cultural competition, for us a kaleidoscope of primeval times. Warriors armed with stone axes, spears, bows and arrows marched past and demonstrated riches, power and fighting spirit. All-day dancing, drumming and singing followed. The tribesmen danced to the rhythms of small drums made from hollow tree trunks, covered with snakeskin or lizard skin. Slow movements alternate with jerky twists and fierce stamping. Muscular bodies rubbed with pig's fat, vegetable sap and ashes gleam in the midday sun. Clothing consists simply of a cloth at the front, which is called laplap in pidgin English and a bush of leaves at the back, the ass grass. The leather apron is decorated with exotic pictures of faces: whilst the forehead, nose, cheeks and chin are decorated with glorious colours. These strange, terrifying faces serve to scare off enemies and demons. Feathers, bones or teeth are stuck in their pierced noses. The symbol for virility is the boar's tusk, as long as a thumb, worn as a nose ornament. You can see huge headdresses made of animal skins or braided human hair, in which are stuck gloriously coloured bird of paradise feathers. When thousands of members of the surrounding mountain tribes meet up once a year for the traditional Sing-Sing, they celebrate the customs and rituals of their ancestors. They keep up their traditions! But also during these three days they have their first brush with civilisation's drugs, which lead to further addiction to these: chewing gum, cigarettes, T-shirts and beer.

We planned a "warm up" on a couple of smaller rivers before the main expedition on the Lagaip and Strickland rivers. We hired a native to drive us to the hinterland in his truck. Our route passed villages with typical houses of worship and sacrificial stones to their forefathers, and standing by the roadside little ghost houses containing the small coffins in which the mountain-based Papuans bury the bones of their dead. The journey led through the Mendi area. When asked our driver, Jishi, answers that he comes from this tribe with "Yes, Mendi man", and then he adds, smiling, "Cannibal men" and spat out an arc of blood-red chewed buai, Papua's "Red Bull". The Areka palm tree's red betel nut is a slight stimulant and is chewed in the whole of Asia as well as in Papua New Guinea.

Ahead of us lies the valley of the River Mendi and the provincial hamlet of the same name. As we passed natives with grunting pigs on lead, and Jishi coolly continued to crack cannibal jokes. The sight of these swine reassured us: their presence means that their consumption has superseded that of the *longpig*, the latter, according to local under-standing, being nothing other than a human being. In pre-missionary days the enemy's heart and forehead would be eaten so as to augment one's own bravery with that of the vanquished. Numerous explorers and adventurers' skulls were smashed with clubs and the brains used to make sago pudding. Gruesome by-products of this cannibalism included necklaces made of human fingers. Uninvited government officials were not infrequently received with arrows, spears and stone axes, some of them were even killed. Some of the mountain tribes additionally indulged in the ritual head-hunt: a man was only considered a man, if he had beheaded someone and hung the head on his house built on stilts.

This was the region of the Highlands we had picked for the first phase of the expedition! To add to our feeling of unease, though ours was to be a second descent of the river, we had been warned that the excitement might not be only on the river. Several years earlier when the Mendi was paddled for the first time by Australian rafters a native lost his life. Although the deceased's village received money from the rafters as "damages", the sum was considered to be insufficient. The

Dressed for battle. *Jonas Noker*   Waterfall on the Erave river. *Jonas Noker*

Papuan women dressed up for a *sing sing*. *Jonas Noker*

disagreement was not resolved and the Australians took to their heels to reach freedom. Since then the area had been avoided by paddlers as they feared the ancient custom of the blood feud. Theft of land, pigs or women always required belligerent atonement. If caught the wrong-doer was thrashed or killed, but a member of the same tribe as the guilty person was also sufficient as expiatory sacrifice. Whether the Mendi people would differentiate between different paddlers or lump everyone together as one tribe, no one wanted to find out in person. Maybe we too, like the hated Australian rafters, belonged to the "boat-travelling clan". As kayak paddlers we had been warned to be on our guard. And so when we jumped from the truck on arrival it was with butterflies in our stomachs. We were, however, greeted with a friendly excited jabbering and not a hostile shower of arrows. We wanted to paddle the Mendi, Angurra and Erave rivers. This network of rivers is navigable as a group and should prepare us for our real expedition target. We sorted all the gear for the trip, which would last several days, and loaded it into the boats before dragging the heavily laden Prijon Tornado kayaks to the river.

Sparkling water carried us through a gloomy gorge. The Mendi enchanted us with its wild beauty. Round moss-covered rocks formed the obstructions and slowly the stream became a topographical big dipper. Despite its steep gradient the Mendi remained runable with great clean lines. We graded the river at IV - V and estimated the volume at around 30 m³/s. The Mendi is without a doubt one of the most beautiful rivers I have run. With our necks craned we could run almost everything by sight, and only once during the two-day descent did we have to shoulder the laden boats. We reached the confluence with the Angurra, where we were greeted by a considerable increase in the force of water. This drove us on from finishing one first descent into the scenic Erave and the start of another first descent. Here, tropical fruits grew alongside the river: mango, papaya and coconut. A fog of forest covered the Erave valley like a heavy blanket. Beams of sunlight only occasionally penetrated through the dense roof of leaves to the shady ground. The jungle's breath lay heavy over the river. Moist musty odours mixed with the clamour of wild animals. The scenic high point was the Imani Falls which fell from a height of fifty metres into the Erave like a white curtain. Here we came across friendly Papuans: the children particularly went out of their minds with excitement. They swarmed over our kayaks and wanted to go with us. Lukas was almost captured but just in the nick of time he shook off his half a dozen passengers before paddling into the next rapid. A few kilometres downstream a small path led out of the ravine; a makeshift, made-up track led back to Mendi, the nearest village. This take-out signalled the end of the warm-up. From now it would be more serious, and we devoted ourselves to the real aim of the expedition.

The Lagaip river rises in a high valley in the central chain of mountains; it joins with the Ok Om river to become the Strickland river and carves through the Highlands in the Strickland Canyon. This river network is one of the least explored areas in Papua New Guinea. It was only in the 1950s that the Strickland was first reconnoitred by some exploratory patrols. Nothing has happened in the surrounding countryside since then. The river is still surrounded by nothing but jungle for hundreds of kilometres. Neither roads nor villages exist. The valley remains virtually uninhabited. There are merely a few huts belonging to tribes living there.

The river network has still not been completely mapped. In 1970 a 32-strong team under W A Cawthorne tried in vain to map the Strickland's course but even with the aid of aerial and satellite pictures the area was not completely clear, as parts of the valley are permanently cloud-covered. The blanks on the map remain with the note "relief data incomplete". Lieutenant John Blashford-Snell attempted the first navigation of the Strickland in 1979, but the attempt failed after forty-five kilometres because of the rapids. This military-style expedition was part of the two-year long "Operation Drake" - a British youth development program and circumnavigation of the world in the foot-steps of the explorer Sir Francis Drake under the patronage of Prince Charles. The heavily-financed "River Strickland phase" was to be supplied with provisions every week dropped by parachute from military planes. After losing one of the two rafts together with equipment, the eight-man team had to wait three days on a ledge, before it could be flown out by two helicopters to Nomad.

It is this part of the river's course that is still unknown. In this very stretch all we could deduce from the neighbouring contours, was that there appeared to be an enormous fall over the length of the canyon. Aerial reconnaissance was imperative. We had to fly over the mountain region in a helicopter to judge the feasibility of the venture. We knew that navigating the Lagaip and the Strickland should only be undertaken with proper air support. We had to make sure that the river did not become a "dead end". It would be catastrophic to be stuck in the middle of the jungle, surrounded by four-thousand-metre mountains and an un-runnable river ahead. So dense was the jungle that th narrow strips of banks also had to permit landing and scouting and maybe portaging. Papua New Guinea's porous limestone is notorious for its extreme hidden dangers: its caves and subterranean river courses, and its sinkholes (holes formed by stepping on a fragile surface which then caves in beneath you). Several sinkholes, which made us sit up and take notice, are drawn on the maps in the canyon that the Strickland voraciously etches into karst. A few years ago in Indonesia in the similar Baliem valley members of an expedition fell through into a cave and drowned.

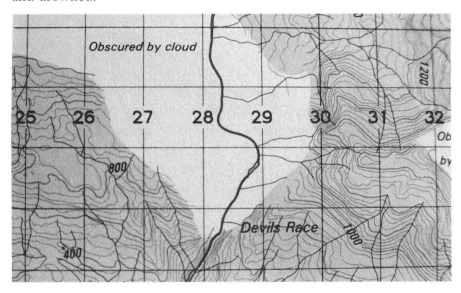

After the helicopter pilot had run through the pre-flight drill and showed us how to get in and out and places to be avoided, we discussed the altitude and route for the journey. Verbal communication on board was checked and we took off and flew up to over 3,000m. and contoured just above the mountain ridge. About 100 km from Mendi as the crow flies we landed in Tari to refuel the chopper. What a country! There are many more rivers than streets here. Between the gigantic mountains are high hanging-valleys, shaped like bathtubs, which, isolated for thousands of years, have developed into islands of evolution. Also the rugged mountains, raging rivers and dense jungle are responsible for around 750 tribes developing independently from one another. The result is a variety of more than 700 languages and 300 dialects. There are tribes settled less than fifty kilometres apart whose languages are as different as English and Chinese. This "Babylonian babble of languages" is today reconciled by "pidgin English". This is a severely cutback hotchpotch of languages with approximately 1,400 words, three quarters of which come from basic English, simple grammar and which uses Western transcription. When we made our second stopover after 200 kilometres in the small village of Nomad, my altitude meter indicated precisely ninety metres above sea level. Whilst we refuelled with kerosene canisters which we had brought with us, the village's headman told us that the last helicopter, and therefore the last outsiders, had landed there more than half a year ago.

From the River Nomad's confluence we flew up the Strickland river. Now it was becoming clear why it was only fifty years ago that the first white men succeeded in venturing into the centre of Papua New Guinea. Rough mangrove forests and swamps extend to both sides of the massive central mountain. Gradually the lowland plain was replaced by chains of hills and smaller mountains. After half-an-hour's flight, wooded mountain slopes gave way abruptly to pitch black rock walls. Ahead of us lay the most striking point on the Strickland, so striking that the bush pilots use them for orientation; the Falls Gorge. We flew into the heart of this massive granite canyon. It is probably the most unspoilt spot that I have ever seen. Over twenty-five kilometres the river seemed to be well and truly hemmed in between perpendicular

walls reaching up over 100 metres. The canyon stretched through the jungle like an oversized gutter. The rock was shiny and wet as the jungle's ground water ran down over the gorge walls. The noise of the motor rebounded muffled in the narrow gorge. I felt lost like an insect swallowed in the gullet of some monster. On both sides numerous waterfalls cascaded over the edge of the colossal chasm into the depths. Mighty rapids with powerful awkward eddy lines lay at the bottom of this seemingly endless gorge. Now in August with low water levels favourable for an attempt and we guessed the rapids to be Grade V. This could change suddenly despite this being the dry season. In Papua New Guinea only the following is true: in the rainy season it will rain and in the dry season it possibly will not. At this level the Falls Gorge was voted OK by all. The pilot flew further upstream at our signal.

Further to the North the blue sky changed to pale clouds. With every kilometre I became more restless, just one or two more bends in the river and we would reach the blanks in the map. The rain forest was strikingly lush and damp. It was raining and visibility was poor, but that was to be expected from a place that was labelled "obscured by clouds". The Strickland wound on in a huge S, hemmed in between the mountains.

The first patrol that had managed to penetrate this far consisted of three white men and 150 Duna and Huri porters. In 1954 their three-month expedition headed by D J Clancy reached this magnificent ravine which the Australians, without further ado, called the Devil's Race. It is a truly diabolical breach.

The Strickland is bounded by the Black Mountain to the East and the White Rock Mountain to the West. In the gorge there were colossal cataracts and solid white water for kilometres. We followed a tight horseshoe course to view the gorge at low altitude. Individual rapids seemed passable, but we would definitely need help with orientation in this wild water chaos. Even from the air there were scarcely any clues in the jungle to locate points on the river. I turned on my satellite navigation equipment which we had linked to the helicopter's network. The GPS (Global Positioning System) receives signals from satellites and thus calculates the current position in a flash. Whilst the helicopter hovered over the river like a humming bird, the GPS stored co-ordinates which would help us to form a useable sketch of the river to guide us later.

Further upstream, the Strickland, a broad bloated river, squeezed itself into a corset of granite. Here the entire river flowed mercilessly over an

221

impassable six-metre fall; upstream of this fall were tall steep banks without any reasonable eddies. To paddle unsuspectingly into this would have fatal consequences. The pilot changed course for us to inspect the waterfall in detail, this time at low altitude. Now for the first time I felt the hot breath of the Strickland: warm, sticky air hit me in the face. Two more impassable slits in a narrow gorge followed behind the waterfall. We stored take-out and get-in points on the GPS to identify the start and finish of the unavoidable task of carrying the boats round these falls. We would have to cut a way through the jungle with machetes and calculated 48 hours for the portage. After half-an-hour's flight we reached the confluence of the Ok Om and Lagaip, the sources of the Strickland. We landed on a broad gravel bank and unloaded the second of three re-supply depots. These contained groceries and cooking fuel so we could minimise the weight in our kayaks. Then we flew eastwards up the Lagaip. Over 100 km in length this offered everything there is in wild water: from steep and narrow to wide open boulder gardens to heavy white water. The view was indescribable. Brown water ate its way though the green of the jungle, plunged over powerful cataracts and carved a path through narrow ravines. We were probably looking down on regions where no explorer, missionary or adventurer had set foot. In 1968 white hunters were still coming across small tribes of natives, the Pagaias for instance, who were convinced that they were the only human beings in existence. The dense jungle now opened out and gave way to banks of fog and mountain cloud forest. These top kilometres of the Lagaip consisted of steep staircase rapids with innumerable siphons where the river disappeared underground. We flew as far as the source, and then veered off and returned to Mendi after 600 kilometres. In the camp we analysed the data. The stored co-ordinates of the supply points and path routes were transcribed to American Tactical pilotage Charts and Australian army maps to complete the white areas. That evening we decided that the river was "on".

We transported the boats as close as possible to the Lagaip by truck, which saved us a few thousand dollars in helicopter rental. However, for the last section into the wilderness we could not avoid this expensive fun. A rough tarmac road from the Mendi basin led north into the mountains. Beyond Mendi the road became worse and the countryside more primitive. We arrived in the Enga province which has been open for only 20 years. Here occasional tribal feuds still take place: these are fought with spears, bows and arrows and are known locally as "highland football". A local sing-sing was taking place at the side of the road. Whilst these festivals are marketed for the tourists in Mount Hagen, traditional sing-sings take place everywhere in the country, to celebrate the payment of a dowry or a wedding, or on reaching a peace agreement with a neighbouring village with which they had been in conflict for years. We drove on without stopping. It is nice to know that there are still sing-sings without white men and cameras. The asphalt gave way to a gravel track with potholes. The police had provided us information on topical "tribal and rascal problems". We had been warned that currently there were problems with thieves (rascals) in this area. The track went over a pass about, 3000 m high, and then led through an area frequented by "street bandits". Despite barred cab windows our driver stopped only at open places. He also feared the so-called road blocks where rocks or trees laid across the road were manned by aggressive Papuans. The Engas are known to be particularly belligerent; there are many muggings here. The Enga province is the last Stone Age enclave in the country.

You should never be surprised by anything on these trips. Even well prepared and with some experience there is always a residual risk. This you have to weigh against how much more you experience than at home in front of the TV. Dicey encounters are just a part of an expedition. (On a previous occasion on the Pan-American Highway in Latin America we hitchhiked from Costa Rica to Nicaragua for three days with kayaks. In the hinterland we had to keep watch at night and once we were taken hostage by drunks who were armed and had set up a roadblock.)

But this time everything went as smoothly as the road would allow and after two strenuous days we finally reached the Porgera gold mine where we chartered a helicopter. I enjoyed the breezy space of the loading area compared to the claustrophobia of the jungle. At least here you had room above you if you played leapfrog! All of the equipment, - including GPS, radios and flares - was tested one last time. We arranged meetings and agreed on radio frequencies with the gold mine pilots for checking flights. These helicopters flew over the river every few days and would be our only connection to the outside world. Apart from these "casual communications" we also agreed on exact co-ordinates of checkpoints which we would mark when we reached them. If we had an accident these would help in searching for us. The next day with the kayaks suspended from a steel rope we were dropped at the put-in for the upper section. 1095 metres above sea level.

Ahead of us lay the Lagaip river, our path through the jungle. The valley is covered in dense rain forest – a lush tangle of creepers and climbers. In the next few days we would go where nobody with a kayak had gone before us. Ahead lay wild water littered with obstacles. The valley soon became narrower, rugged limestone walls towered above us. The river disappeared in a jungle gorge. Slender tree roots clung to the ledges like cobwebs. Ferns and moss grew rampant every-where. And we were in the thick of it, on heavy wild water with a gradient of up to 80m per kilometre. Despite luggage weighing 25 kg the high-volume Prijon Tornadoes proved to be a sound investment. The prototype had already given us good service in the Russian Caucasus on a previous expedition. We completed the first leg, to the confluence of a side-stream, by late afternoon. On a bare sand bank we pitched camp and put together a tasty stir-fry of rice and dried vegetables. It gets dark fast and early on the equator and we were in bed by eight. Yet it was not possible to think of sleeping. The tent became a sauna with the heat radiating from the jungle; but the tent not only kept out the rain but also leeches, snakes and mosquitoes. For hours we listened to the noises of the jungle, the frogs croaking and the cicadas chirping. I fell asleep, despite the heat, towards midnight – only to be woken up again by thunder and lightning. Noah's Ark-style rain set in.

The coolness of the morning caused the damp air to condense and the fog which formed only broke up when the first rays of the equatorial sun, still low on the horizon, warmed the air. For breakfast there was rice pudding with dried fruit and cinnamon, served with tea or coffee. Loading the boats took all morning and required care and time. If you live in your boat all day you develop an especially intimate feeling for your kayak. After all, the "polyethylene Samsonite" enabled you to be completely self-sufficient. On the other hand, you are also dependent on it. Losing your boat in this wilderness could be fatal.

The Lagaip welcomed us with fabulous wild water and fantastic scenery. Flanked on both sides by jungle giants it raced in a natural slalom down the valley. The heat of the jungle built up in the river valley. We cooled off in an enchanted side–canyon at the foot of a waterfall. Drinking water was prepared with a ceramic filter and refined to "jungle juice" with vitamin tablets. After an hour we set off again and left this picturesque gem. Shortly afterwards we stopped to draw the first of our markers using aerosol paint. We had agreed on these co-ordinates as one of several checkpoints. The helicopter company could follow our progress in this way during their checking flights. On the next bend of the river a path crossed the Lagaip. A hand-woven suspension bridge, roughly fifty metres long, stretched across the river. Thin liana fibres are shot by bow and arrow from bank to bank, to start building the bridge, then thick lianas are then pulled behind. Finally the floor is made from pieces of bamboo held in place by rattan palm branches up to twenty metres long.

The next morning the jungle was steaming once again after the nightly downpour. They were the heftiest showers so far and the river had risen by around one metre. The swift-flowing river carried us to Pori, a side river, with unexpected speed. We discovered a clearing in the jungle at this estuary and landed carefully. A handful of people lived here in a traditional shared longhouse. This building on stilts is made from bamboo and rattan, the roof covered with branches from the fan palm. Dense smoke from the cooking fires pours through the cracks. The extended family shares the space with their most valuable possession, pigs. As a result these costly animals are always under observation and on top of this they give out warmth if the fire has burnt down. Though the Papuans are primarily hunter gatherers, they tend gardens and swine too. They slash and burn a bit of the jungle, build a fence to keep out the wild animals and lay out hillside vegetable patches. These plantings yield sweet potatoes and plantain, the basic foodstuff of the river-based Papuans. We were received cordially but also at a significant suspicious distance. From the behaviour of the children it was obvious they were seeing white men for the first time.

As I got back into my kayak I felt I had seen something of the peace prevalent in primitive people rarely disturbed, people who had some-how been ignored by those outside of their habitat throughout their evolution. It is not always my aim on an expedition just to attempt further extreme first descents. Contact with local people can be just as exciting and the diverse insights into their culture just as rewarding; being included in events that are everyday occurrences for locals often turn these trips into unforgettable experiences. I have eaten cooked marmot in the Asiatic Steppes with Mongolians served with simmered horse's milk; dined off monkeys and caymans (South American alligators) with Piaroa Indians in the South American Amazonian terri-tory. You never forget something like that. These impressions are for me the most important memories – more intense than coping with the largest rapids or highest waterfalls. This is why countries in the so-called "Third World" are of more interest me and I am less interested in "civilised" North America, Australia or New Zealand; although there is of course fantastic wild water there too.

That afternoon the Lagaip became more demanding as huge rapids stacked up closely one after another in a gorge. We began to think that we were already on the larger Strickland. Clearly the river had risen even higher during the day. We had to land time and again to scout steeply falling cataracts and paddle across the boils and vicious eddy lines that required extreme concentration. To us this seemed to be the limit of what you would want to tackle with a laden boat, especially in the Papua New Guinea outback.

Finally we arrived at 415 metres above sea level and the Ok Om confluence – ahead of us lay the magnificent Strickland ravine. This region, the tribal ground of the primitive Hewas, was penetrated by the first white man, J.P.Sinclair only as recently as 1956. Even up to 1971 the region remained an official no-go area owing to "hostility and cannibalism". Access was allowed only with a Government escort. However, our problems stemmed from the river and not from the people who live by it. According to the GPS, our second re-supply point was located within the next few kilometres. When we found it we did not believe our eyes: the gravel bank on which we had landed by helicopter only days before was flooded, covered in several metres of water. The rucksack deposited some forty metres from the river now lay directly at the water's edge. It would have been washed away within a few hours. Admittedly we had noticed the river rising but we simply were not aware of the extent of the rise. Pensively we stowed the provisions in our kayaks and paddled on. Nervousness took hold. Time to pitch camp – but it was difficult to find a campsite. The gravel banks had disappeared beneath raging floods; the water stretched up to the dense jungle. Eventually we pitched camp on a stony slope. The number one topic at the campfire was the water level – up till now it had poured every night and the river seemed to be permanently rising. It did not look good. Next morning there was another rude awakening. The surrounding mountains were covered in cloud after a torrential downpour. Reality outdid our worst fears: the Strickland had continued to rise – by three metres. We estimated that the volume had quadrupled since we had scouted from the helicopter. From now on we were playing in another league whether we liked it or not.

Suddenly from behind a bend in the river we were greeted by a loud fluttering and calling. Hundreds of flying foxes, which live along the river in large colonies, sailed though the sky. Usually they were to be seen hanging headdown in the massive treetops or nibbling on fruit and flower pollen. Flying foxes are large squirrel-like mammals whose "wings" have a span of up to 1.40 metres and are formed by a web of skin stretched between the front and rear legs. They calmed down after a while and, suspended from branches, returned to sleep. As they are particularly appetising they occasionally end up in a Papuan cooking pot. They also have a symbolic significance and head hunters only are allowed to wear the flying fox fur as a sign that they have killed.

Foaming rapids reminded us of our present problem. In the middle of the jungle the river had suddenly turned into a psychological night-mare. Even sections that we had graded as flat water had become swirling, boiling water. The current was crazily fast. As soon as you broke out into the current you were sucked along as if on a conveyor belt. Crossing by ferry glide resulted in travelling an enormous distance down-river. Prior to this I had only experienced such dimensions during a trip down the Maypur & Atures rapids in Venezuela when they were in full flood. At that time the Orinoco was flowing at $60,000\text{m}^3/\text{s}$ – an impressive one and a half million c.f.s. – and blessed us with similar problems. But on this occasion floodwater flotsam was added to the equation. Huge tree trunks uprooted by the river made the whole experience even more dangerous. The river seemed to strike out at us with branches, as if the seething river could not reach us. We had, how-ever, no choice other than to continue our journey. Together with the driftwood we were swept along on this tidal wave. With this amount of driftwood you could only talk about paddling for your life. But that was not all: in contrast to the cool highlands, tropical heat and extreme humidity now reigned in the Strickland gorge. Our stamina and concentration drained away, soon we were totally exhausted. We were stretched to our absolute limit.

Suddenly we became icy-cold from fright: we found ourselves hurtling headlong towards a gigantic rapid – a combination of huge breakers and deep holes. Two 400 cubic metre stoppers blocked the river in front of us. Lukas and Dirk made big vertical reverse somer-saults with the fully laden boats. Lukas flew threw the air upside down headfirst, as if looping the loop on a big dipper. Wolfgang was the only one to find his way through, slipping through the gap between the enormous stoppers and was out of danger. I touched the right stopper on its extreme left and clipped the left one on the extreme right. After two major capsizes I surfed off the last wave and found myself next to Wolfgang and Dirk in an eddy and rubbed the sand from the river out of my eyes. We looked at each other. Where was Lukas? There he was: his boat rushed, bottom up, over a large rock and into an oval hydraulic. Helpless, we had to watch as he was violently sucked back into the hydraulic and held for ages. Again and again he tried to right himself. Then he bailed out. His head disappeared in the brown waves. He reappeared a few times but was immediately drawn down under the water again. We lost sight of him and I clambered out of my kayak and on to a rock to spot him again and to grab an idea of the river further ahead. I caught sight of Lukas; he had been swept on much farther downstream. Dirk sprinted after him on my directions. Waterborne once more I caught up with and clipped Lukas' boat using the towline on my lifejacket's rescue equipment. A boat full of water weighs a good quarter of a tonne. It dragged like crazy, and at times I was almost pulled out of my boat. Finally I succeeded in dragging Lukas' boat ashore to Wolfgang but it was only by paddling at my limit. Dirk had to land before the next rapid on the opposite bank. To paddle on without careful scouting would simply be suicide. There was no sign of Lukas. We could not do anything else. Dirk found himself at a dead end on the other bank after his rescue attempt. We communicated our next moves across the river by radio. First of all he had to carry his equipment and then his boat several hundred metres upstream before he could dare to cross the river to us. In the meantime we scoured the bank on foot for kilometres. Nothing. None of us thought Lukas had a chance of survival in the powerful cataracts and raging current he must have swum. Dirk finally crossed safely to on our bank. We collected flotsam and levelled out some boulders and built an acceptable emergency bivouac. Night fell.

Silently and in the glow of the torch we cooked ourselves something to eat. Everyone was sunk in his own thoughts, going through the dramatic events once again. Later, despite the extreme situation: the loss of a friend, trapped in the middle of a gorge and the high water, Wolfgang, Dirk and I, sober and composed, discussed the next step. No sign of resignation or gorge madness. It shows just how important it is to have mentally strong companions. We analysed the situation and worked through possible solutions. The next contact point with the helicopter might not be far. With the aid of the GPS equipment we fixed our current position. In two days a helicopter would land at a point downstream during a check flight. That was our only chance to get out of here. There was only the question whether we would get there in time to catch the helicopter. So we decided to paddle to this checkpoint, the one we had named "Strickland Gorge 3," wait for the helicopter and then look for Lukas' body from the air and then to fly out. None of us slept properly that night. Each of us tried to digest what had happened. To me the situation seemed like a deja-vu experience, only that it was me who was lost that time. A few years earlier I made a similar mistake in the Ethiopian highlands which almost cost me my life. Exhausted and alone I capsized in a pour-over on the Blue Nile. I finally swam and was swept for miles through crocodile-infested water. Just short of drowning I escaped to the bank with bruised ribs and collapsed unconscious. But luckily you are seldom totally alone and natives found me and dragged me into their group. I hoped that Lukas was just as lucky as I had been.

The following morning there was still more water - a metre higher, and seemingly still rising. The colour of the Strickland had changed from milky coffee to black tea. The river was so heavily clouded with sediment that even the waves and stoppers ceased to froth white. From the bank we could hear the muffled rumble of rocks striking one another in the river. However before we set off, we carried Lukas' boat up to the top of a hill where a helicopter could land and stored the GPS position. We wanted to come back to collect the equipment and a few personal items for the bereaved family. We got into the boats with mixed feelings: the river was our only escape route but also our biggest threat. The whole of the Strickland seemed to be a colossal rapid, the water pressure was terrifying even for us experienced paddlers. Exploding masses of water plummeted boiling down the valley. Where possible we hopped from eddy to eddy. Then pok-pok-pok. A dry roar penetrated above the thunderous noise. The helicopter! Before I could let off a flare we were spotted. The pilot hovered a metre above the steep bank. The door opened and somebody clambered out. It was Lukas.

The tension and dejection dissolved in boundless relief. The proverbial rocks fell from our hearts by the tonne. Lukas, visibly marked by the strain, reported feebly that after he was swept downstream for miles he found himself on the bank again with water in his lungs and totally exhausted, washed ashore on a bend in the river. He had spent the night in a cave and drunk water from puddles. The following day a helicopter pilot, who was just checking for our aerosol paint markers, had spotted him. Lukas was standing naked on a rock waving his arms; he had just taken his clothes off to dry them. At first sight the pilot thought that this poor crazy guy on the rock was the only survivor of the four paddlers he had flown to the river with their kayaks. What had happened to them?

The pilot, still hovering above the river, urged him to get on board. Lukas got back into the helicopter and flew off in the direction of civilisation. We carried on kayaking to the checkpoint, as it was not until there that the helicopter was able to land.

265 metres above sea level – Finally we reached the meeting point SG3. A few hours later the helicopter arrived as arranged. It took us back to the "bridgehead of civilisation": the Porgera gold mine. To go on was out of the question. The river, having risen in total by seven metres compared to the river gauge at the outset, now flowed at 1500 m^3/s . We had already risked life and limb and ridden a lot of luck. Despite that we had succeeded in navigating one of the most difficult and logistically most awkward and costly rivers of Papua New Guinea for the first time. All in all it had taken nine flying hours to reconnoitre the river and to transport us together with our kayaks in and out. I looked down on the black foaming chaos called the Strickland from the air, a long, wild channel in a huge wild country. We had wrested 150 adventurous river kilometres from the wilderness in the last seven days. The pilot flew round another bad weather front bringing more rain in a wide arc. With the sun behind us we pushed a perfectly circular rainbow in front of us.

WOLFGANG HAIBACH
MARCUS SCHMID

When Wolfgang led this Homathko expedition he already had a reputation: from descents in Corsica, the first man - an eighteen year old upstart - to run the big drop on the Ritzenaze; from manic high water runs in the Austrian and Bavarian Alps, including a ridiculous high water run on the Schwarzbach where a particular drop had to be portaged because the snow bridge over the river was too low to paddle under; from the Fraser where he, literally, drew the short straw for the running order for Overlander Falls (a month before I did, much to my chagrin). Often people would say "Oh Wolfgang, you know, well he even looks like a bear..." But this would give the wrong impression of the man, as it implies brute strength and no finesse.

I missed out on this trip down the Homathko by days, catching up with the triumphant group on their return from the river having spent the previous week driving around BC looking for them. They were wide-eyed and shattered and my suggestion of a quick run down the nearest river was met with exhaustion.

Marcus was the young upstart on this Homathko expedition and had just embarked on his career as a student. Later Marcus became the driving force for the expansion of the AKC, the German based Alpine Kayak Club, to include paddlers from around the world.

I had first met the two of them when they gave the evening lectures for the Jones Weekend in 1985. They, along with a Scot, Eric Thompson, all members of the then infamous AKC, came and told tales of derring-do, of paddling the Tamur in Nepal, with a super 8mm film showing Wolfgang rolling just above a horrendous drop which had the audience gasping.

Then they gave a further twenty minute talk about safety: about the AKC attitude to safety, their theory of boat design, about why they had round ended boats, why the end loops were running lengthwise along the boat, about the AKC designed "Multisafe" life jacket. They introduced the British paddler to safety as a positive concept. Up until then the British attitude to safety had been a negative reaction, an almost "if it is new, it is dangerous dogma". (Remember the "new plastic kayaks = new dangerous kayaks" theory. The same argument as was used against fiberglass when it was new.) They corrected the commonly held belief that the AKC was a bunch of suicidal nuts who were sure to drown, either trying to become a member or once they had joined.

Then we went and drank some beer.

ERIC, MARCUS AND WOLFGANG   THE "GOLDEN BOOTS" THEY WON IN THE CHARRIOT RACE AT MIKE JONES RALLY.

SCENES FROM A FIRST DESCENT

Translated by Marcus Schmid

When we drove into Alexis Creek gas station with our heavily-laden Fords on a hot August afternoon in 1987, a strange scent must have hit the owner. A mixture of wet neoprene, dust, rotten vegetables and gasoline. One of the vehicles had a leaking tank; it must have been holed by our driving too fast on the endless dirt roads in Western British Columbia.

On the telephone at "Joe Denby's Bar", opposite the gas station, we organised the final details of our latest adventure: the first descent of the Homathko River. In the Yellow pages under "H" for helicopter we found "White Saddle Air Services - Tatla Lake." Though their best price of $550.00 per hour seemed pricey, split between our group of ten kayak paddlers it would be reasonable, and we definitely didn't want to attempt the descent without heli-scouting. It would be a nightmare to end up in one of the narrow inner canyons with an un-runnable drop and no possible portage in front of us. Apart from the scouting the helicopter would enable us to drop off supplies in bear-proof, we hoped, caches. Next, under "A" we found Dean Air who could fly us back in a float plane from Bute Inlet at the mouth of the river where it flowed into the Pacific Ocean. The voice at the other end of the line sounded reliable, and so we felt happy that they would pick us up at the end of our trip.

August 28th, and we were at the put-in at Tatlayoko Lake, with about a four mile paddle across the lake to the outlet that marks the start of the Homathko river. The water was clear and warm and after packing all our gear in the boats we eagerly set off on this warm-up paddle down the lake.

A small, friendly, crystal-clear, stream, just deep enough for our heavy boats, welcomed us. It was hard to believe that this little creek of around 300-400cfs. would develop into the huge thundering raging ruffian of a river of perhaps 12,000 cfs. we had seen from the helicopter. With no real appreciation of what it would become, yet babbling contentedly, the stream started to grow. A few side creeks joined and the stream became river. Up above our heads giant uprooted trees were jammed into the banks giving us a warning of the possible force of nature that the river could unleash. More and more tributaries joined with their cloudy ice-cold water until the Homathko had turned milky green.

The first day's twenty kilometres were easy, entertaining white water. That evening we camped in a small wood by the river bank. According to our maps the difficult part of the canyon was about to start; the gradient was shown at 20‰ and the volume was already up to 1500cfs.

"Let me lead," Marcus shouted at Stuart and disappeared over the horizon line. From above, all we could see were the tips of Marcus's boat flipping hectic enders. After a short while he was washed out and rolled up and, exhausted, pulled into the eddy below. "Let Me Lead" became the name of this opening of the canyon. From here on the trip was a fast-lane ride to the Pacific Ocean. The volume, gradient and the difficulties of the river all increased significantly. Some of the "innocent" paddlers, new to paddling outside Europe, were amazed at the size of the stoppers and performed unintentional flying enders. However little things like this could not dampen our enthusiasm. One rapid on a fast right hand corner seemed to have an irresistible drag towards an unfriendly-looking monstrous hole for Lukas and this produced a rather unconventional but spectacular route. A few corners later it was Holger's and my turn to be made to look like complete beginners. Swirling waters and boils caused our boats to disappear in wicked whirlpools. In between the rapids of the upper part of the "Grand Canyon" however short flat sections gave our nerves a chance to recover.

Unfortunately the views of the highest peaks of the Canadian Coastal Mountains which surrounded the river here were obscured by the smoke of a forest fire raging up above our heads. This would anyway have been a distraction - our attention was focused on the river ahead, a crucial section, a brutal quarter-mile long rapid with several ugly-looking holes and a couple of mean pour-overs. Stuart was the first to attempt it. He got a terrible hammering, getting "window-shaded" in one of the holes before managing to extricate himself and make it to the last eddy in one piece - just. My run was not much better, but it was left to Lukas once again to provide the highlight for the spectators. Not liking the sight of the giant holes he ran most of the rapid upside down, "deliberately of course," he later laughingly tried to convince us.

As the river dropped steadily towards the ocean, white water continued to crash over us and some of the more notable rapids even warranted our giving them ephemeral names like "Detergent Added" and

"Little Corsica". Another, an entrance rapid of big glassy waves, was named "Birthday Canyon". Ivor celebrated his anniversary by deliberately swimming down this beautiful stretch of the polished limestone canyon while we all sat on the bank singing "Happy Birthday" before joining him in the waves.

BIRTHDAY CANYON *Marcus Schmid*

This frivolity ended when we arrived at Doran Creek. This was the Homathko's biggest tributary to date and added another 1000 cfs. It marked a definite portage; we hoped the only one on the river. We stopped here for lunch before the portage began. We knew from our helicopter inspection that right after Doran creek joined the Homathko the river entered a short limestone gorge that ended in a seven metre waterfall. It was not really a waterfall; a better description would be a "compression", the canyon walls being so close together that the water backed up before it squeezed through. For four hours we grunted through the B.C. undergrowth losing blood to the ever-present mosquitoes. Invective filled the air as boats snagged on branches and bushes again and again. Eventually the portage was over as canyon walls mercifully allowed us back to the river. The final stretch of the Great

Canyon compensated us for the tiring and painful effort of the carry with straightforward big bouncy rapids and by the time we reached the evening campground the sunset was painting the Tiedemann glacier a bright purple.

The next morning the skyline of Mount Waddington was sharp and clear in the cool morning air and by eight o'clock we had our kayaks packed and ready for our final round with the Homathko. On passing Mosley Creek, the main river had now risen to 6,000 cfs. and another outstanding rapid awaited us around the corner. The river was compressed into a twenty metre wide channel which ended with a right-angle corner into a giant hole. "With all that pressure the hole can't be a keeper", Stuart stated, and before we could challenge his logic he snapped shut his spray deck and set off. His run down the entrance rapid all the way to the hole was fine, but the hole destroyed his theory: it got taken apart in spectacular fashion, using Stuart

STUART SMITH IN 'THE BET'   *Marcus Schmid*

as the example for a comprehensive "proof by demonstration". The resulting wagers on who would make the rapid upright led us to naming this quarrelsome ruffian "The Bet". The bookies refused to take bets on Lukas and true to form - upside down as usual - he was flushed straight through.

A half mile limestone gorge with 100 metre high sheer walls was the next obstacle on the river. From high above we were able to see two big rapids which would be impossible to portage inside the gorge. With

236

no way of rigging any safety, it would have been like performing a high wire act for the first time, without a safety net. A short breathtaking portage was the better option. However below this gorge the Homathko entered a further series of limestone gorges. Here we realised that the previous four days of solid hot sunshine which we had enjoyed so much had caused the river to rise unexpectedly. All the tributaries had added more melt water than usual and the Homathko did not look like the same river we had scouted from the helicopter a few days earlier. Indications of the serious difficulties ahead could be seen: swirling pressure waves, large boils, currents disappearing through undercuts along with whirlpools and river wide stoppers, made a descent impossible.

If we had thought the first portage around "Falls Canyon" had been hard we were wrong. By comparison that was an evening constitutional walk. This forced-march was a couple of kilometres long but we had to complete it; our next food cache lay at the end. If we wanted to eat then we had to reach this supply depot - also we had a plane to catch. The portage was a brutal grunt, a true torture of mosquitoes, horseflies, heat, sore feet, and dehydration. Shouting and swearing gradually faded as exhaustion overhauled us. Dehydration took its toll on everyone; by the time we finished the portage my knees and arms were shaking. We all gulped river water like desperadoes in the desert reaching a water hole.

Finally we reached "Murderers' Bar". In April 1864 a group of hated road workers were slaughtered by the local Chilcotin Indians. The workers were trying to push a road though the Homathko gorge; fortunately it was never completed and the wilderness took back what had been built.

The final canyon, Waddington Canyon, lay not far ahead. Our original study of the maps of the region had led us to believe we would have to portage it and we would have to allow an extra day for this carry. The helicopter scout had proved otherwise and the pilot had explained that in 1984 there had been a huge flood caused by a glacial lake bursting its ice dam. This flood was the cause of the uprooted trees we had seen all the way down the river. At the same time it had filled Waddington canyon with silt and so this was now a rather flat stretch of water. Dead tree tops reached out of the waters indicating the depth of the old channel. Dangers still existed as the large volume of water created whirlpools and huge boils and large boulders could be heard rumbling below. Ifor's sudden disappearance in one of these boils prompted us to proceed with more care. Finally we reached the end of Waddington Canyon where all the stored-up gradient was released in a horrendous mile of white water down an open gravel river bed. We managed to run this and a further ten kilometres of extreme white water with only one energy-sapping portage. That night, starry bright and relatively warm, we camped on an island listening to the roar of the river and hoping that it would not rise. "Beer" was the most often used word around the campfire that night.

The following day we paddled the last 50 kilometres down a fast but flat Homathko to Bute Inlet where our plane was to meet us. Here, finally out of the claustrophobic gorges we could see the scenery and the incredible variety of nature's richness that had surrounded us for the previous days: breathtaking views of huge glacier fields, bizarre rock formations, fish otters, a lonesome grizzly and a few wolves. Just before the start of the inlet we passed a logging camp but we decided to paddle on and find a suitable campsite on the shores of the inlet. We smelt the sea; the Pacific Ocean lay ahead. Relief and joy were on everyone's face, forgotten were the endless portages, sore feet, aching joints and tired limbs. There was no time for reflection; a campsite had to be found. The muddy swampy inlet failed to provide a suitable spot and we paddled back to the logging camp. Here we were welcomed politely and to our good fortune the men who were to have flown in that day had failed to show and so the kitchen offered to feed us at rock bottom prices. Spare ribs, steaks, fresh baked potatoes, but no beer because of camp regulations, were on offer. After days of noodles on rice with canned tomato sauce, we were in paradise. Later the chef brought warm apple pies and vanilla ice cream. In the morning we confirmed our flight with Dean Air, and two planes duly came humming down the valley and collected us in a side arm of the inlet.

DON WEEDEN

For years I had heard of Don Weeden, but not by name. I had heard the story that someone on a Sun Kosi trip had stopped at the mouth of Dudh Kosi. Here he met the local to whom Mike Jones and Mick Hopkinson had entrusted the kayaks they were abandoning at the end of the 1976 Dudh Kosi expedition. The local had been so amazed by this whole episode: two kayak paddlers coming down the river then a very large very noisy whirly thing arriving on his beach and whisking them all off, that when Don arrived some six years later the villager was still looking after the kayaks. The story goes he was washing the chicken shit off the kayaks once a week and giving the boats a polish every month. Don rescued the boats and relieved the villager of his weekly tasks.

Before I started compiling this book this was all I knew of Don. I also had heard the story of a bandit run down the river below Niagara Falls resulting in arrests and hand cuffs but I had no idea that the perpetrators were such an illustrious pair of paddlers!

A little more research and I discovered that he was a contemporary of Whit Deschner at Evergreen college. Here Willie Unseold, the famous mountaineer, was a professor and was running a program to study the effect of tourism on the Sherpas. This was why Don went to Nepal for the first time. He bumped into Hans Memminger, the German kayak explorer, in 1975 and joined him for a paddle down the Trisuli thus joining the second (as far as I was aware) kayaking expedition to Nepal; the first was by a group of Czechoslovaks who attempted the Dudh Kosi in 1972.

I finally met up with Don and discovered that he was not a knarled old man with a beard that I had grown in my imagination as I heard more stories of khukri rum sessions in his house in Kathmandu. I also found out that he started paddling in 1972, another climbing convert who got fed up with not climbing in the rain of the Pacific North West. He later worked for a stint as a guide at Nantahala Outdoor Center. He paddled the Marsyandi from Khundi solo in 1976 making the second descent (Hans Memminger had made the first but from lower down earlier that year) and later led, from his kayak, the first commercial raft trip down the Sun Kosi in 1979 which is where we came in.

Kayakers defy Niagara's fury

By MICHAEL CLARKSON
Standard Staff

NIAGARA FALLS —Niagara was in a good mood Wednesday. Ken Lagergren was thankful. He didn't get dumped into the maelstrom.

On a beautiful fall afternoon, with the soft foliage of the deep gorge providing a colorful backdrop for television cameras, Lagergren and three friends cruised down the bubbling lower Niagara River rapids in small plastic kayaks.

"The river was friendly to me today," said the soft-spoken 32-year-old structural engineer from Hailey, Idaho. "The current and the waves broke just right."

It isn't always so. In an illegal rapids run in 1977, Lagergren fell out of the boat and had to swim for his life, a mile above the whirlpool.

And, during the first of two runs before the ABC-TV cameras yesterday, three of the four American kayakers tumbled upside-down, but were able to right themselves during the five-minute, two-mile trip.

"There is tremendous energy in that water; it's intimidating," said Chris Spelius, 29, operator of raft trips in Chile, making his fourth trip down these rapids in as many years.

This one was sanctioned by government officials, but the other three were not. Spelius managed to avoid police and $100 fines that were levied against two of his comrades for earlier adventures.

Spelius admitted that he and Lagergren illegally made a trip through the same rapids in the summer of 1980.

"I guess nobody saw us that time," he said.

Two other times he was spotted by police but eluded them.

"Each time I managed to duck into the woods with my kayak," said Spelius, a nine-year veteran of the sport. "I think I know every trail in the area. This trip was more relaxing, though, with police not chasing me."

Among the four expert kayakers was Carrie Ashton, 29, director of an outing club in Sewanee, Tennessee, who placed ninth in a women's division in the 1972 Olympics.

Because it was her first time in the river (considered to have the best kayaking rapids in North America), Carrie was "extremely nervous" and chose a more conservative route in the water than the three bearded men.

She hesitated at comparing the ride to a roller coaster. "I prefer the kayak, since you only have to put faith in your own ability, not in someone else's," said the attractive brunette. "It's the ability to react to a situation that I enjoy."

Six people have died in barrels and commercial rafts in the rapids since 1861, but Lagergren says the kayak is the safest means of travel there.

"Rafts and barrels are like oak trees; they can break, but a kayak is more like a flexible pine that bends with the water," he said.

"And you can exert control with skill, finesse and total body coordination."

Donald Weeden, 25, of Ann Arbor, Michigan, explained the tactics of the 35 m.p.h. run in his $500, 13-foot craft: "You try and pick a good, consistent line of current and stay with it. If you're not careful, this river can control you.

"Unseen arms can grab your arms and paddle."

The kayakers have broken the river into such an art, they have given names to various waves and parts of the rapids — Max Throb (maximum throbulation of 120,000 cubic feet per second), Himalayas, Helter Skelter and Deep Throat.

Lagergren stressed that the rapids are only for skilled boatsmen and that they couldn't even be used for kayak racing. "The waves are too high to be able to spot the racing gates," he said.

Films of yesterday's trip will be shown on ABC-TV's American Sportsman next spring.

Perhaps shooting the whitewater was the easy part yesterday. When the adventurers climbed out at the whirlpool, they were faced with carrying their kayaks 300 steps up the steep gorge.

NIAGARA

"Many have come to pitt their strength and cunning against the churning waters of the Great Niagara Gorge. Some made it. Some didn't."

Niagara Daredevil Museum placard.

Thirty shirtless river guides were packed into the sweltering dormitory room; the machismo was almost as overpowering as the stench. Chris Spelius (known as 'Spe' to almost everyone) was excitedly narrating a ridiculously poor quality 8 mm film. Shot from a bridge high above the rapids, the grainy, often out of focus, footage gave it the look of an expedition documentary from the turn of the century. The two kayakers - Spe and another western boater, Ken Lagergren - were barely discernible in the maw of white water. Their runs had the appearance of small skiffs battling through a typhoon. Spe would occasionally point to a section of fuzzy turbulence and tell us, "That's the section we've named the Himalayas. Twenty-five-foot waves. Tricky if one collapses on you." The year was 1978. The footage was the duo's descent of the Whirlpool Rapids in Niagara Gorge, which, of course, is most famous for its Falls two miles upstream.

This crowd of Nantahala Outdoor Centre guides, mainly creek-runners and racing types, weren't terribly impressed. That figured. In the late seventies, before white-water videos, country-wide rodeo circuits, and the Internet, American kayakers generally took a provincial outlook on the sport. The steep, technical, low-volume rivers that surround the Centre, based in North Carolina were the perfect training ground for the world-class racing talent the Centre still produces. A guide in the corner jeered, "No holes, no rocks, it's a clean flush through". But the few of us who had paddled the big water of the West - the Colorado, the Salmon or Snake rivers in flood - fully understood the scale and immense power of what we were watching. For Spe there was no question. Niagara was the simply the biggest set of rapids in North America. To confirm this he had bestowed the run with a "10" on his big water thrombulator scale.

Spe embodied his origins as a western U.S. river guide: six foot four, pectorals larger than most women's breasts, a shock of blond hair, and a habit of calling everyone "little buddy". Like Spe I was also a recent import from the West, and we soon became good buddies. (I remained little buddy, however.) As "big water" boaters, we had both experienced the ridicule of the racer types for our looser, more reactive boating style. (Mind you by this time Spe had already been at the centre for a couple of years and was gaining a reputation as a slalom racer.) Our base was the Chattooga river, famous as the Deliverance river, where we conspired against each other to secure the day's slot for safety kayaker: getting paid to kayak with the trip. But our favourite paddle was to take off after work to a blown-out dam on the Savannah River, known as Greg Shoals, and get back to our big water roots. At low water the former dam site resembled a graveyard of jagged concrete blocks. But when the evening's release of 10,000 cfs arrived, the Shoals would be transformed to a Colorado-sized rapid with massive keeper holes and surfing waves. Typically, there was a macho competition between the carload of guides, particularly between Spe and me. I can still remember his intense disappointment when I pioneered the "hairy ferry" at the top of the dam site by jumping the gun while he was describing the move to a group of us in the adjoining eddy. The move was gutsy because if you slipped off the upstream diagonal wave it was certain carnage in an ugly keeper hole below. Little buddies weren't supposed to show up the ultimate stud.

At outings to Greg Shoals over the next two summers, Spe constantly belittled the rapids in comparison with Niagara. Typically, he'd say, "this wave reminds me of "Pipeline" (the first section on Niagara), but imagine it being 10 feet higher". Or, after I'd just been thrashed in a sizeable hole, "Hey stud, that was only a five on the thrombulator scale". And throughout he would constantly remind me that this was merely a training exercise for the ultimate run, where a screw up or a swim could mean biting the big one (death). I was hooked. It was not a matter of whether to run Niagara, but when.

In fact it was a newspaper clipping describing three deaths on Niagara that first called Spe's attention to the gorge. A 37- foot, so-called unflippable raft, designed by Cornell University engineers, had been stood on end and capsized, throwing 29 people into the rapids. The article stated that if it had not been for helicopter rescue from both shores, the death toll of three and several serious injuries would have been much higher. Spe immediately did the sensible thing: quit his guiding job on the Colorado and flew East with a buddy to take on Niagara.

The last summer I worked guiding alongside Spe was wedged between two years of graduate school, and cut short at that for having to attend a summer session. Marooned in the flatlands of Southern Michigan I could already feel my kayaking skills slipping away. I knew I had to act on Niagara soon, before sedentary academia wasted away what kayaking prowess I had left.

The opportunity came suddenly. Two months later, in August 1981, Spe was going to be in Upstate New York for the National Flat-Water Kayak trials, not too far from Niagara. He wouldn't be taking a white-water kayak with him, so to further entice him I offered to let him use my new Perception Mirage, one of the first plastic high performance kayaks on the market. I'd kayak in my ten-year-old "Easy Rider", a Fibreglass pig with loads of volume. Perfect, I thought, for the big water of the gorge.

I planned to arrive at the gorge by midday so that I would have time to scout the rapids before Spe showed up that evening. We'd make the run next day, and I'd be back in classes the following day, nobody the wiser.

Niagara Falls, New York, is an unlikely setting for one for one of the continent's greatest stretches of white-water. Famous as a budget honeymoon destination, Main Street is lined with hotels arrayed with flashing neon hearts and cupids. Las Vegas of the East.

Spe had told me that the best place to scout the rapids was along the riverside Daredevil Gallery Museum on the Canadian side. To get there I drove across the gorge on the Whirlpool Bridge, nearly driving into the side of the bridge attempting to get a peek of the rapids two hundred feet below. No place to stop, I'd come back for the aerial view later. A quarter mile downstream the museum is situated at river level. You descend by elevator tube. The small museum at the bottom houses a Rogues Gallery of daredevil stunters: The Great Blondin, Daring Dixon, tower leapers, barrel-shooters, publicity-mad swimmers, bungee jumpers. For over 150 years, Niagara has been a magnet to the lunatic fringe. We would be in good company. The catalogue of survivors and non-survivors was a fascinating monument to human folly. But soon the roar of the river pulled me forward.

Outside the museum they have constructed wooden boardwalks

which run alongside the river. My initial reaction upon approaching the rapids was one of relief. After the years of build-up, the white-water didn't appear all that bad. From Spe's descriptions I figured the exploding diagonal waves slightly upstream to be the "Pipeline". Big stuff- well, actually REALLY BIG. But, at first look, not beyond the realm of some other big water runs I'd done in the past few years: high water on the Bio Bio, monsoon runoff on Nepal's rivers, Lava on the Grand Canyon. But this initial impression was wrong. As I walked down river, first to the succession of six impossibly huge exploding waves known as the Himalayas, and beyond that to Helter-Skelter, a long, chaotic section of irregular explosion waves, I began to appreciate the extraordinary scale of these rapids. Their speed (clocked at 35 miles per hour), turbulence and sheer power were beyond anything I'd seen before. I was mesmerised; I was also having trouble placing my kayak in this maw.

The statistics of whirlpool rapids (as the gorge rapids are sometimes called) stand up to the comparisons. Lava Falls, the biggie on the Colorado, drops the equivalent of 35 feet a mile with a river flow of between 10,000-30,000cfs. Niagara Gorge drops at over 60 feet per mile in its 1.5 miles with a cfs of 100,000 – 120,000. Besides, Lava does not have THE whirlpool, the mother of all whirlpools.

The daredevil gallery gives access to the upper part of the rapids, but to get a look at the crux of the rapids, the infamous whirlpool, for which the rapids are named, you need to walk down river and take the aerial tram ride which spans the river at that point. I must have done the round trip four times that afternoon, staring in awe at the swirling 10-foot-wide black hole that formed every thirty seconds or so just below the apex of a giant Vee wave. On my last trip, I clocked the whirlpool from the time it formed, to when it finally dissipated 100 metres downstream (with its replacement already in full rotation above): sixty seconds. Long enough to implode your sprayskirt, peel back your eyelids, strip you of your lifejacket and helmet, and eventually suck you thirty feet under the surface, probably drowning you. (As Spe would say, "I was suuuuucked out of my boat"). Clearly, the whirlpool was to be avoided at all costs.

Finally, to get a sweeping aerial view of the rapids, I walked upstream to Whirlpool Bridge. Built at the turn of the century, this single-span black iron relic is part of the history of the gorge. I walked across the bridge on foot to where a sign in the middle says, "You are now entering the United States". Two hundred feet below the rapid has just begun its acceleration. Consistent with overall scale, the rapid's tongue stretches an interminable 100 metres downstream. Waiting at the bottom, like the fire-spewing dragon at the end of a castle gangway, is a twenty-foot-high explosion wave. But that's not all: forming the left hand side of the rapid's "Vee" is "Pipeline", a 30-meter-long crashing diagonal wave named after the treacherous North Shore Oahu surfing spot.

High above the river, the rapids below appear diminished. But I ignored this illusion, knowing better. I'm focused on one thing: the route that's required to thread the needle between the angry Dragon and the all but expert surfers' nightmare. It's a gap of about eight to ten feet, like a high pass between two white summits, except that these summits' heights are constantly changing, (explode-collapse-explode), while the dark green pass between them contracts and expands with the explosions. A moving target further complicated by the wildly surging approach to the pass. But hitting this bull's eye allows you to slice through the rapids' first defences, lined up well for the lead into the Himalayas. Miss the target and there's a chance you'll get pounded and have to roll, and stray from the line. As with most big water rapids, it appeared that success at Niagara would be partly determined in the initial moves at the top.

In all, I spent over four hours scouting the rapids, by far the longest scout I've ever done for a single rapid. I'd gained a new appreciation for the kamikazes who knocked off first descents here over a hundred years ago - in an assortment of craft. After all, for how many class five rapids could it be said: "Yeah, too bad, the first descent was bagged by a guy in a steam-powered launch"?

Actually, the first descent of Niagara Gorge was more a commercial proposition than a stunt, but that doesn't take away from its shear ballsiness. In 1861, the steam-powered "Maid of the Mist," the tourist boat that plied the pool below the falls, was sold by auction on the very sensible condition that the vessel be delivered ten miles downstream. For $500.00 (a lot of money in those days) Captain Joel E. Robinson agreed to take the boat through the rapids. For much of the run the Maid disappeared from sight. The pounding white-water sheared off funnel and deck fittings as if they were plastic, but Captain Robinson and his crew of two came through unscathed. But it can't have looked that easy - twenty-two years were to pass before anyone repeated the trip.

Captain Mathew Webb, the first genuine "stunter" to challenge the rapids would have easily qualified for Spe's Ultimate Stud Club. He had already gained fame as the first person to swim the English Channel, and Niagara Gorge, considered one of the roughest sections of water in the world, would add another feather in his cap. He should have stuck to the ocean. Swimming without a lifejacket, Captain Webb was swallowed by the rapid's first huge wave and was not seen again until the whirlpool, at which point spectators were unable to say whether he was dead or alive. (As Spe would have said, "He was suuuuucked out of his swimsuit!") His body was recovered four days later.

Spe might be getting the best kayak but no way was he going to get the best lifejacket.

Captain Webb's folly ushered in the craze of stunting. Over the next thirty years a parade of on-the-fringe adventurers shot the rapids in everything from wooden barrels to eighteen-foot skiffs, including an assortment of strange contrivances. In 1901, an entrepreneur even tried to start a passenger service in a motor vessel appropriately named, "The Fool Killer." It sank on its second trip, after spinning for hours in the whirlpool minus smokestack, rudder and propeller. As the placard at the Daredevil Museum succinctly put it, "Some made it, some didn't." The list of attempts on the Niagara Gorge reads like a chronology of Mt. Everest climbs, with the occasional "(died)" attached chillingly to a name. In fact, the odds at Niagara are much the same as climbing Everest. Of the forty or so trips on the Gorge prior to 1981, at least six had ended in death. Spe had told me of a group of Idaho boaters who had flown all the way to Niagara to join him on his second descent only to back out after taking in the museum's morbid displays and the scout from the boardwalk.

Mentally exhausted from scouting, I called our local conspirator, Walter Funk, a college professor at whose house we'd be spending the night. Walt lived on the American side, so I crossed back over the Whirlpool bridge, checking out of Canada and back into the US . Two officers manned the US immigration booth and most vehicles were waved through the single lane checkpoint. Not surprisingly, I was stopped. Glancing at the two kayaks, the attending officer jokingly asked, "You're not thinking of running the rapids are you? You know you'd be breaking about 25 local, state, federal, and international laws if you did. Not to mention you'd be dead. Ha! Ha! Ha!" I told him I was a model boy scout who wanted to live a long life and drove through.

Spe arrived and we discussed tomorrow's commando operation over the dinner table. Walt would stash our fisherman outfits–complete with poles and fish baskets - in a small cave just up the trail from the planned take-out on the Canadian side. Spe and I would exchange our boats and kayaking gear for the outfits and when the police came we'd point downstream and tell them, "The lunatics went that way...I hope you catch them." I thought about calling my parents, as Spe had done on the eve of his first run, then decided against. Why give my mother a sleepless night?

The mood was sombre around the Funks' breakfast table. The weather was dismal - thick fog and drizzle. As we poked at our five-egg omelettes, Walter said, "You know, you guys can just come here and hang out. You don't have to run the gorge."

I made it clear, between mouthfuls, that I didn't drive all the way from Michigan for a world-class breakfast, nodding in appreciation to Mrs. Funk. After breakfast we began preparing our boats in the garage. To my amazement Spe asked Walter for some contact cement and began gluing his sprayskirt on to the cockpit cowling. "There's no way I'm getting sucked out of my boat", he explained. During Spe's most recent attempt, Ken had taken the swim of his life after his sprayskirt blew somewhere in the Himalayas. I thought about it for all of ten seconds and asked him to pass the can over. (Hell, the guy may be a lunatic, but he'd run Niagara twice before.)

Following our plan we drove to a small parking lot under the Whirlpool Bridge. Walter slipped the kayak-laden car between two semi-trailers. Already dressed in full gear, we quickly shouldered the boats and headed down the breakneck steep trail to the big eddy above Butterfly rock, upstream of the bridge. I slipped once or twice on the slick trail, once grabbing a root, fully stretched, to save myself from careering to the gorge bottom. I told myself, "this has to be the most dangerous part of the run" .... but I failed to convince myself. On the bank next to the eddy, we wedged our boats among shoreline rocks and began to wiggle through the top opening of our spray skirts. Spe completed this awkward manoeuvre first and disappeared behind the rock. I was halfway through the sprayskirt tube when I heard voices above me on the trail. Without turning around I shoved off into the eddy, suspended precariously between cockpit rim and seat.

"You're under arrest. Come back on shore son." It was two

uniformed men in fluorescent rain jackets and official State Park Smoky-the-bear-like hats. Each has a rifle. I had to bite my lip not to laugh.

"That trail's a bitch, isn't it", I manage to say. One of them repeats that I am under arrest, the other adding, "Don't be crazy. You'll kill yourself down there."

Meanwhile, I continue to wiggle down into the tight sprayskirt, rocking uncomfortably side to side. I ask them, "What if I turn myself in? Am I still under arrest?"

"Yes, son. Just come on in now", one of the rifles informs me.

"Well (and I loved saying this) I might as well get my money's worth. See you at the take-out! If you're lucky!" I finally manage to work through the sprayskirt tube. I put in a reverse sweep and head into the current.

Over my shoulder I hear one of the officers yell, " We'll see you in court, if not at the undertakers."

As I pass by Spe in his hideout, I motion him forward. Looking downstream, I feel as if I've entered a dream: the fog, the black silhouette of the bridge, the bridge's emergency siren, the surreal acceleration towards explosions of white foam below. Spe joins me and says, "Let's get out of here."

I let Spe get about twenty metres ahead. I want a guide through the Pipeline. It isn't easy following him. Surges in the current propel him right then left. I see he's on line to hit the "pass". Then he disappears, and it's my turn to thread the needle. I'm right on it, a slick glassy wave, foam on either side, then air time, and a clean landing.

I know from the scout that the Himalayas are 80 metres below, which, at the river's speed means I have less than ten seconds before reaching the initial explosion wave. I want to hit that first wave head on, but I have no vision downstream; I'm lost in an ocean storm of crosscutting swells; my paddling is wholly reactive; I struggle simply to keep my boat pointed with the current. I see Spe - a blur of yellow - shoot behind me to my right and suddenly the first towering wave is before me. I fly up the wave, bracing hard into it, and just as suddenly I'm speeding down the back of the wave.

"Like North Atlantic storm waves" is the best description I've heard of the Himalayas. The waves are steep, as high as twenty-five feet from trough to peak, and although widely spaced, the speed of the current occasionally cuts the bottom out of a wave, and causes a sudden, explosive collapse. You do not want to be on, or even near the peak of a Himalayan wave when this happens.

Like any small boat weathering a gale, my only object is to avoid a capsize. I climb the next wave head on, and fly over its crest. But while climbing the third (or is it the fourth? I've lost track) I'm met by a wall of foam, start surfing backwards, then grey sky, green water, grey sky, I'm cartwheeling, and finally green water. Oh shit, I've got to roll. Brain screams: WARNING! WARNING! GOT TO ROLL! I feel the surge of the next wave. TIME TO POP IT! I'm up! Brace into the next one. I'm through the Himalayas.

You know you've entered Helter-Skelter not because the waves are slightly smaller but because they're no longer regular. They're wildly irregular. It's like when a jazz number slips from a deep pounding beat into improvised weirdness, as if the players finally succumb to musical entropy. Helter-Skelter is the chop you often find at the bottom of floodwater rapids, only on a Niagaran scale. Got to keep your balance. Brace right. Brace left.

We had originally planned to eddy out on the right above the whirlpool. Still in the current, I look over my shoulder for Spe. He's just behind. I learn later that he has rolled somewhere in Helter-Skelter, but all he says while passing me is "Let's keep going; cops will be on us". I want to take a breather, share with Spe the excitement of the run, and regroup for what's below. But I know he's right, and besides, I want to follow his line through the final drop.

The river perceptively slackens after Helter-Skelter, piling up and forming two football-field sized eddies on either side. However, the current's tongue remains wide and soon guns the accelerator again for the final abrupt drop. The rapid is a classic Vee with a crashing twenty foot wave at the bottom, which every several seconds dumps a swimming pool of water off its face. The diagonal fences on either side of the Vee are six feet high and moving fast towards the centre, essentially acting as a funnel into the crashing wave. All this is classic big water stuff and the wave is the kind you'd pump yourself up to try and surf head-on, the river equivalent of the North Shore break on Oahu .... if it weren't for the mother of all whirlpools directly downstream.

This is what makes Niagara so potentially dangerous: enter the Vee out of your boat, having failed to claw your way into one of the two football field-sized eddies, and forget it, you're history. But in our kayaks and mostly in control it's not difficult to avoid. I follow Spe's line to the far right, working hard left to right, and then explode over the six-foot-high "eddy fence" and oh thank you God! - miss getting flushed into the eye of the whirlpool.

Miller Time? Not yet! Although the far right route avoids the mother of all whirlpools, there are smaller whirlpools forming along the eddy line, but this is Niagara and they aren't small. Soon after I jump the eddy fence only to find myself spinning in one. A metre or so below the surface, I'm wondering if I haven't screwed up after all and been sucked into the unspeakable one, when suddenly I'm back on the surface and I've rolled back up...... and WHOOSH!

WHOOSH! Because 30 feet directly above me is a helicopter. I nearly lose the grip on my paddle to its rotor down draught .

A voice bellows through a megaphone, "Proceed to shore, proceed to shore!"

I see Spe not far downstream. I paddle to him.

"Gotta split up. Our only chance!" Spe yells above the rotors.

"Which shore you want?" I yell. Spe hesitates, or perhaps I don't hear him. "All right..... I'll go American," immediately regretting my generosity. It's like this: the helicopter probably came from the American shore - called by the State park guys at the put-in - and our getaway plan was set up for the Canadian side. As consolation, at least I won't be cited for an illegal border crossing. As Spe paddles away, I yell across to him "Don't get caught", knowing well that he'll do everything in his power, short of throwing rocks at the helicopter, to avoid capture.

The river makes a sharp right turn below the whirlpool. Spe begins working across the current heading to our originally planned take-out on the Canadian side. I paddle hard with the current. I'll choose a place to pull out once I know what the helicopter is doing.

Moving fast downstream, I look over my shoulder to see the helicopter following Spe. Ha! Ha! Well, it's his turn to get caught. I'm now in racing tempo, going for speed, using the adrenalin pumping through my body to keep the RPMs high. I'm aiming to put as much distance between the helicopter and myself. The river remains powerful, the current fast; the riverbanks fly by. And then I spot the helicopter, still on the other side, but it appears to be heading down-stream towards me.

Damn! It couldn't have already picked up Spe. I figure my only chance is to get to shore - the American is far closer - before the helicopter reaches me. That way I can get into the trees at the gorge bottom and perhaps work my way unnoticed down river. No way can I outrun the helicopter if I continue on the river. Besides, Walter had told me that there's the coast guard station at Lewiston, around the next bend. They've got big, fast boats. Better bail now.

I sweep my bow upstream and surf a wave or two diagonally before reaching the slower water along the shore. The helicopter is not far upstream, bearing down fast. Damn! Hitting the rocky shore, I scramble, dragging my boat into the sparse forest. I find a hollow underneath a large tree and stash my kayak and paddle, and continue running. Helicopter's above me now, Thwock-Thwock-Thwock, presumably calling in my position. It continues to hover; I'm sure I've been spotted.

My situation is pretty hopeless. For one mad moment I consider running back into the river and swimming for it, but then remember again the coast guard at Lewiston.

Running downstream changing direction frequently to try to confuse the pilot, I spot a fluorescent jacket-rifle-Smoky-the-bear-hat through the trees, and then another. Their walkie-talkies are squawking; helicopter's calling in my co-ordinates. (Squaaawk .... lunatic proceeding downstream off right flank, now turning to shore .... squaaawk.) Two more Smokey-the-bear hats coming from my right. They see me. I run towards the river. One of them trips in pursuit. I double back upstream, spotting a couple more patches of orange closing in. I double back again. The helicopter returns overhead. I'm thinking: this could go on for awhile. Then someone yells behind me, "I've got his boat", and suddenly I realise it's time to give up. I like that boat, I like my Iliad paddle, and besides if we keep going like this someone is likely to get hurt, and it will probably be one of them.

"Over here!" I yell in no particular direction.

The closest two amble up. They're overweight, panting, and not very happy. One of them grabs my arms, and the other handcuffs me.

"Son of bitch - huh - coulda killed ourselves - huh - after you", exclaims one of them, still panting heavily. It's clear that the Niagara Park Police aren't in the habit of chasing deviants like myself on foot. The other four officers arrive, all in standard Park police outfits. I have to bite my lip. A couple of them pick up my boat, and we begin the march back to civilisation, and I presume the local gaol.

Like the put-in the trail out of the gorge is steep with switchbacks. The two park police carrying my kayak are having trouble negotiating the turns. I persuade them to take off my handcuffs and have me shoulder

251

the kayak the rest of the way. I tell them, "If I try to escape, shoot me."

I'm not prepared for what greets me at the top of the gorge. The trailhead is abuzz with people (I guess seventy-five to hundred), blazing squad cars, and three television crews. I'm immediately approached by a newscaster in a brown polyester suit. (You always think of the best answers two hours later.)

"Here's the kayaker right now. Why did you kayak the whirlpool rapids?"

I answer lamely, "Because they're there?"

There are other questions. I play the role of sports hero (they're thinking deranged daredevil) and answer the questions as inanely as possible.

The police put my handcuffs back on and usher me to a waiting squad car. Having seen my share of cop shows on TV, I remember to duck when they push me through the door. I'm thinking, what I really need is a big plate of Mexican food washed down by a six-pack of Carta Blancas, but somehow I feel this won't be on the menu where I'm headed. The two officers in the car aren't very helpful about what happens next. To them I could be a shoplifter or sex offender.

Our first stop is the Niagara Frontier State Parks Office. I'm booked for "creating a disturbance while operating a water craft and disobeying the request of a police officer." A photographer from the Niagara

APPEARANCE TICKET
Niagara Falls Police Dept.
Niagara Falls, N. Y.

Gazette shows up to document the event. In the background, two maintenance workers hold up my kayak and paddle, like some drug runner's confiscated escape vehicle.

The next stop is the holding pen at the County Jail. Still handcuffed, I'm led into a cell block containing about twenty, mostly scruffy, criminals, awaiting bail, trial, execution, whatever. I should mention at this point what I'm wearing: a full "Captain America" wet suit, resplendent in red, yellow, and blue, with white stars on the shoulders. Completing the outfit are one pink and one blue plastic sandal. The wet suit is still damp. I ask for a blanket, but don't get an answer. To keep warm I begin doing chin ups on the bars. After all the twists and turns of the day, perhaps this is the strangest moment of all: not one of my companions in crime even so much as glances at me. No appropriate and expected questions as, "Bank job through a sewer?" "Spiderman beat you this time?" or even, "Hey aren't you the lunatic I just heard about on the radio who boated the Niagara?"

My one phone call went to Walter and Edith. Edith answered. She'd heard about my capture on the radio. But Walter didn't show up with the bail money for three hours because he was busy getting Spe out of the state.

Predictably, Spe was overjoyed when the pursuing helicopter hovered momentarily once he'd reached the Canadian shore and then doubled back for me. The Canadians were caught napping, or couldn't have cared less about our escapades, and Spe boldly walked up the trail with his kayak to where Walter had the car parked. The contingency plan (an extremely stupid one I might add) was to rendezvous at Burger King on the American side in the event that one or both of us ended up on this shore. The two of them were sitting down having a meal - Spe ordered four whoppers and six fries - when two squad cars pulled into the parking lot, sirens wailing, having obviously spotted the kayak on the car. A glance around the restaurant told them who the likely owner was. They headed straight for Spe and Walter's table. A dicey moment, but Spe, in true form, managed in a matter of minutes to convince the slack jawed cops that he'd just come from the National Flat water Championships in Schenectady, New York, that the kayak on top of the car was a flat water kayak which would sink in all of five seconds if it were to attempt the rapids, and that the kayaker who was caught got what he deserved, because Spe had seen the rapids and believed that running them was sheer lunacy.

As soon as the cops left, Spe and Walter jumped in the car and headed for the airport. Spe knew when it was time to get out of Dodge. He told the counter attendant, "I don't care if I have to fly through Los Angeles, get me to Atlanta (closest major airport to the Nantahala Centre) tonight."

I was arraigned the next morning. The judge was Italian and about four foot eleven. He clearly didn't know what a kayak was and I decided it was better if he were none the wiser. I began to protest the charges, saying something like, "The only disorder to be found were the rapids themselves," but Walter, who was standing at my side, gave me a sharp nudge, prompting me to mumble, "I plead guilty."

Outside the courthouse a TV crew asked whether the $50 fine was worth it. The obvious answer was, "Hell, yes. You can blow $50 on a night in the Big Apple, but I got world-class white-water, a James Bond style chase, and a spot on the evening news. This is America. Crime does pay."

Indeed it does. Two days later I got a call from a producer at ABC sports. A stringer in Upstate New York had seen my interview on the TV, knew the rapids, and thought it would make a great show for "American Sportsmen". ABC was able to get one-time permission for a contingent of four to run the gorge. Spe, Ken Lagergren, myself, and the Olympic paddler, Carrie Ashton. (We felt that three beards were enough.) We enjoyed every minute of the escort through town by the Niagara Frontier State Park police. To top it off, I sold my "Easy Rider" pig kayak to the Daredevil museum for $500 Canadian. It would be in good company.

My only regret is that I've never been able to persuade Spe to pay his half of the fine!

E.W.MANBY

I refuse to write a full introduction to my mum.

Surfice to say Mum taught history. I remember these history lessons, not that I was ever formally taught by her in a class room. I would come home for the weekend from University and find my room was being used as a store room for her teaching props. One weekend I returned to find Egypt on my bedroom floor, not literally but the model mud huts and such like built by her pupils as part of the lessons. A large one metre by two metre chicken wire and papier-mâché model of mountains and flood plains to explain the birth of civilisation in the area and why the Nile flood plain was so fertile, took up the rest of the floor space. Lively history lessons. Hardly a date to remember in my Mum's lessons.

I will say that she tends to see things through rose tinted spectacles at times!

THE BIRTHDAY PARTY

It all began years ago when David, aged thirteen, joined the kayak club at school and one Saturday afternoon invited us, his parents, to come and see him roll his kayak in the canal. We had no experience of fibreglass, and certainly not the resilient plastic boats to come. Picture-Book, feather head-dressed Red Indians paddling through the forests of the New World was kayaking to me. David lowered himself into his boat; put the spray deck on around the cockpit, and set off fairly competently along the calm canal water. We hurried along after him and when we caught up, he said he wanted to show us a roll and immediately - oh dear - he turned his kayak upside down, a spluttering face appeared, the tip of his paddle showed, the face disappeared again. Then more frantic paddle splashing. "Get him out! Get him out! He'll drown!" I called and prepared to jump into the canal. David's father, however, remained unconcernedly calm and eventually, after more paddle splashing and a final paddle swish, the kayak was upright and a triumphant, but breathless, face appeared. David could roll!

We enjoyed those years of kayak slaloms, when as parents we were needed to transport schoolboys and their canoes. Wellington boots at the edge of flashing rivers, tents in muddy fields, slalom poles dangling, eager young brothers and a small sister with us; this became our weekend world, always with happy people, other parents for new friendships for us. The years rolled by and David's focus moved from careful slaloms to white water kayaking. A different anxiety for parents. No longer poles but jagged rocks to miss.

It was quite sad when he grew up and we were no longer needed for transport; but we still enjoyed the kayaking friends who called in, for we were on the way to North Wales and the Dee at Llangollen and a bed or floor at David's parents' house on the way was welcome! (As was the home brew! Dad.)

Many years rolled by, all our children were grown up and we had retired and were settling down to a quiet old age gardening and growing vegetables in the summer and reading and nodding time away through the winter months when the invitation to the birthday party came! The invitation was to a fortnight's kayaking and rafting on the Çoruh river in Eastern Turkey. We accepted. How could we fail David? We all accepted – father, mother, two brothers, a sister in law, a sister and three nephews and a niece.

Yes – we accepted, how could we, the parents, fail David by chickening out of such a party, but we saw ourselves as an elderly pair travelling in the van carrying the tents and equipment along the track that winds down the Çoruh valley, whilst the younger ones went by raft and kayak.

We were instructed to fly to Erzurum in the middle distance of Turkey where David and his current-not-so young van would meet us. We all arrived in Erzurum on the correct date and that evening, the evening of the actual birthday, a party was held in an upstairs room in a restaurant chosen by David. We English admitted afterwards that when we arrived we felt very Western, hygienic and doubtful. Would our love for David, who can as you know be, well, eccentric, would our love be enough to carry us through? Then upstairs we went into a large dining room where a long table with spotless white cloth was attractively laid ready for the birthday party. We had such a welcome. Turkish worlds are still closely tied to families. Here was an English family. How natural that they should all gather for the eldest son's birthday. The food was delicious, subtly spiced, and no one hurried us; grandchildren, one by one, fell asleep, heads on parents' laps. We drank our birthday toasts and the waiters smiled with pleasure at the family ceremony.

The next day further Northwards to the Çoruh, a lovely fast-flowing river rising in the Pontiac Alps and flowing Eastwards until turning Northwards and heading through Georgia and into the Black Sea. It is set in a steep valley with a narrow winding track squeezed in next to the river linking the small villages quite untouched by the mass holiday world. The villages – well, groups of houses – still belonged to themselves, sheep and goats on the hills and vegetables in the terraced fields along with apricots to harvest later, though in that hot summer world, Coke in cans and ice cream could be gratefully bought in the larger villages from the small family-run shops. For us, the grandparents, who had taken our four children on very economical camping holidays in France and Italy, it was the most luxurious life, for David had the help of Horace and Alan who had kindly agreed to stay on and help with the Birthday Party trip. We crumblies were waited on hand and foot.

When we accepted I saw the elderly pair being driven by van down the road, so we were a little shocked to be given a paddle, lifejacket, and helmet! Aged inhibitions melted and we found ourselves steady paddlers on the raft. "Paddle on the right! Paddle on the RIGHT!" I dug my paddle into the water with sharp jabs as we seemed to be swooshing straight towards a jagged cliff. It all depended on me! Oh no, it didn't: the raft flowed with the water and I remembered a slide-show given by David when he explained to his audience that the raft or kayak would move with the flowing river warded off the rocks by the cushion of water. It was just so. And we, the grandparents, were eager for our time in the front of the double topolino. I'd seen the joyous faces of the small grandchildren on their turns in the front cockpit of the double kayak, holding on very tightly to the rim and letting go with one hand very quickly to wave with pleasure to the raft passengers. And we, the oldest, had our turns too. It was all very exciting and such an adventure and so relaxed but we all reacted very quickly to any command!

For the first few days we moved camp down the river stopping at the best campsites that David knows. He also knows the river well too and no doubt he could tell how the falls and rapids come, the twists and turns, the rocky white water interspersed with easy drifting flat bits. After three days we arrived at the small village of Yusufeli where we camped at the "Greenpeace" campsite on the outskirts of the village. From here we would drive to the put in and back from the take out for the next day's run. The villagers in Yusufeli know David well and loved the family party. One day "the Father" went to have his hair cut. The barber, Mustafa Engin, cut properly with scissors clicking very fast but so exactly against a comb. No hand clippers, and very definitely, no electric clippers. News spread that David's father was having his haircut and soon a steady stream of visitors called in on the barber's, sitting down on the stiff chairs to watch. Click, click, click, the scissors snipped. It was the shortest hair cut I'd seen him have for ages, reminding me of the post war years when we had met each other more than forty years before. And the haircut lasted for ages, never losing its excellent shaping.

Then, really rather reluctant to leave "our" world of the Çoruh, we set out for the Euphrates. Miles and miles and miles across the wheat fields of Eastern Turkey. The corn was ripe and though we did see the occasional combine harvesters munching up the fields and pouring a steady stream of grain into the following trailers, most of the huge fields were harvested by fathers with scythes and head-scarfed mothers binding the sheaves and the children carrying them to stand them in stooks, for the carts to gather in later to stack in the yards. It was just like my history lessons about farming in the Middle Ages.

The Euphrates was the second half of the expedition. Up until this lovely holiday, the Euphrates and its fellow the Tigris, had, for me, been two semi-diagonal lines sweeping across the blackboard to reach the Persian Gulf at the bottom right hand corner! In history lessons this was Mesopotamia, the land of two rivers, rivalling Egypt in being the first place in the world where mankind could, on the deep alluvial mud, grow so much food that there was time over from surviving to think and invent and move out of the Stone Age. And here I was floating not in the imagination on a reed-bundle raft across the blackboard but in reality down the river in a raft with David!

"Our" part of the Euphrates was way way upstream from the reed beds and mud. Our Euphrates flowed mostly between high rock-faces of the canyon. The water was calmer than the Çoruh so we all, but mostly the children, could swim from the raft or be towed by a rope as we drifted along. The kayaks were in constant use for "water fun" and were often roughly roped to the raft to make a jolly, riotous platform, or the lovely warmth would make us all somnolent, even the children, and we would drift between the cliffs with occasional paddle strokes to keep us on course.

The cliffs on either side seemed to encase the river in a contented world. As we looked way ahead , the river in the warm haze looked as if it had disappeared, gone forever between the cliffs, but as we paddled and floated on, we'd come to the end of our reach and find another reach, presenting, in the distance, the same illusion. Birds nested on the cliffs and cold fresh water springs spouted out from them, and it proved great fun to paddle in as close as possible under the projecting rock so under a veil of icy-cold water. A very cold shampooing of hair took place! On and on we paddled and drifted, and we camped at night, sleeping out on the pebbly beaches in the small bays, waking at sunrise, to shower perhaps under the icy-cold springs.

My holiday pleasure was definitely increased by interest in and the teaching of history - Mankind's emergence from the Stone Age - The invention of the first machines - Shaduf and Sakkia. I had seen Shadufs on other holidays, man's scheme whereby the heavy stone bound onto one end of a pole balanced in a forked upright pole planted in the mud, would, seesaw-wise, lift the weight of a bucket of water from the river, so that all that man had to do was tip the water lazily into the irrigation channels: the principle of the lever at work for mankind. The first machine! And we were floating down the Euphrates millennia later and the same ingenious machine was still at work. Just as easy as two children lifting each other on a seesaw! Unfortunately David did not know of any "Sakkias" an ancient invention incorporating a cog wheel for the first time to enable an ox to lift water from the river by walking round and round! He took us, however, to a most ingenious water-powered flour mill. The same springs of water spouting out from the cliff that made showering such fun, supplied the power. The force of this water falling from high above supplied the power to turn the upper millstone round and round , grinding the corn against the lower millstone. I heard the same content-making rackety-clack of the wooden parts moving as I had heard in an old windmill in England. But I also saw women grinding corn by hand between the stones of a quern. Does one long for them to be liberated from this chore, or stay still contented in village life?

We were very content with our lives as we slid down the Euphrates and were sad when we reached the take-out point at a rather drab flat area of waste land over which we carried our possessions to a road and waited for David to negotiate the price of a Dolmus minibus to take us on the first stage of our journey back to our other life. We waved and thanked and waved as we drove away leaving David, Horace and Alan to get all the equipment back to the van and drive it all the way home!

KITSCRIPTS

In 1994 I went to Turkey with Dave and met up with my cousins Michael Alexander and Pippar. I can remember that the allder one's called me perma grin because I was always grinning and having so much fun. When I was in Turkey I made friends with one of the groen ups called Horace and in the raft he was stering one of the days and he shot up into the air and splashed into the water at the other side.

In the dubell topaleyno it was rilly fun, I was in the front and Allan Ellard was in the back and I did a escamow roll. One of the best things was camping. We climbed up to a castle and explored it but there wasn't really anything to explore. One of the days we were going down this river and I put my hands in the water and the water was absolutely roasting because it had come down from the moutain and the sun had been on it. One day we went swimming in the river with the Turkish boys. When we were in the white water I could hardly see most of the time and when I was in the raft we got caught in a stopper.

We couldn't stay the last week when Dave and the others went to the Euphrates so my Dad and I and James and Anita went and camped up beside a castle and the next day I sat on the top of a lorry coming down from the mountain. The week had been really fun but I was glad I was coming home to see my Mum and my little brother.

by Kit MacInnes-Manby Aged 5 at the time.

PIPSCRIPTS

I remember the trip to Turkey really well, it was my first ever rafting trip and I was really excited about going. We spent the first night at a really nice campsite where I drank vast amounts of 7-up and the groan-ups drank vast amounts of beer!

The next day we set off down the Coruh and I was the lucky child who got to ride in the front of the double topolino, I got very wet and had a brilliant time! Afterwards I was rolled (when the canoe rolls over and back up) and I boasted about my "roll" all week. We slept in tents and every morning my brothers told me off for kicking them during the night.

When we were bouncing up and down on the raft, when we were on *safe* dry land, my brother Michael was clumsy enough to fall off and break his arm (Bounced off was more like it. Uncle Dave) The nice man at campsite drove Michael for miles to a hospital and I got locked in the loo and couldn't get out!

At that same campsite, where we stayed for a few days for Michael's arm to heal sufficiently so we could all proceed, we managed to drink 39 bottles of Fanta between the four children!

My favourite part of the trip was walking down the river in the shallows at the top of the Euphrates when the water was still warm enough, but I also liked the making Euphrates Mud Pie later on when the water was cool enough to cool the pudding (mess) in[1]. My dad washed his hair under a mini waterfall while in a canoe and holding a bottle of shampoo.

I enjoyed the trip to Turkey because we were never in the same place two nights in a row and we had some brilliant nights sleeping under the stars. I'll definitely go back sometime.

Pippa Manby. (aged 9 at the time)

---

[1] The Euphrates in August is warm, but as the river flows through the canyon below Kemah the sheer volume of fresh water springs is sufficient to cool the river till swimming in it is no longer pleasurable. Euprates Mud Pie comes out of a box labeled "Misssisppi Mud Pie"!